IMAGES
of America

LIMESTONE COUNTY

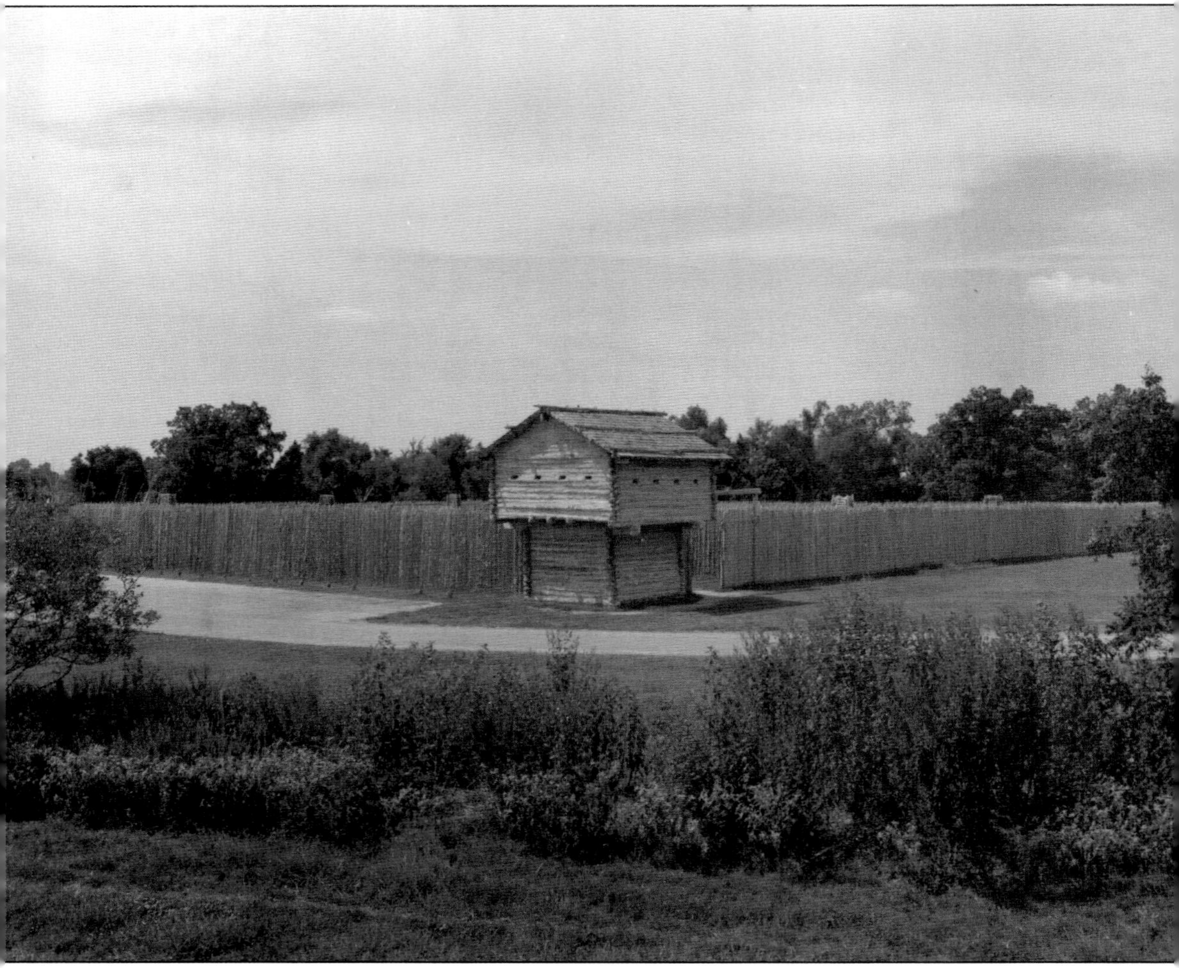

This 1980s photograph of Old Fort Parker shows the second reconstruction of the fort, which was built in 1967. Originally part of the Texas Parks and Wildlife Department, Fort Parker is currently owned and operated by Limestone County and the cities of Mexia and Groesbeck. The story of Fort Parker is known worldwide, and thousands of visitors tour the site annually. (Old Fort Parker.)

ON THE COVER: Shown is a performance of the Oglewanagi Dance Group at Old Fort Parker. Based in Mexia, this group was made up of area youth who were interested in learning Native American culture and dance. It was organized in 1956 by Ken Pearson, area Boy Scouts executive, and continued until 1967. This well-known group traveled across the United States, performing and participating in various competitions. (The Texas Collection at Baylor University.)

IMAGES
of America

LIMESTONE COUNTY

William F. Reagan and the Limestone
County Historical Commission

ARCADIA
PUBLISHING

ISBN 978-0-7385-9639-6

Published by Arcadia Publishing
Charleston, South Carolina

Printed in the United States of America

Library of Congress Control Number: 2012949184

For all general information, please contact Arcadia Publishing:
Telephone 843-853-2070
Fax 843-853-0044
E-mail sales@arcadiapublishing.com
For customer service and orders:
Toll-Free 1-888-313-2665

Visit us on the Internet at www.arcadiapublishing.com

To the memory of the early pioneers of Limestone County,
who had the courage to leave safety and comfort to seek
a new life for themselves and future generations

Contents

ACKNOWLEDGMENTS

The Limestone County Historical Commission appreciates all of the help and support that it received toward the completion of this project. This book would not have been possible without the contributions of photographic material from so many individuals, including Bill Bond, G'Ann Smith-Tilley, Bob Crider, Faye Dunn, Logan D. Wilson, Karen Parten, Sue Mills, Bobbie Muhlinghause, Carol Webb, Dick Flatt, Frank Seay, Harry Walters, Louis York, Helen Matthews, Larry Sewell, Claude and Mildred Monk, June Archer, Peggy Champion, Ethel Porter, Tommie Rhodes, Katharyn Gray, Judy Lipsey, Terry Don Roach, Karl Shiflett, and Tom Hawkins.

The Limestone CHC reached out to several museums, libraries, university archives, and other organizations for assistance. Many interesting photographs that have been included in the book were discovered in their collections. Expressions of gratitude go to the Gibbs Memorial Library; the Limestone County Historical Museum; Fort Parker State Park; Old Fort Parker; the History Room at the Mexia State Supported Living Center; the Kosse Heritage House; the Confederate Reunion Grounds Historic Site; the Mexia School Museum; the Groesbeck School Museum; the City of Groesbeck; Mexia Rotary Club; the Brazos River Authority; Incommons Bank of Coolidge; the City of Coolidge; the Cushing Library at Texas A&M University; the Texas Collection at Baylor University, Waco, Texas; the DeGoyler Library at Southern Methodist University, Dallas, Texas; the Panhandle-Plains Historical Museum, Canyon, Texas; Trinity University; the Oklahoma Historical Society; the Texas Ranger Museum, Waco, Texas; the Texas Archeological Society, University of Texas at Austin; and the Fred Hutchinson Cancer Research Center.

Appreciation also goes to the Limestone County Commissioners Court and Judge Daniel Burkeen for their continued encouragement and support.

The Limestone County Historical Commission (2011–2012):

Tom Hawkins
Bruce Jordan
Linda Jordan
Donald "Bubba" McDonald
Sarah McReynolds
Dolly Merryman
Cindy Pollard
William Reagan
Brandon Smith
Eric Turrubiarte
Janelle Whiddon
Logan D. Wilson

INTRODUCTION

The first Anglo settlers in present-day Limestone County were the recipients of Mexican land grants. The first settlement, Fort Parker, was established in 1833. On May 19, 1836, the fort was the site of an Indian attack. Five of the inhabitants were killed and five were taken captive, including nine-year-old Cynthia Ann Parker. She grew up as a Comanche, married a Comanche chief, and was the mother of Quanah Parker, the last great Comanche chief.

The town of Springfield was established in 1838 and soon became the commercial, social, and political center of the surrounding territory. On April 11, 1846, Limestone County was created by the state legislature, and on April 18, Springfield was designated as the county seat. The first courthouse was constructed in 1847. Other communities established prior to the Civil War include Tehuacana, Personville, Eutaw, and Horn Hill. The settlement of the Springfield area began in earnest following the arrival of Logan A. Stroud. He became the largest slave owner in Limestone County, having 156 slaves prior to emancipation.

In 1861, ninety-eight percent of Limestone County voters followed the rest of the state and voted for secession. It is estimated that three-fourths of the county's eligible voters fought for the Confederacy. Several companies of men were organized in the county, one of the most well known being the Eutaw Blues, organized at Eutaw by Capt. Anson Moss. Some Limestone County men were conscripted to stay at home to serve in the Home Guard, while other men organized independent groups and traveled to other places to enlist.

The Emancipation Proclamation was read from the front porch of the Stroud's plantation home on June 19, 1865. Freedmen from the area began to hold annual Juneteenth celebrations at a site along the Navasota River called Comanche Crossing. During the early years, the Honorable Ralph Long was the featured orator, speaking at times from the bed of a wagon with as many as 20,000 gathered for the occasion. Juneteenth celebrations still continue at the site, which is now named Booker T. Washington Park.

In the 1880s, small groups of Limestone County Confederate veterans began to meet informally to socialize and reminisce about the war. In 1888, they began meeting annually at the site where Jack's Creek enters the Navasota River, and the following year they organized the Joseph E. Johnston Camp of the United Confederate Veterans. The annual reunions at the Confederate Reunion Grounds were weeklong affairs. An estimated 7,000 people from all over the county and from different parts of the state would meet at the site in late July or early August during the time of the full moon. Tents were erected and brush arbors constructed so that entire families could camp out for the duration. These annual reunions continued until the 1940s.

The most horrific period in the county's history were the years immediately following the Civil War. Arson, lynchings, and racial tensions eventually led to the governor's declaration of martial law in the county. So terrible was this period of time that most people who lived through it refused to talk about it in later years.

Better times came when the Houston & Texas Central Railroad began construction of a line through the county in 1869. The railroad company established several new towns: Kosse, Thornton,

Groesbeck, and Mexia. Bypassed by the railroad, Eutaw and Springfield soon disappeared. With the demise of Springfield, the county seat was moved to Groesbeck in 1873. In 1903, the Trinity & Brazos Valley Railroad constructed a line from Cleburne to Mexia and later extended it to Teague in Freestone County. This led to the establishment of the town of Coolidge by the railroad company in 1903. This line was abandoned in 1942. In 1906, the Houston & Texas Central Railroad built the Nelleva Cutoff from Mexia to Nelleva in Brazos County, and Personville became an important stop on this line. The cutoff was not profitable, however, and was abandoned in 1933. State Highway 39 was later built on the cutoff bed.

The coming of the railroads to the county accelerated the production of cotton. Many family farms raising cotton as the cash crop were established. Communities developed in all parts of the county, each with a school, one or two churches, one or two stores, a blacksmith shop, and a cotton gin. Following World War II, cattle production began replacing cotton as the major agricultural endeavor in the county, and the small communities began to disappear. As the populations of the rural communities dwindled, many lost their schools. At one time, there were over 100 schools throughout the county. Through the process of consolidation, only three school districts now remain: Groesbeck ISD, Mexia ISD, and Coolidge ISD.

Limestone County has also been the home to schools of higher learning. Tehuacana was the home of Trinity University (1869–1902) and Westminster College (1902–1949). College-level courses were also offered in Thornton at the Thornton Male & Female Institute from 1877 until 1891. In the early 1970s, Navarro College began offering classes in Mexia.

Prosperity came to Limestone County following World War I, when oil was discovered in the Mexia area in 1921. Mexia went from a peaceful community of 4,000 to a raucous boomtown of 50,000 in just a few weeks. In addition to honest job seekers, gamblers and bootleggers invaded Mexia, prompting the state to send in a company of Texas Rangers and the National Guard to eliminate the criminal elements. The peak year of production in the Mexia oil fields was 1922, when 35 million barrels of oil were produced. Prosperous times continued until the Great Depression.

During the Great Depression, the federal government initiated several programs to put people back to work. It was during this time that the Civilian Conservation Corps undertook the restoration of Old Fort Parker and Fort Parker State Park. Also, many schools in the county were constructed under the Works Progress Administration (WPA).

Limestone County has always responded to the call of duty. In World War I, Company K of the 143rd Infantry was created of Limestone County volunteers under Capt. Scott Reed. A National Guard company was established in Mexia following World War I, and this unit was called into service at the onset of World War II. During the war, Mexia was home to a German POW camp, and an army airfield was located at Prairie Hill.

The post–World War II era has brought many changes to Limestone County. Most of the small farming communities are now gone, and cattle production has become the main agricultural activity. The old POW camp property became the Mexia State School, a residential facility for individuals with mental disabilities. Today, the Mexia State Supported Living Center is one of the largest employers in the area. Energy production has once again brought prosperity to the county. A power plant was constructed in southeastern Limestone County during the early 1980s. Mining operations to supply area power plants with lignite coal and the drilling for natural gas has helped to improve the county's economy in recent years. The construction of Lake Mexia and Lake Limestone has increased recreational tourism.

One

EARLY SETTLEMENT

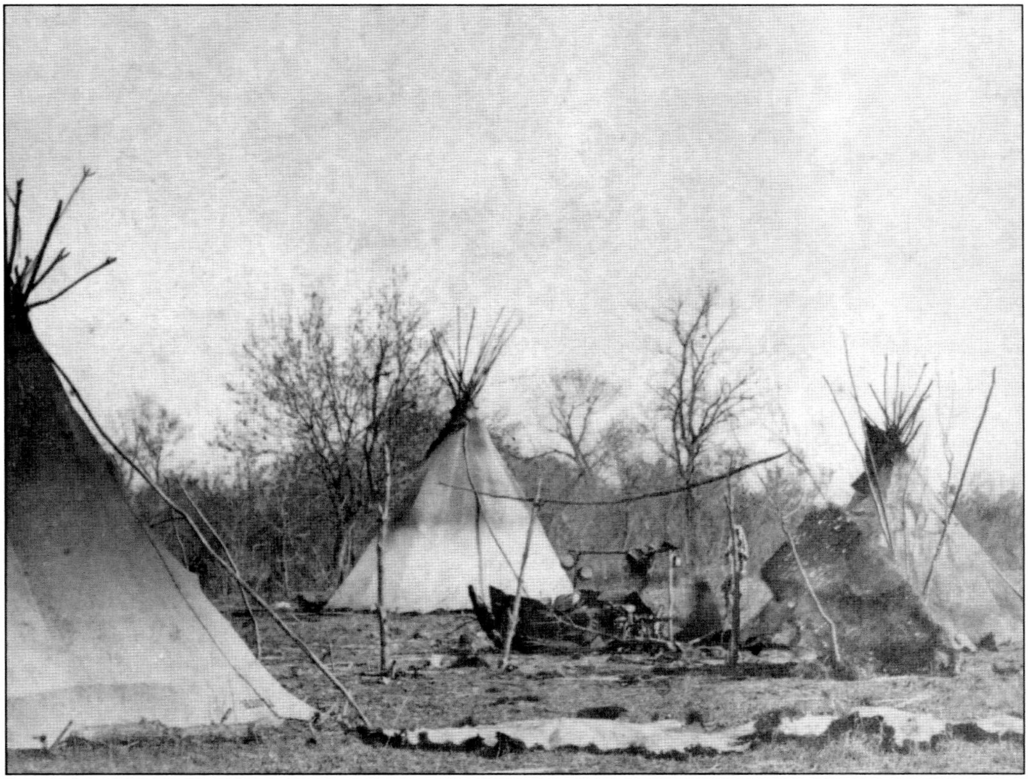

The first Anglo settlers in present-day Limestone County found a land of abundant resources where they could build new lives. However, life on the outermost edge of the frontier meant the possibility of attacks by hostile Indians. The greatest threat was the Comanche. These nomadic buffalo hunters were exceptional horsemen and fierce warriors. This small Comanche encampment with tepees depicts their nomadic lifestyle. (DeGolyer Library, Southern Methodist University, Ag2008.0005.)

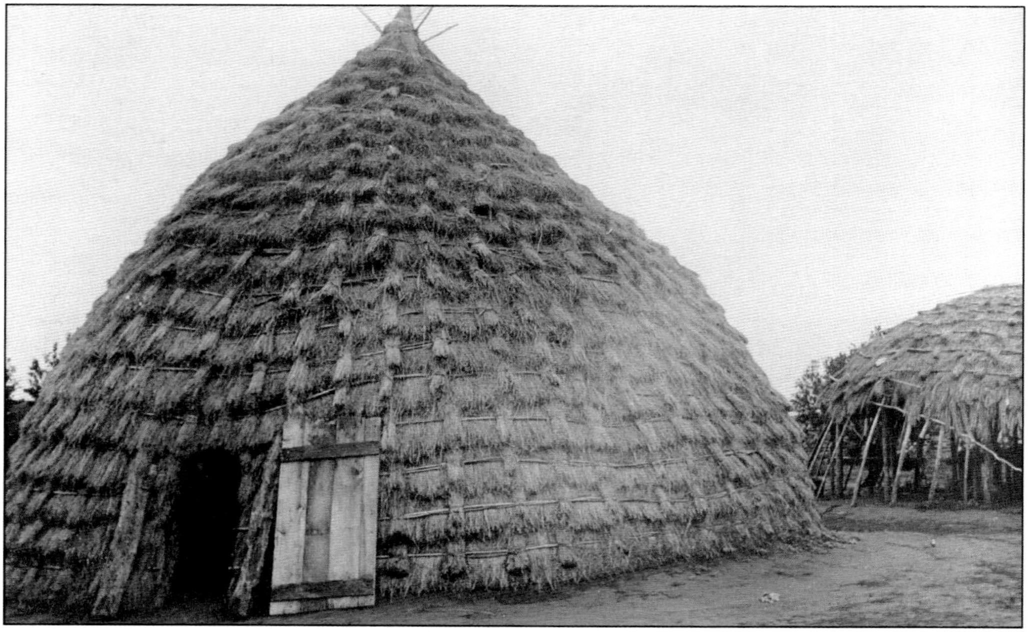

By 1750, Wichita-speaking groups had migrated into central Texas. The Wichita included the Tawakoni, Keechi, Waco, Iscani, Taovayas, and Wichita. They built permanent grass houses like this one and practiced agriculture but left their villages during the winter to hunt buffalo. They were hospitable toward strangers, engaged in trade with the French and the Comanche, and cannibalized Apache and Osage captives. (DeGolyer Library, Southern Methodist University, Ag1982.0152.)

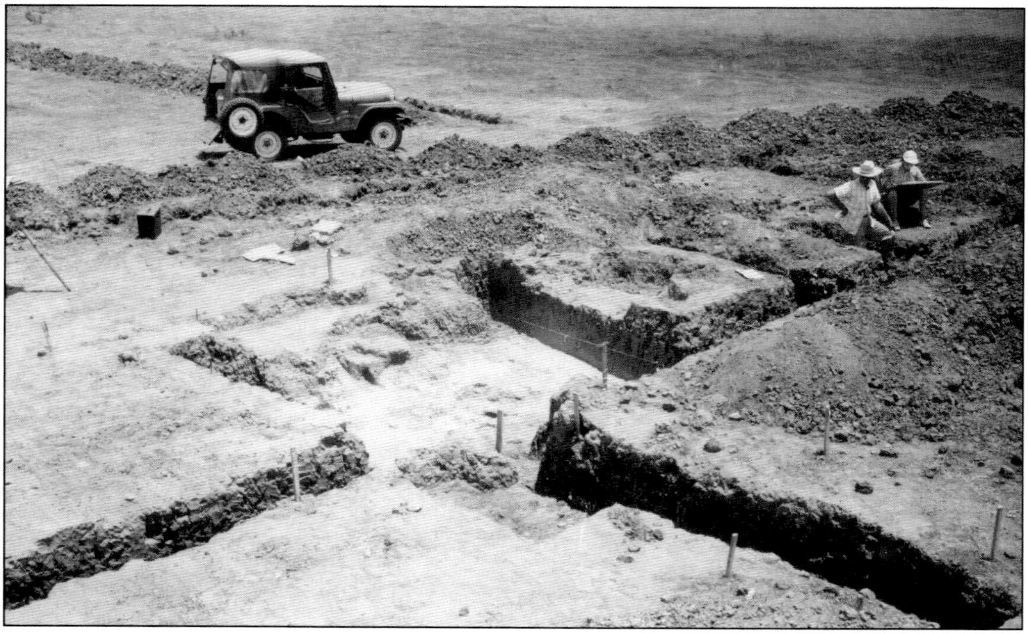

The most prominent Wichita group in Limestone County was the Tawakoni (Tehuacana), who had a large village near the present town of Tehuacana. The Vinson Site was excavated by the University of Texas, the Texas Archeological Society, and local archeologists over a 20-year period beginning in 1961. Overall, eight dwellings, three cache pits, and several other features were excavated. (Texas Archeological Research Laboratory.)

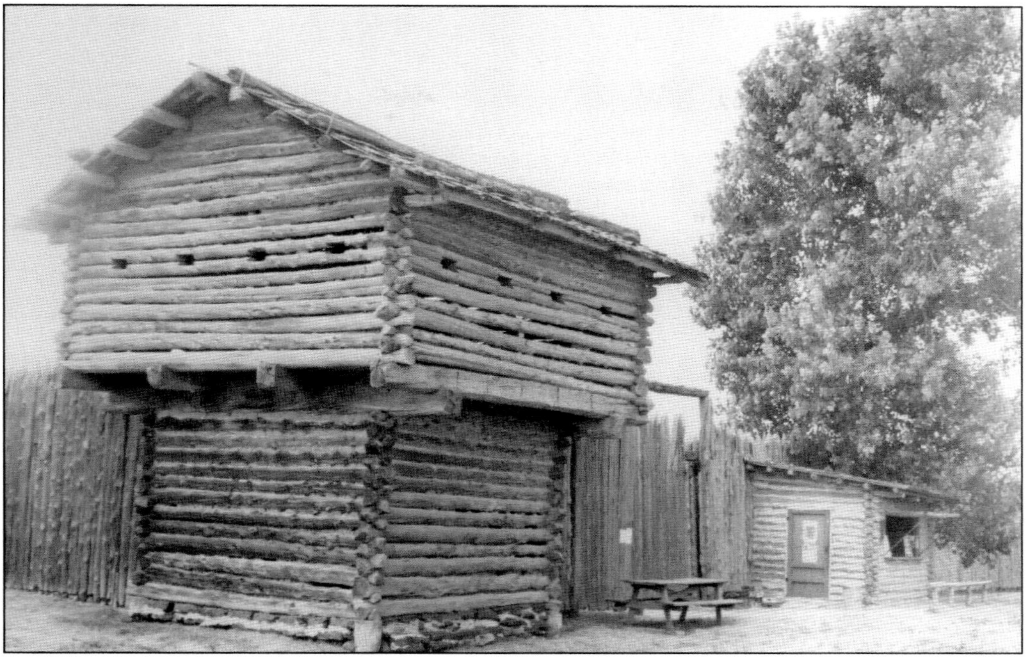

In 1832, Daniel Parker gained permission from the Mexican government to settle in Texas. The Parkers and other members of the newly formed Pilgrim Baptist Church came to Texas in 1833 from Crawford County, Illinois. Daniel and most of his followers settled in present-day Anderson County. The remaining members of the group traveled westward to an area along the Navasota River, where each family in the group had received a land grant. They built cabins and cleared the land for farming. Due to the threat of Indian attacks, they built a fort for protection. Fort Parker became the first Anglo settlement in present-day Limestone County. These photographs show the first reconstruction of the fort, which was built by the Civilian Conservation Corps in 1936 for the Texas centennial. (Both, Limestone County Historical Museum.)

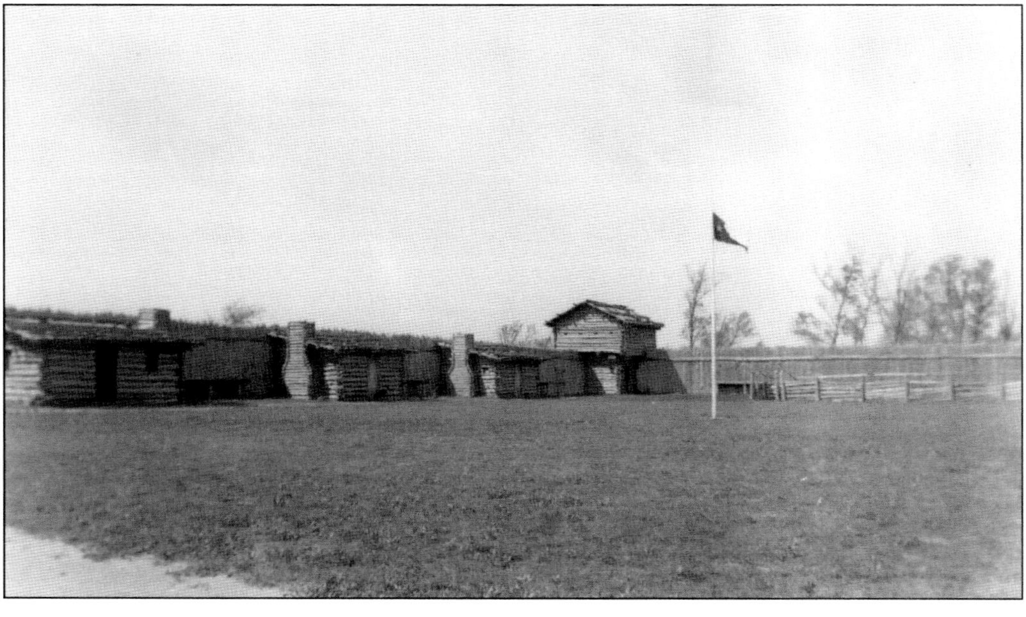

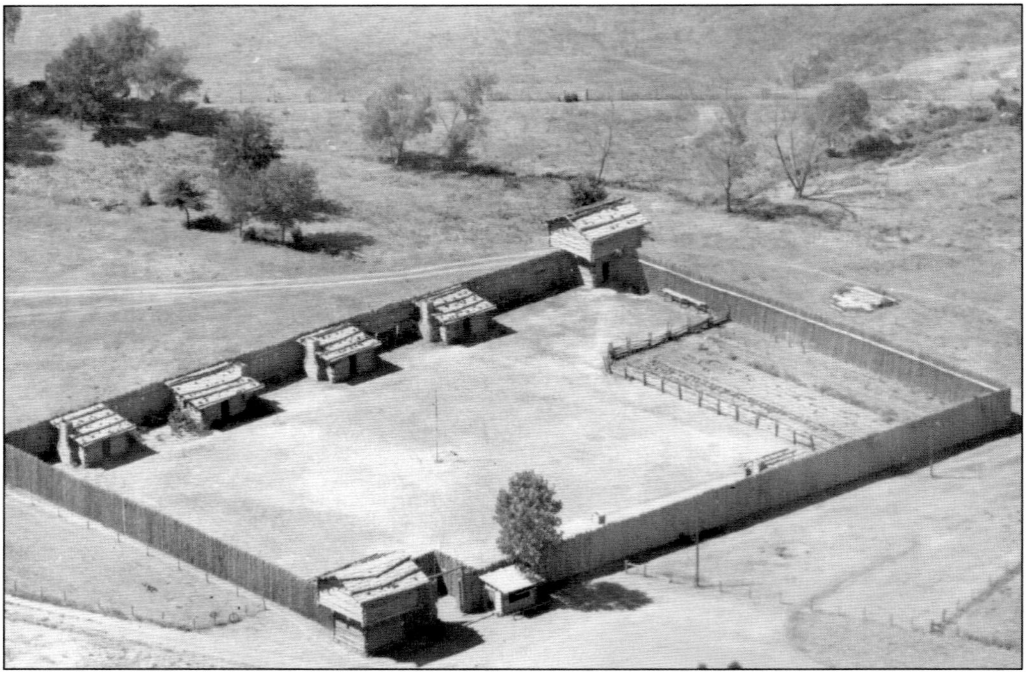

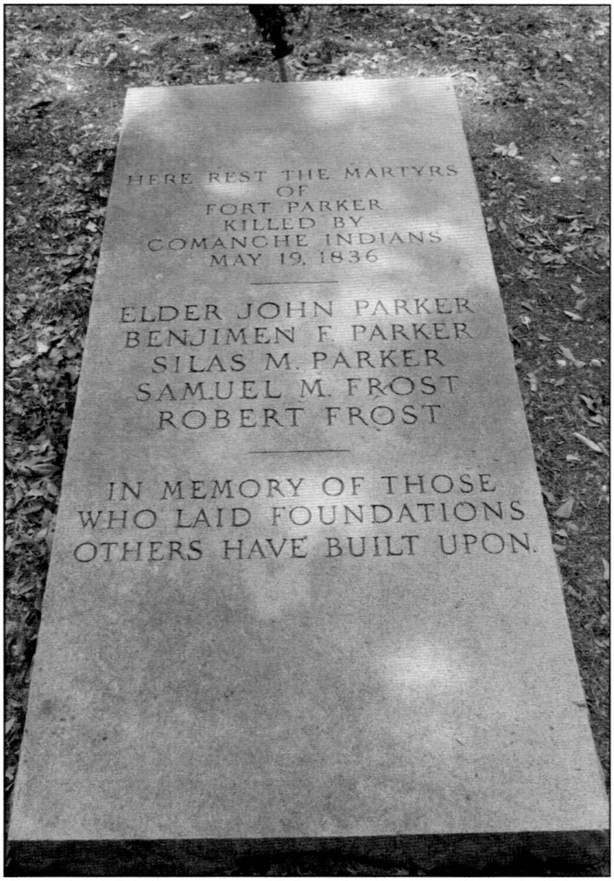

On May 19, 1836, a group of Comanche and Kiowa Indians attacked Fort Parker, killing five and wounding two. Rachel Parker Plummer, her son James Pratt Plummer, Elizabeth Kellogg, nine-year-old Cynthia Ann Parker, and her younger brother John Parker were taken captive. In two separate groups, survivors of the attack traveled to safety at Fort Houston in present-day Anderson County. Shown above is the first reconstruction of Fort Parker. (Gibbs Memorial Library.)

Several days after the attack, men from Fort Houston returned to Fort Parker and buried the remains of the dead in a mass grave about one and a half miles from the fort. Later, as others began to settle in the area, burials continued at the site. Previously known as the Union Burial Ground, Lewisville Cemetery, and Glenwood Cemetery, it has been called Fort Parker Memorial Park since about 1950. (William Reagan.)

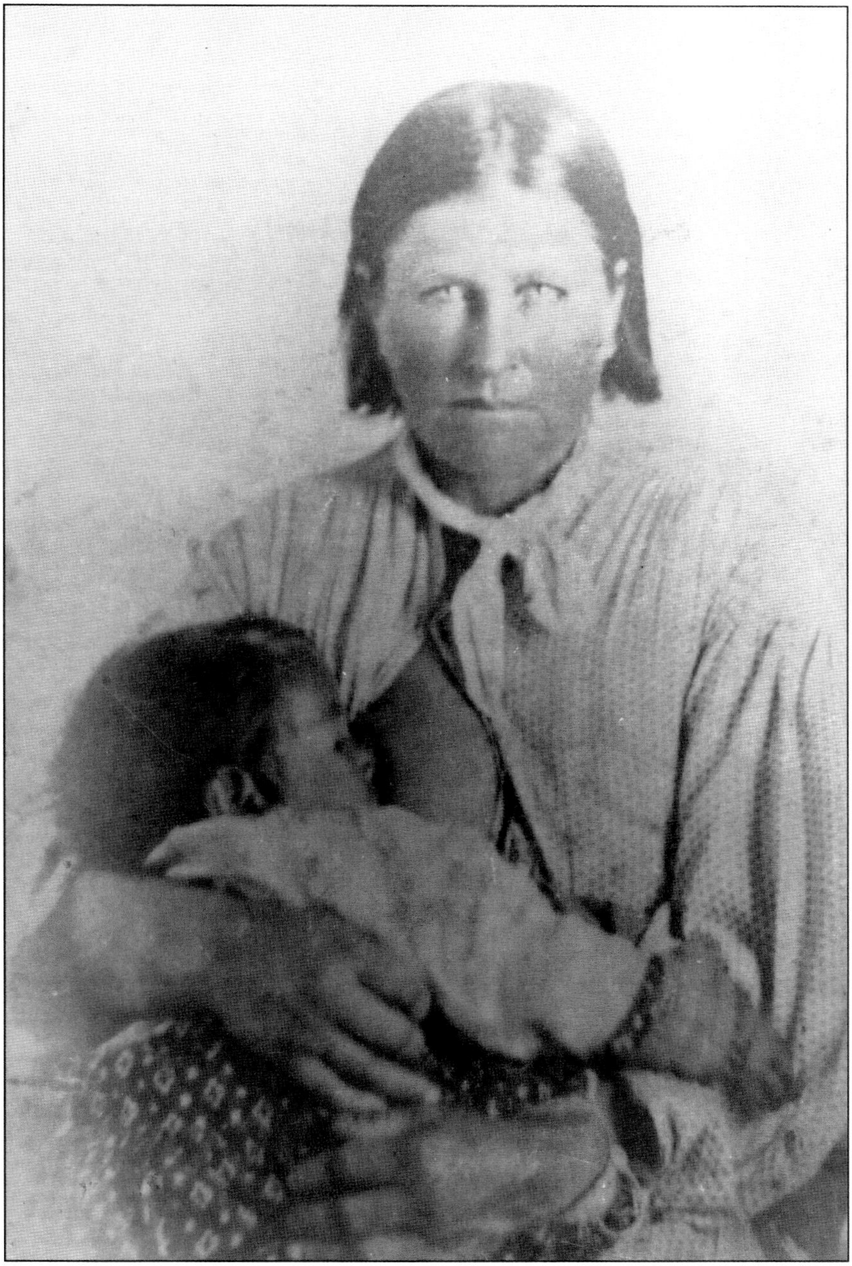

After being taken captive during the attack on Fort Parker at the age of nine, Cynthia Ann Parker grew up with the Comanche. She learned the customs and language of the tribe and even married a Comanche chief, Peta Nocona, with whom she had three children. She was recaptured on December 17, 1860, at the Battle of Pease River by soldiers under the command of Capt. Sullivan Ross and was later identified by her uncle, Isaac Parker. This 1861 photograph of Cynthia Ann and her daughter Topsannah was taken in Fort Worth while they were traveling with her uncle to his home in Birdville. During the Battle of Pease River, Peta Nocona was killed and Cynthia Ann was separated from her sons, Quanah and Pecos. Grieving her husband and missing children, Cynthia Ann followed the way of the Comanche and cut her hair short to publicly display her feelings of loss. (The Texas Collection at Baylor University.)

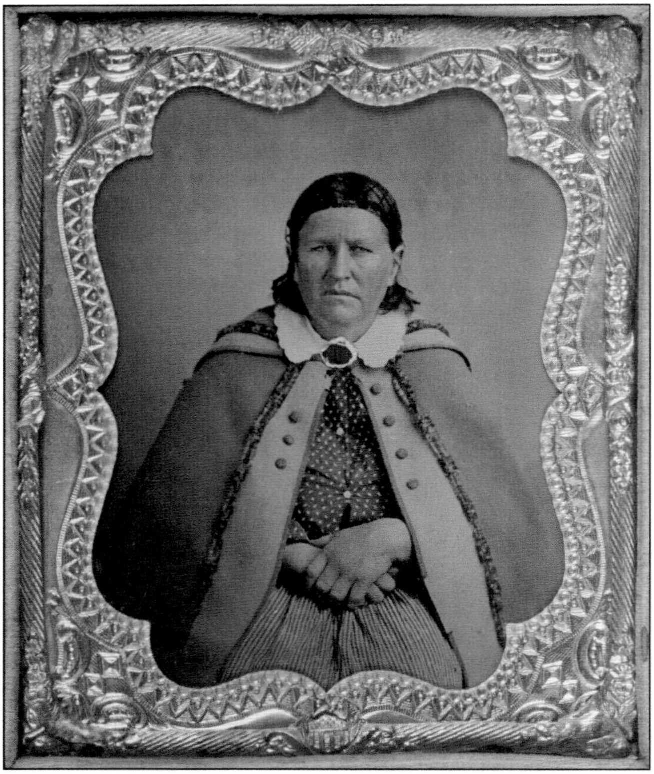

This photograph of Cynthia Ann Parker was taken in February 1861, while she was in Austin with her uncle, Isaac Parker. She lived with her uncle for three months at Birdville, then with her brother Silas until he enlisted in the Confederate army, and finally with her sister Orlena. Sadly, her daughter Topsannah died in 1864. Cynthia Ann died in 1871. (DeGoyler Library, Southern Methodist University, Ag2008.0005.)

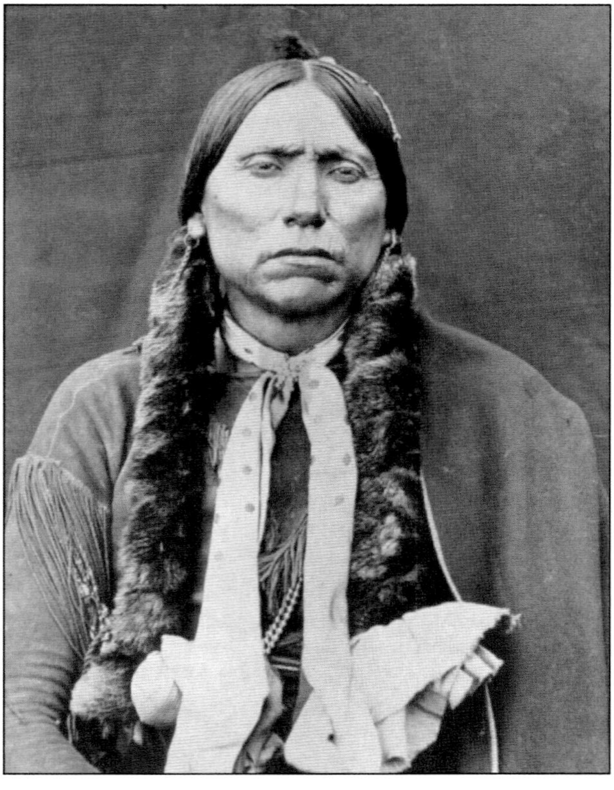

Quanah Parker was the eldest son of Cynthia Ann Parker and became chief of the Quahadi Comanche. Refusing to sign any treaty, he continued to lead raids against settlements in West Texas until 1875, at which time he led his people to the reservation and encouraged them to adopt the white culture. (The Texas Collection at Baylor University.)

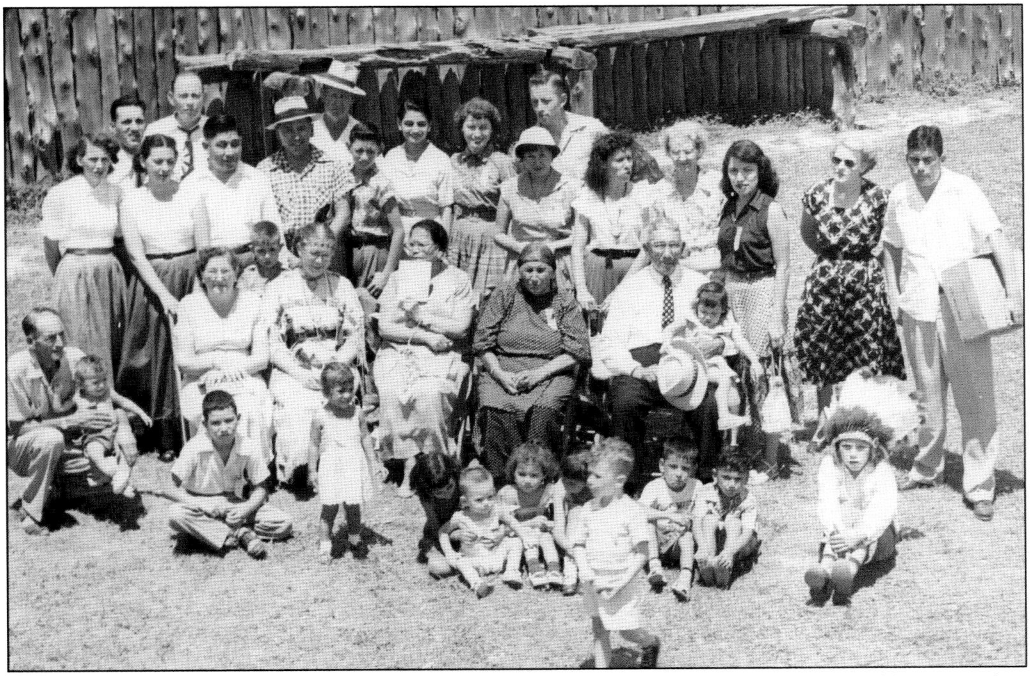

On July 3, 1953, Parker descendants, both Comanche and Anglo, gathered at Old Fort Parker and Fort Parker State Park to hold the first Parker Family Reunion. In the above photograph are Comanche members of the family at the reunion. Seated in the center are three of Quanah Parker's children: Wanada Parker Page (holding paper), Weyoda Parker (in polka-dot dress), and White Parker. Pictured below are the Anglo Parker descendants. The older gentleman sitting at the front is Hinton Plummer, the son of L.T.M. Plummer. Alternating between Limestone County and Oklahoma, the Parker Family Reunions have continued annually to the present time. (Both, the Texas Collection at Baylor University.)

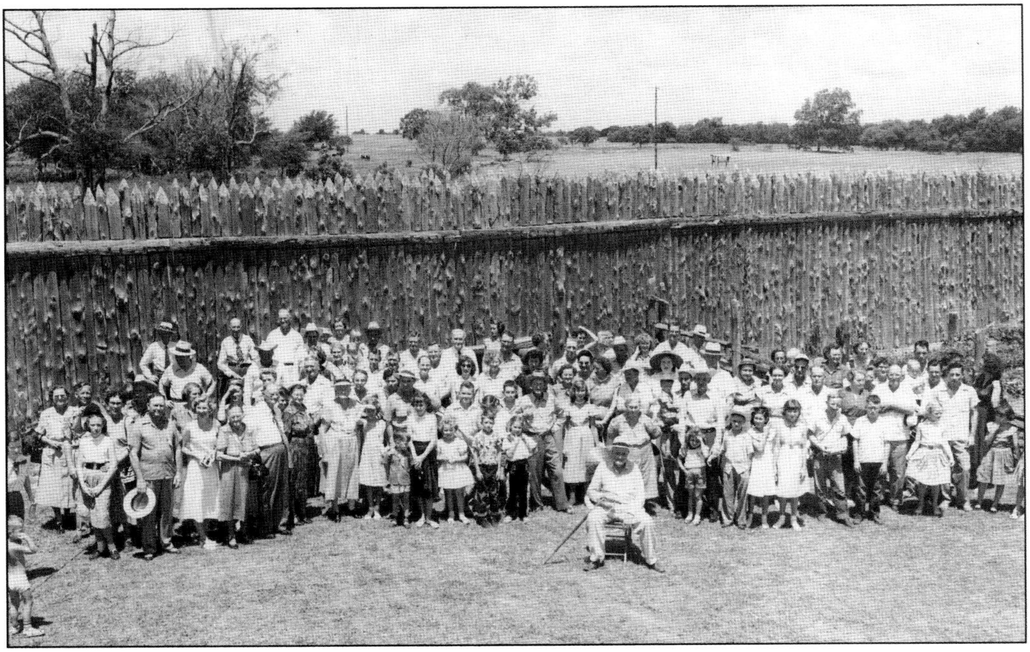

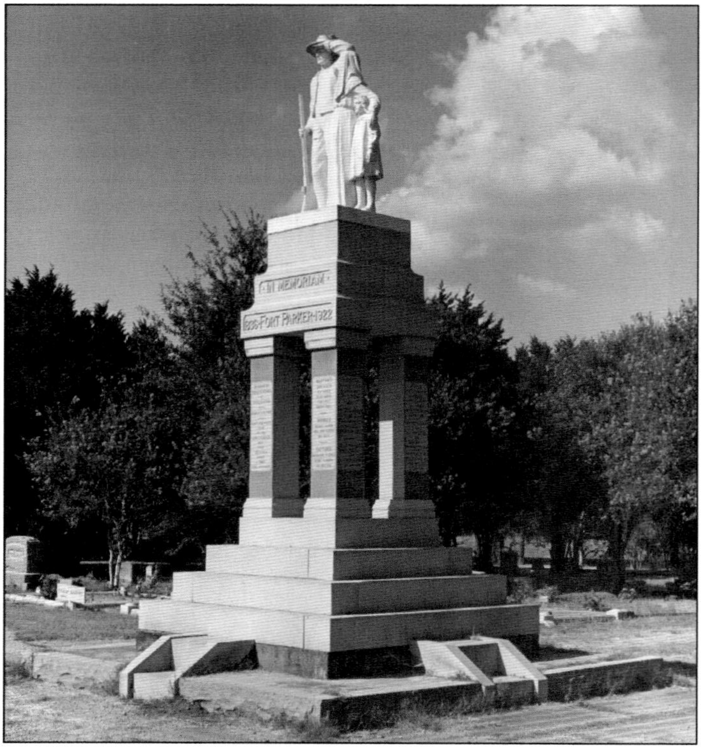

Funded by appropriations of the 37th Texas Legislature and individual donations, the Pioneer Monument was erected in Fort Parker Memorial Park in 1922 in memory of the first pioneers. A statue of Silas and Lucy Parker and their daughter Cynthia Ann was erected atop the monument in 1932. It was funded by the 42nd legislature and through donations from the citizens of Groesbeck. (Limestone County Historical Museum.)

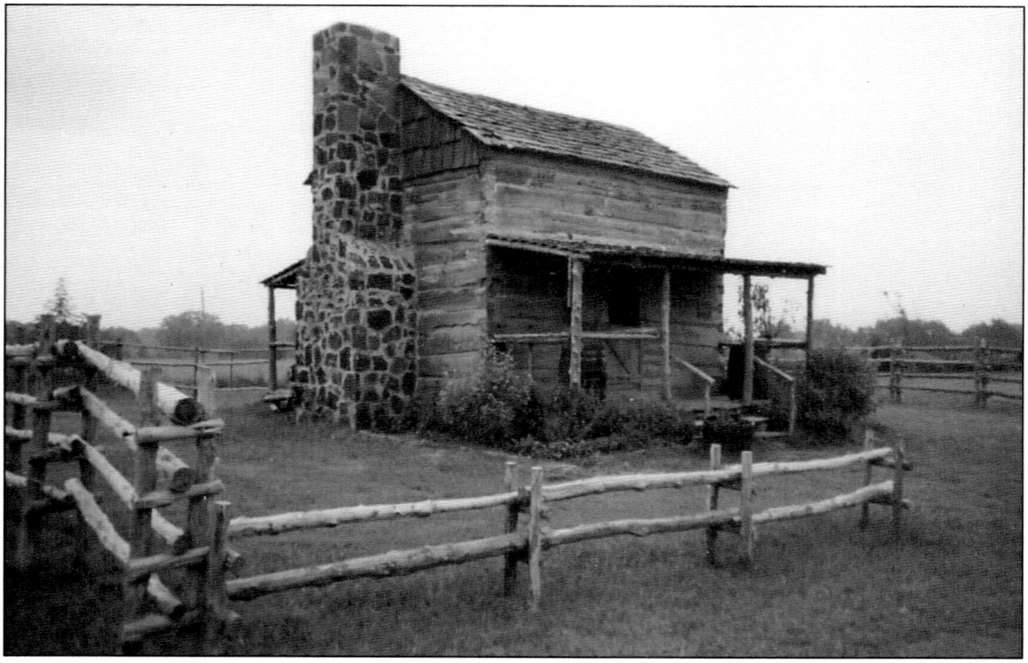

Following the Indian attack, Fort Parker was abandoned. Its logs were eventually carried away by settlers and used as building materials. It is believed that Mordecia Yell, a Methodist circuit preacher, used logs from the abandoned fort to build this two-story cabin in 1850. The restored Yell Cabin, which was relocated to the Old Fort Parker site, can now be toured by visitors. (Old Fort Parker.)

After receiving a land grant, Elisha Anglin and his family came to Limestone County with the Parkers. Except for his son Abram, he moved his family to Fort Houston in early 1836. Leaving the area after the attack on Fort Parker, he returned several times beginning in 1838, helped to lay out the town of Springfield, and permanently settled his family in the county in 1844. (DeGoyler Library, Southern Methodist University, Ag2008.0005.)

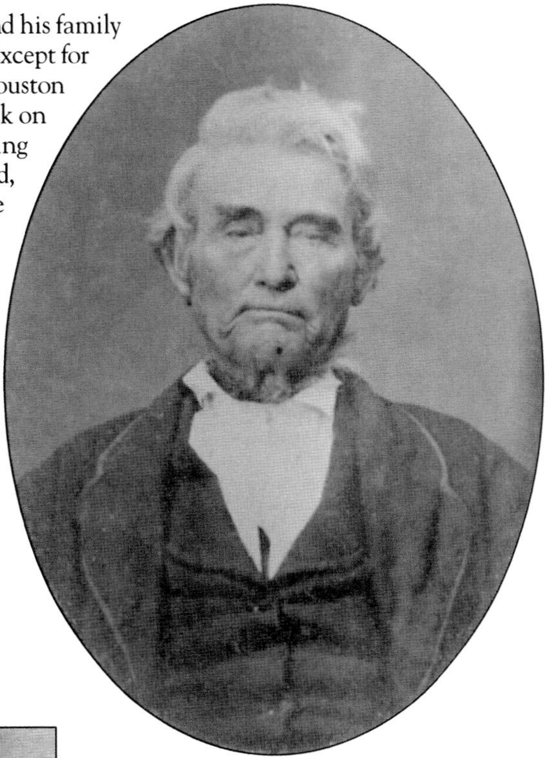

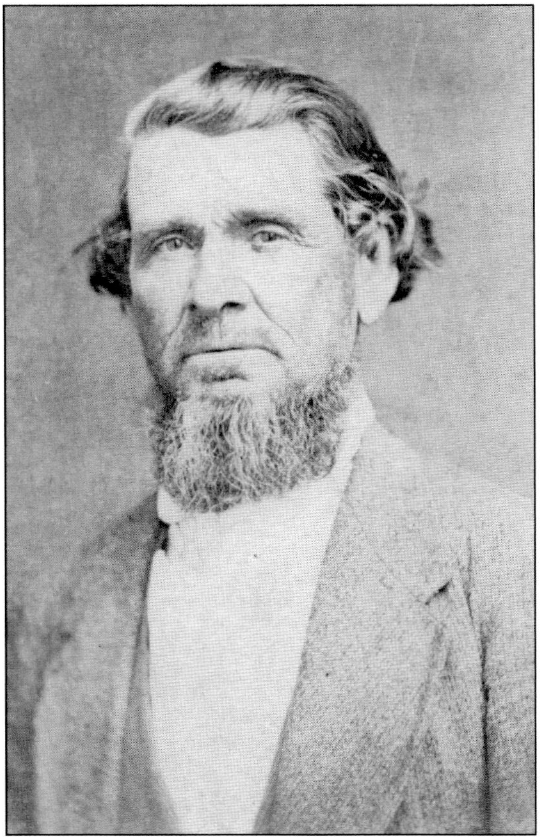

Abram Anglin and his father, Elisha Anglin, were working in the fields on May 19, 1836, when they were informed by L.T.M. Plummer of the attack on Fort Parker. They, along with Plummer, David and Evan Faulkenberry, and Seth and Silas Bates, helped rescue some of the settlers and led one group of survivors to safety at Fort Houston. (The Texas Collection at Baylor University.)

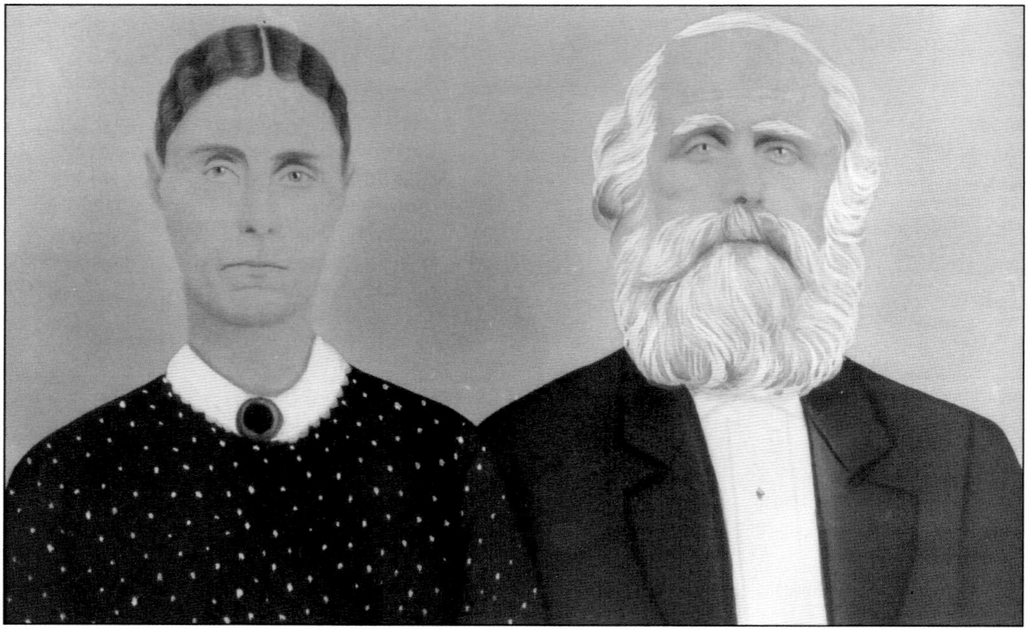

L.T.M. Plummer came to Texas with the Parker group and received a land grant out of the Andres Varela Survey. His first wife, Rachel Parker Plummer, and their son John Pratt were two of the five captives taken during the attack on Fort Parker. In addition to farming, he served several years as a Texas Ranger. He is pictured with his third wife, Ageline. (Limestone County Historical Museum.)

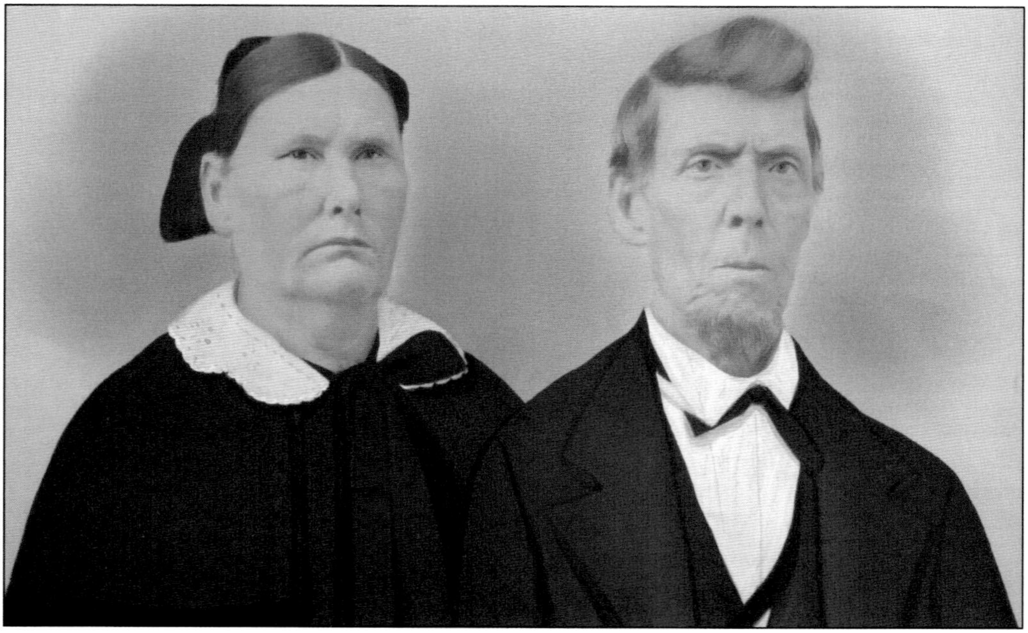

Silas Bates accompanied his father, Seth, to Texas. Silas built his cabin in 1835 at Bates Spring near Groesbeck, where the city park is now located. After the Indian attack on Fort Parker, he helped lead one of two groups of survivors to Fort Houston. The Bates family permanently settled in Limestone County in 1843. Silas is pictured with his second wife, Adaline. (Limestone County Historical Museum.)

In 1836, Alfonso Steele, age 17, came to Texas to join the fight for Texas Independence. During the Battle of San Jacinto, he was severely wounded but eventually recovered. He later married Mary Ann Powell, and their family was among the first in Limestone County when they arrived in 1842. Living to the age of 94, he became the last survivor of the Battle of San Jacinto. (William Reagan.)

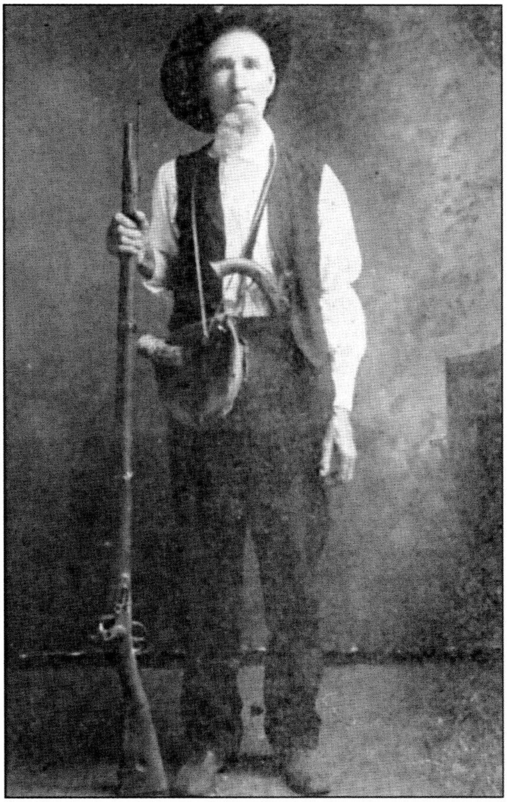

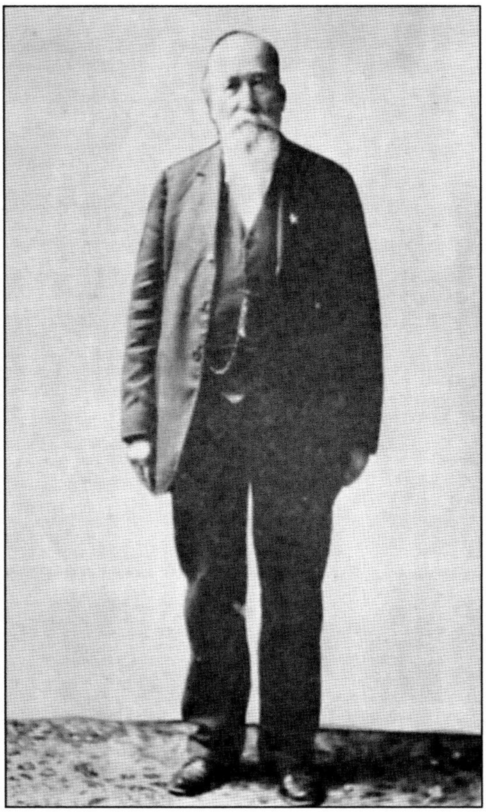

Hampton Steele was the eldest son of Alfonso and Mary Ann Steele. He came with his parents to present-day Limestone County as a young boy in 1842. In 1925, he wrote *A History of Limestone County 1833–1860*, which provides valuable information about Limestone County's earliest settlers, first school, and first courthouses. (William Reagan.)

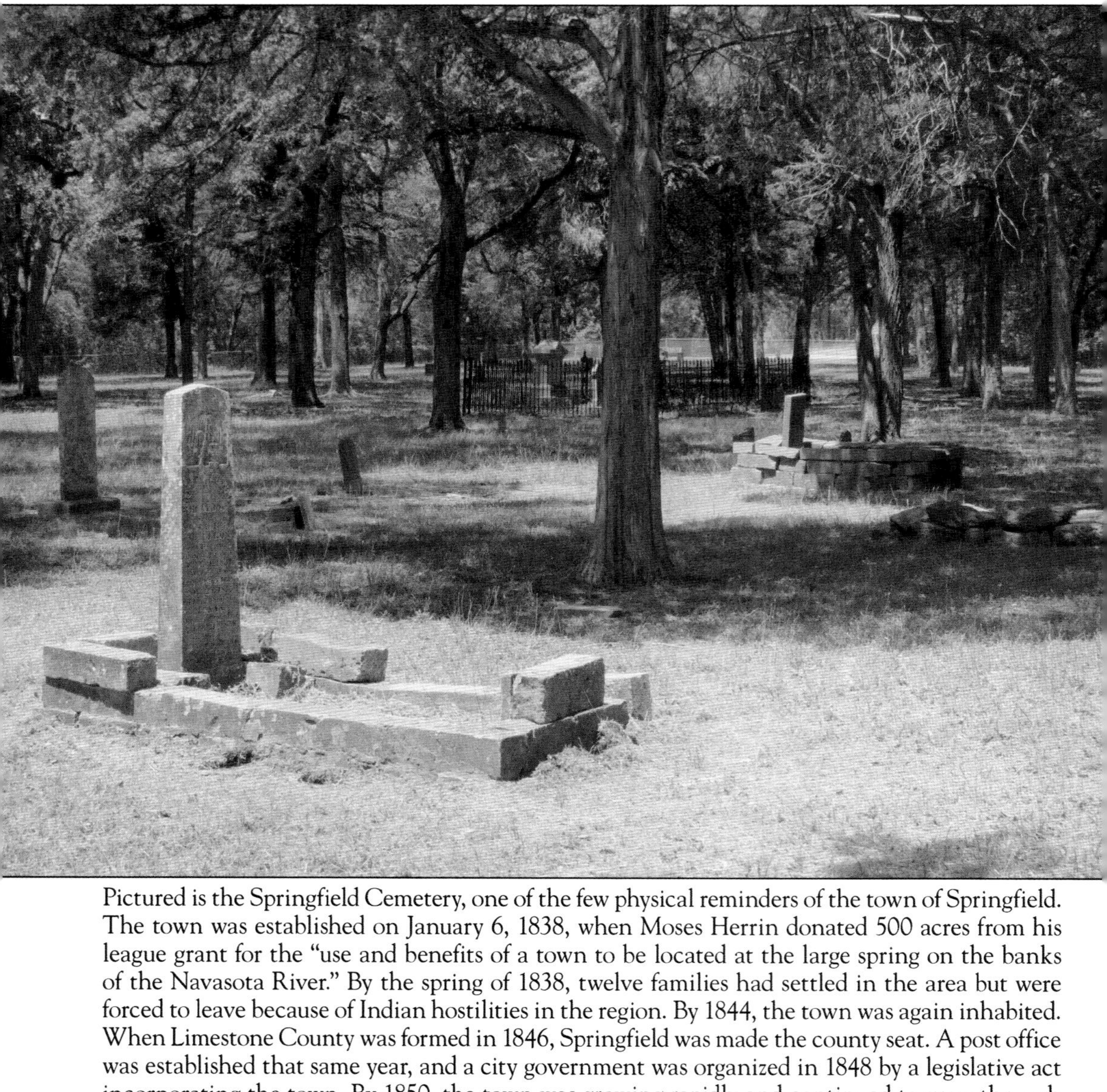

Pictured is the Springfield Cemetery, one of the few physical reminders of the town of Springfield. The town was established on January 6, 1838, when Moses Herrin donated 500 acres from his league grant for the "use and benefits of a town to be located at the large spring on the banks of the Navasota River." By the spring of 1838, twelve families had settled in the area but were forced to leave because of Indian hostilities in the region. By 1844, the town was again inhabited. When Limestone County was formed in 1846, Springfield was made the county seat. A post office was established that same year, and a city government was organized in 1848 by a legislative act incorporating the town. By 1850, the town was growing rapidly and continued to grow through the start of the Civil War. Other Limestone County communities established before the Civil War include Tehuacana, Personville, Lost Prairie, Eutaw, Honest Ridge, Tidwell, Eaton, Phifer Chapel, Head's Prairie, Lewisville, Davis Prairie, Ferguson Prairie, Hog Range, and Sulphur Springs. (William Reagan.)

Two

Civil War to World War

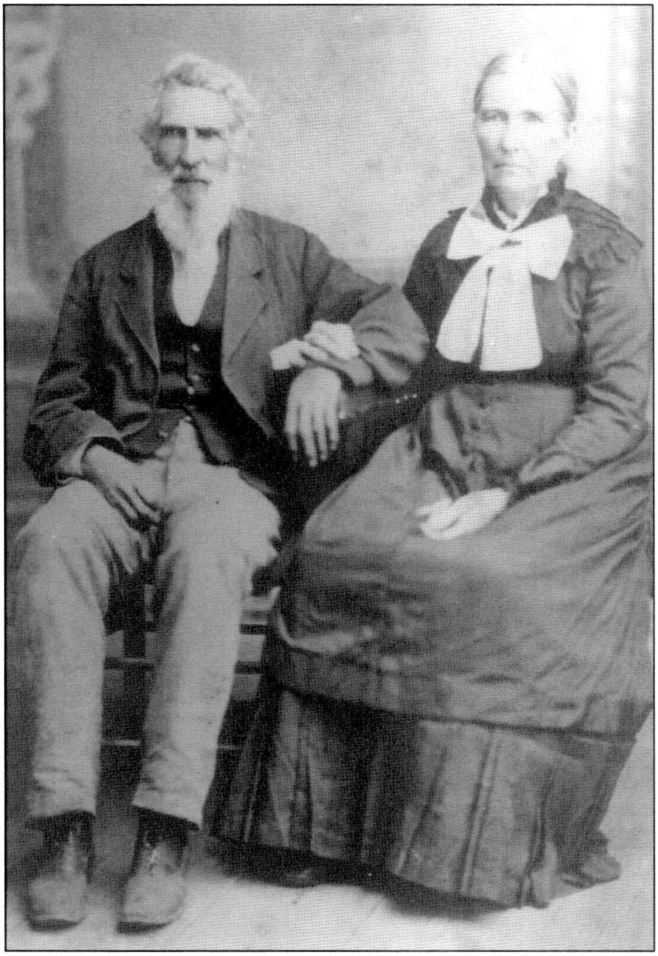

Shortly after his birth in Morgan County, Georgia, on October 10, 1814, Logan A. Stroud's family moved to Alabama and in 1837 to Robertson County, Texas. On May 19, 1842, he married Jane Elizabeth Harlan and moved to present-day Limestone County. Logan Stroud was the largest slave owner in Limestone County, having 156 slaves just prior to emancipation. (Logan D. Wilson.)

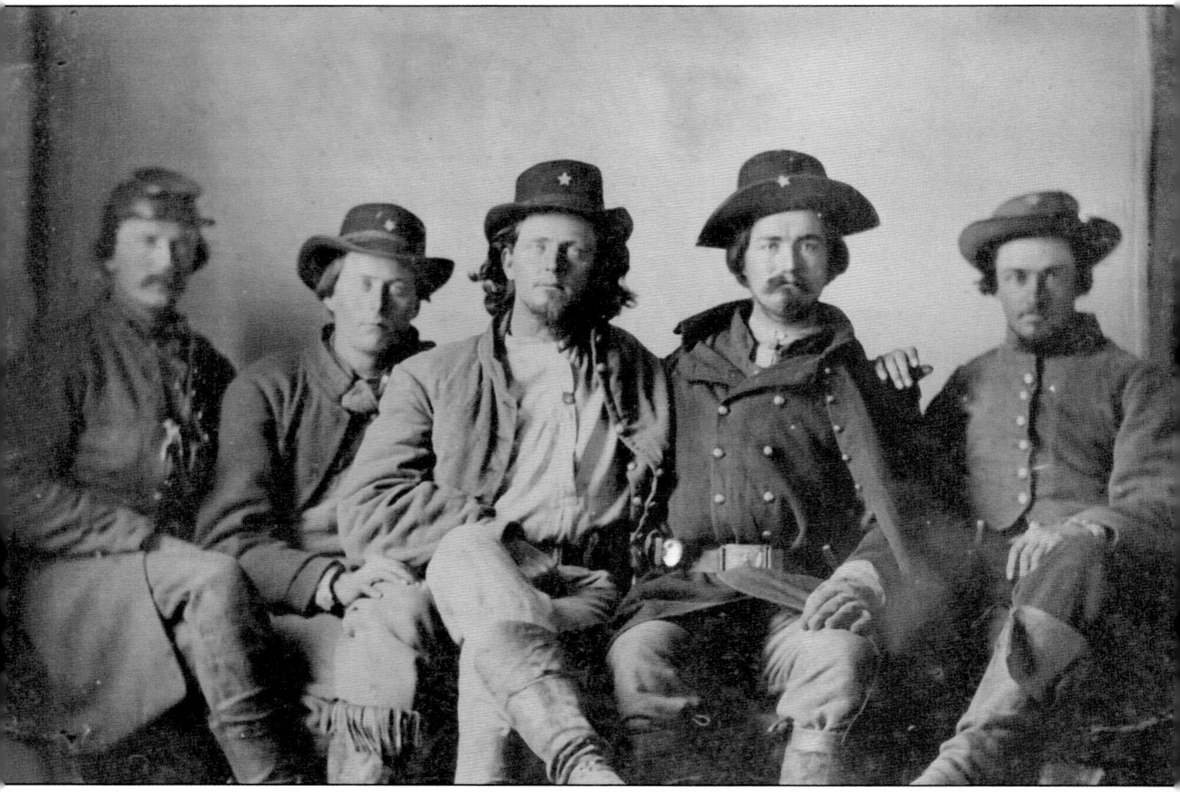

In 1861, Texas seceded from the Union. About three-fourths of Limestone County's voting-eligible residents served in the Confederate army. A company of Limestone County men was organized at Springfield under the command of Capt. Lochlin Johnson Farrar. Another company, known as the Eutaw Blues, was organized at Eutaw under Capt. Anson F. Moss and became Company K of the 12th Texas Calvary. Additional companies were organized by Green B. Duncan, J.L. Billington, Hardy Jones, D.M. Pendergast, William J. Rasco, R.C. Robison, and H.H. Stevenson. Some men were conscripted to stay at home to serve in the Home Guard, while other men organized independent groups and traveled to other places to enlist. The five men pictured here were part of a group of 20 men who traveled from Springfield to Houston, where on September 8, 1861, they enlisted in Company C of the 8th Texas Cavalry, better known as Terry's Texas Rangers. From left to right are Peter Kendall, Dick Oliver, Felix G. Kennedy, William A. Lynch, and Thomas Burney. (Panhandle-Plains Historical Museum.)

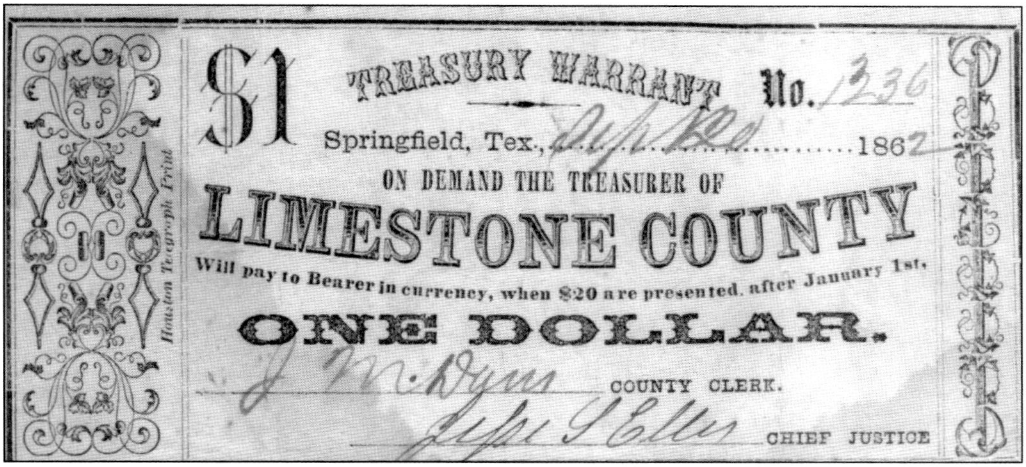

$1 TREASURY WARRANT No. 1236

Springfield, Tex., ...1862

ON DEMAND THE TREASURER OF

LIMESTONE COUNTY

Will pay to Bearer in currency, when $20 are presented, after January 1st,

ONE DOLLAR.

COUNTY CLERK.

CHIEF JUSTICE

Houston Telegraph Print

After Texas seceded from the Union, the people of Limestone County had to wait several months before Confederate currency arrived. In order for the county government to transact business, several thousand dollars worth of treasury warrants in various denominations were issued. This 1862 Limestone County treasury warrant had a value of $1. (Limestone County Historical Museum.)

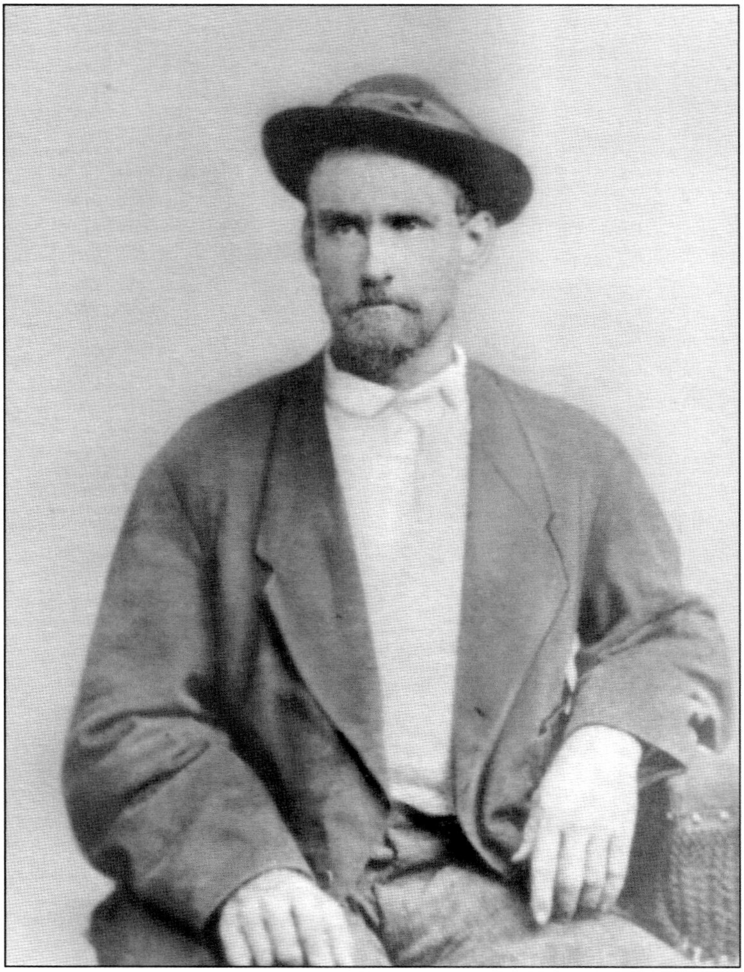

In 1861, Thomas Burney was 19 years old when he left Springfield and traveled to Houston, where he and about 20 other Limestone County men enlisted with Terry's Texas Rangers. This photograph of Burney was taken in New Orleans in 1865 on his trip back to Limestone County at the end of the war. (Harry Walters.)

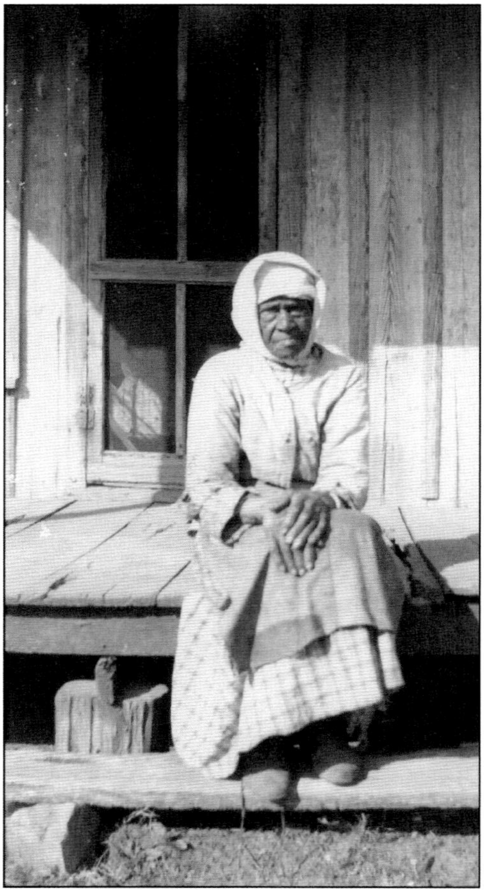

In 1850, there were 618 slaves owned by 114 men in Limestone County; 15 men owned more than half of all the slaves in the county. By 1860, the number of slaves increased to 884, including Kate Curry, who was born into slavery but was freed by Lincoln's Emancipation Proclamation in 1865. She was 103 years old when this photograph was taken in 1936. (Texas Collection at Baylor University.)

On June 19, 1865, the Emancipation Proclamation was read on the Logan Stroud plantation, signaling freedom for slaves in the county. Shown below is Booker T. Washington Park, site of annual Juneteenth celebrations dating back to the 1860s. The tabernacle (foreground) was used for church and educational services. The upstairs of the pavilion (background) was used for dancing. Concessions were located on the ground floor. (Limestone County Historical Museum.)

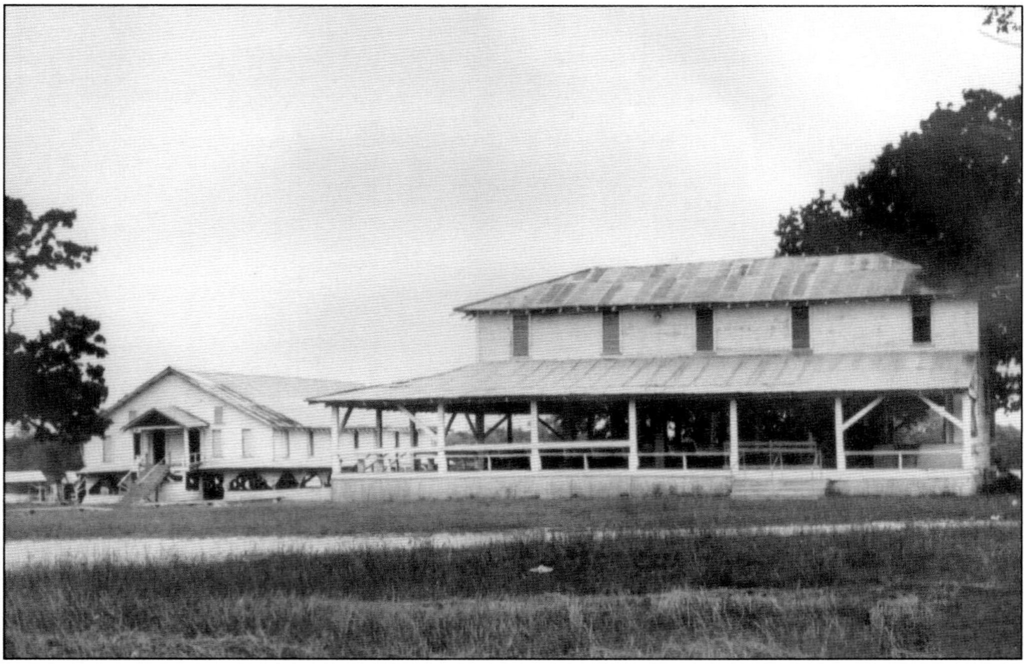

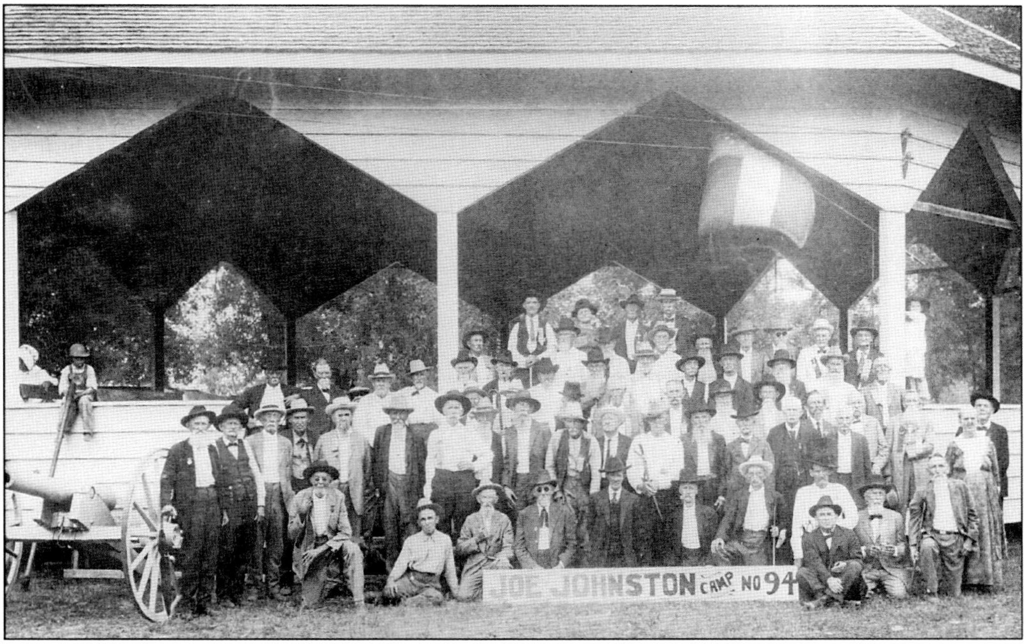

In the 1880s, small groups of Limestone County Confederate veterans began to meet informally to socialize and reminisce about the war. In 1888, they began meeting annually at the site where Jack's Creek enters the Navasota River and, in the following year, organized the Joseph E. Johnston Camp of the United Confederate Veterans. This photograph shows the Confederate veterans attending the 1921 reunion. (Gibbs Memorial Library.)

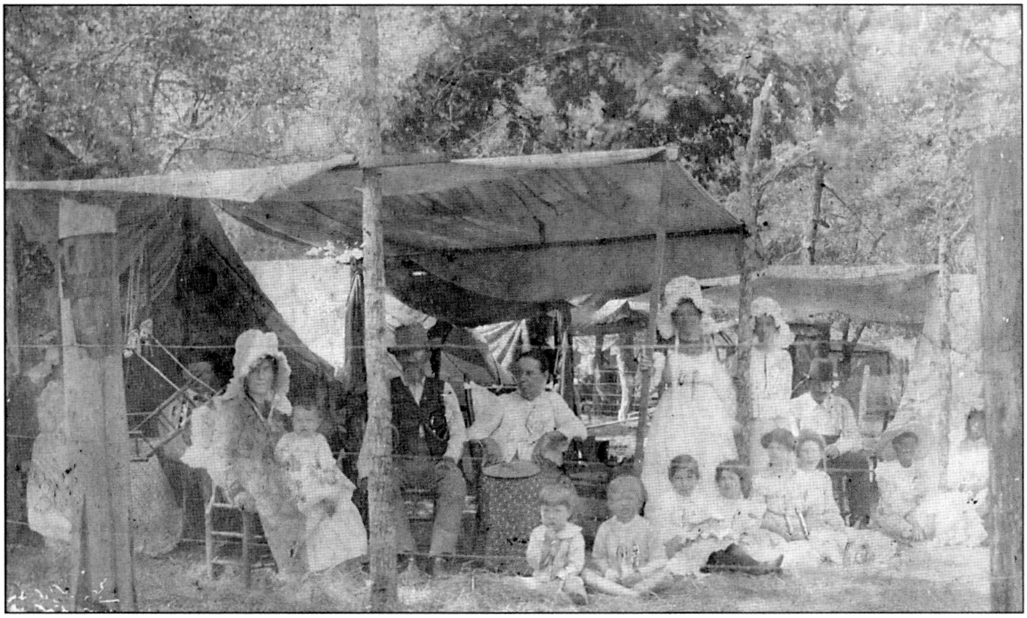

In 1892, veterans and families began purchasing lots at the Confederate Reunion Grounds for $5 each to pay for the first 20 acres of land purchased from the Mexía family for the sum of $200. Each purchaser received a deed for camping privileges at the annual reunions. As the crowds grew larger each year, additional tracts of land were purchased from several individuals. (Limestone County Historical Museum.)

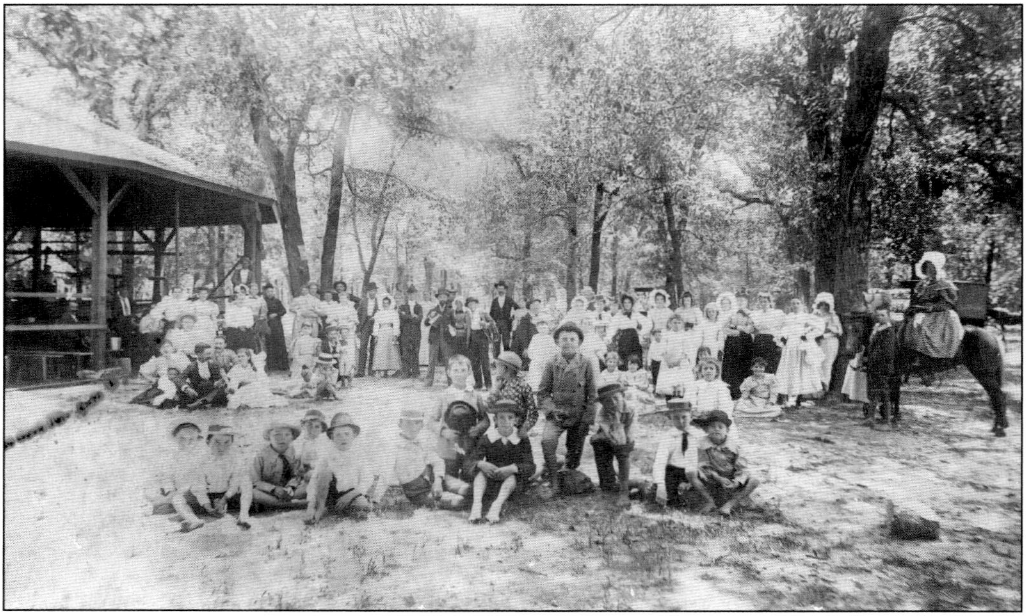

The annual reunions at the Confederate Reunion Grounds were weeklong affairs. Upward of 7,000 people from all over the county and from different parts of the state would meet at the site in late July or early August during the time of the full moon. Tents were erected and brush arbors constructed so that entire families could camp out for the duration. (Gibbs Memorial Library.)

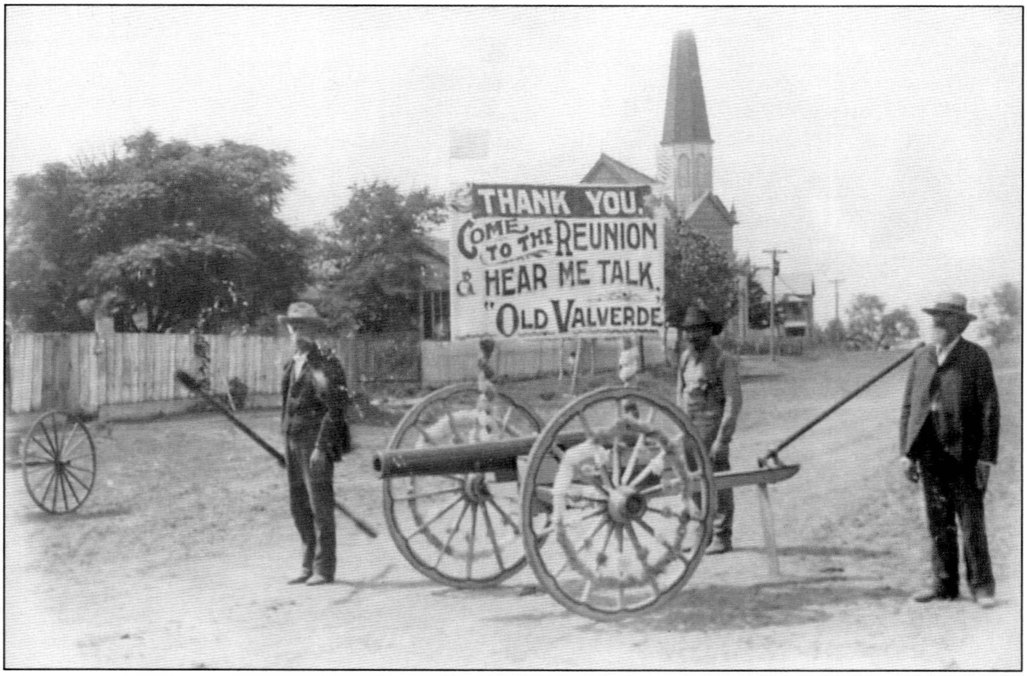

This photograph shows the Val Verde Cannon being rolled out for the annual reunion in the late 1890s. It was one of two Union cannons captured by Confederates at the Battle of Mansfield, Louisiana, in 1864. Today, it is on display at the Confederate Reunion Grounds, while her sister cannon resides in neighboring Freestone County. During the reunions, the cannon was fired each day at dawn and dusk. (Gibbs Memorial Library.)

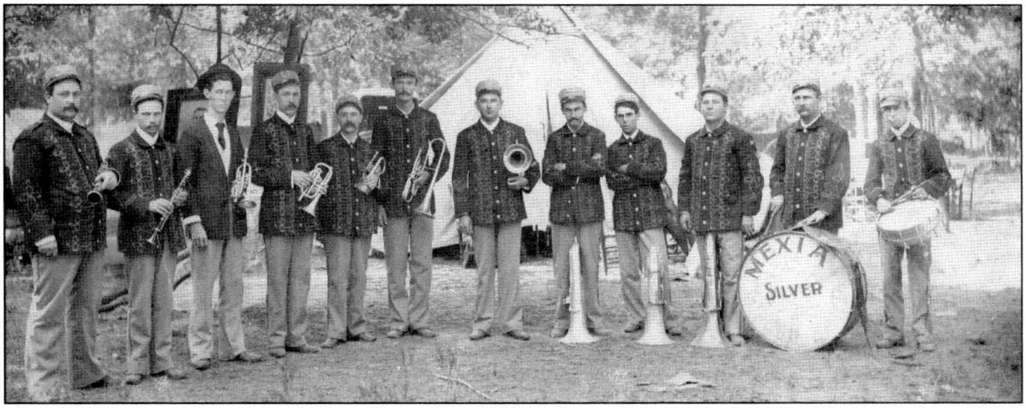

In addition to eulogizing Confederate veterans who had died during the previous year, the annual gatherings at the Confederate Reunion Grounds included parades, brass-band concerts, patriotic speeches, games, and traditional Southern foods. The midway, where carnival people hawked their sideshows or rides, was especially popular with the children. Shown here is the Silver Coronets, who provided the music during the reunion's early days. (Gibbs Memorial Library.)

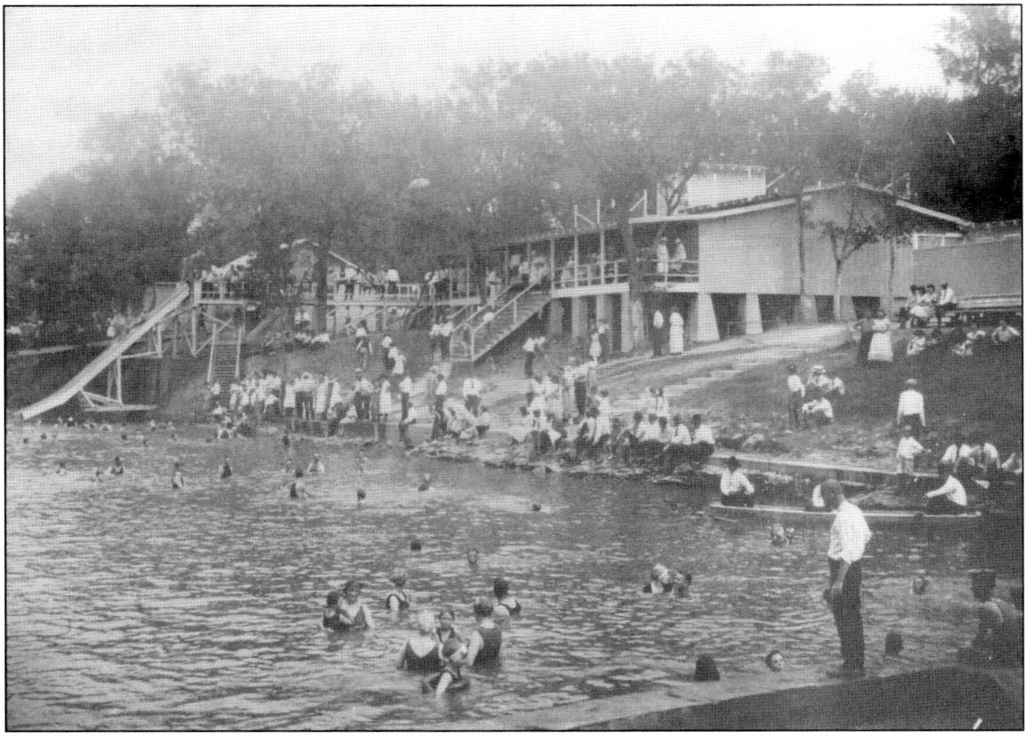

In November 1920, wildcatter Albert E. Humphreys struck oil in Limestone County, and Mexia, with one of the largest oil fields in the world, became a boomtown. While other Texas reunion grounds faded away with the demise of older veterans, Humphreys brought improvements and a surge of renewed activity to the Confederate Reunion Grounds, including the Pure Oil Company clubhouse and a large bathhouse on the creek. (Gibbs Memorial Library.)

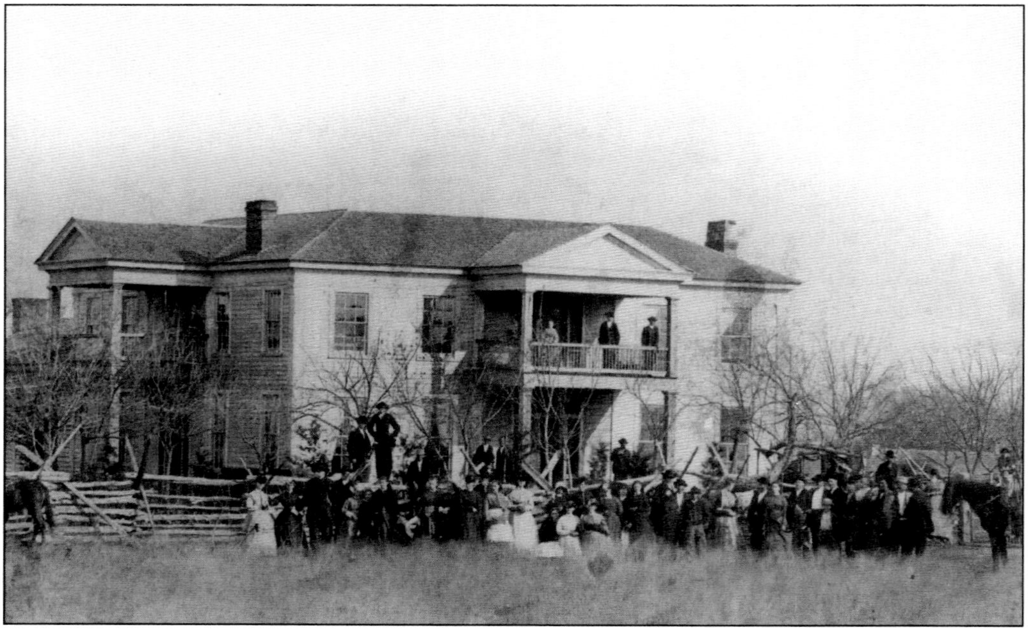

The town of Tehuacana was founded in 1847 by John Boyd on the site of the abandoned Tawakoni Indian village. The town finished third in an unsuccessful bid to become the state capital in 1850, after Austin and Palestine. In 1869, Boyd persuaded the Cumberland Presbyterian Church to establish Trinity University at Tehuacana. Above, the faculty and students of Trinity University stand in front of Boyd House, which was given to the university by Boyd in 1869. This building was used as the first classroom for the university. Later, it was used for the female department and then by the law school. In the photograph below is the original Trinity administrative classroom building shortly after it was completed in 1873. The designer, Alpha Young, is standing in the doorway. (Both, Trinity University Special Collections and Archives.)

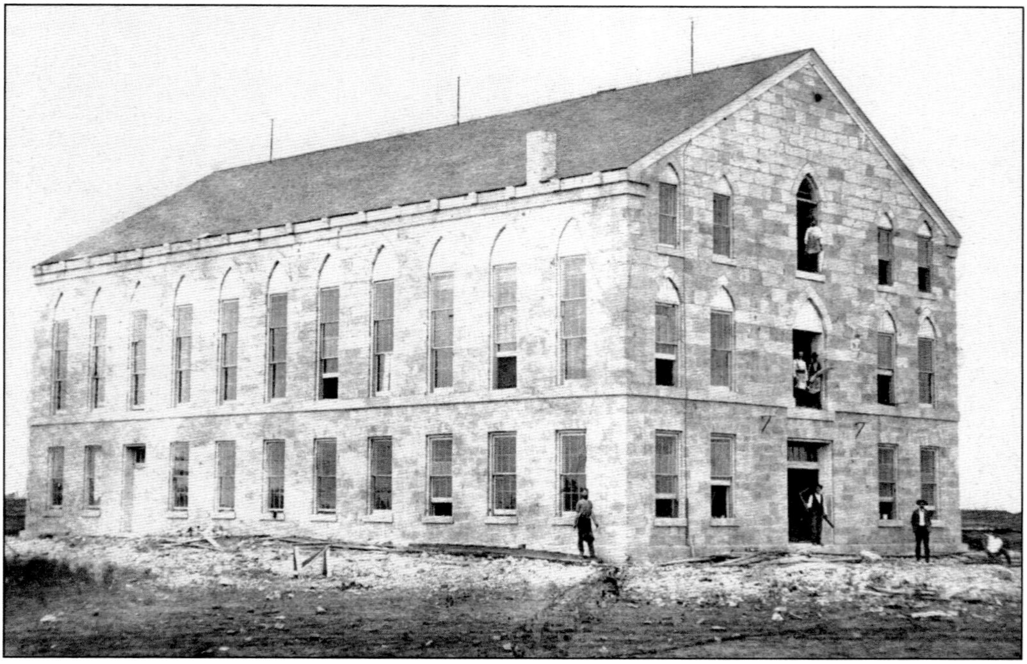

The photograph at right shows the addition of the south wing to the original administrative classroom building that was completed in 1892. In addition to the chapel, which seated 600, the building contained 26 large rooms designed for classrooms, laboratories, society halls, offices, and a library. Even with the passing of time, the building still stands proudly on the hill at Tehuacana. In more recent times, the dome had to be removed from the building, but it is the hope of many county residents to have it replaced in the near future. The photograph below, taken in 1898, shows the interior of the physical science lab in the administrative building. It was said to have had the most modern equipment of the day. (Both, Trinity University Special Collections and Archives.)

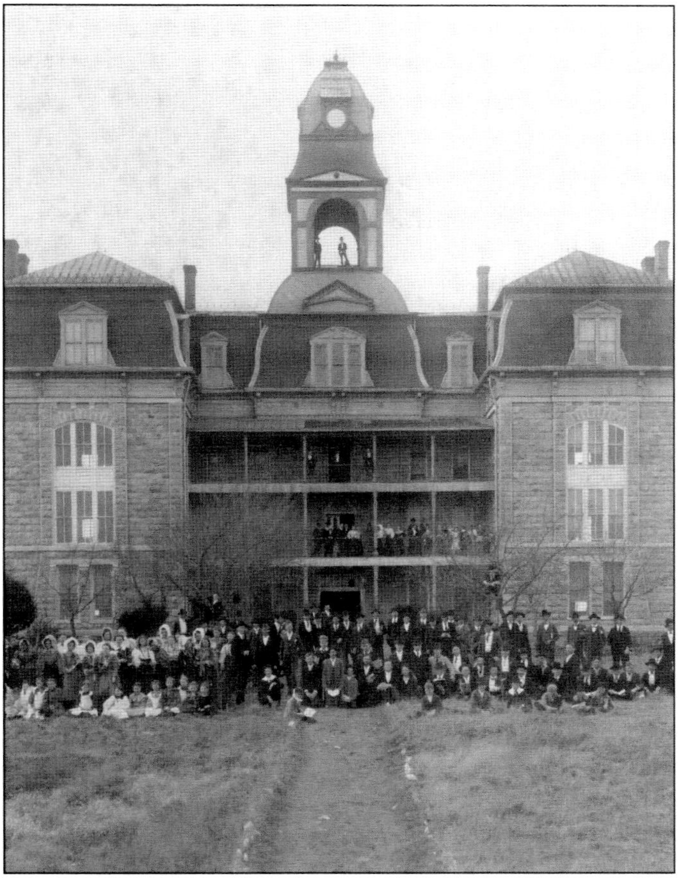

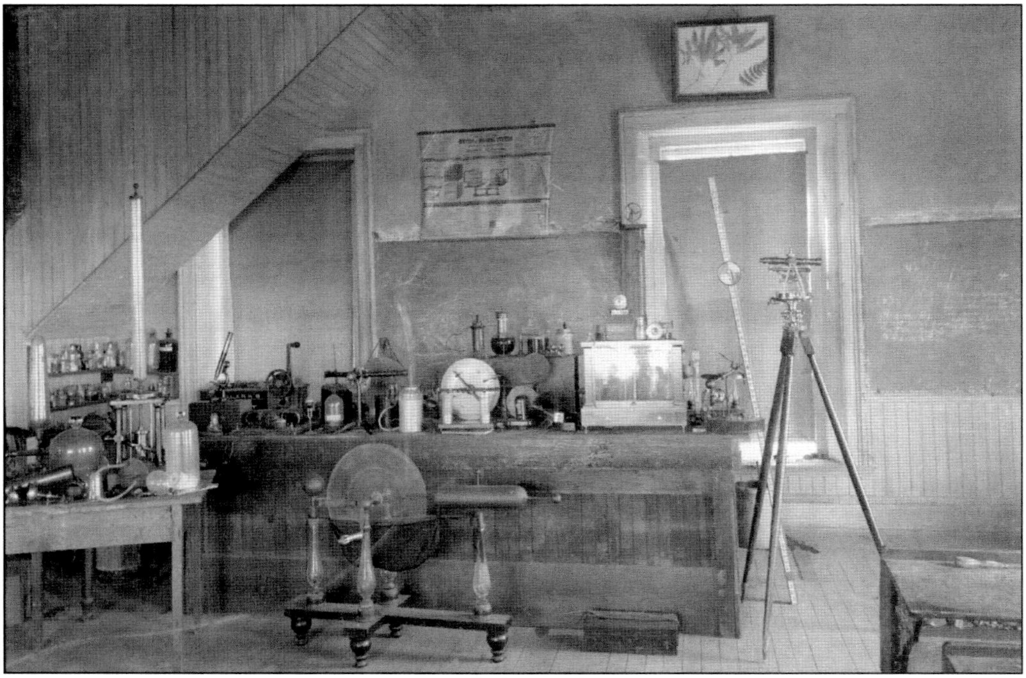

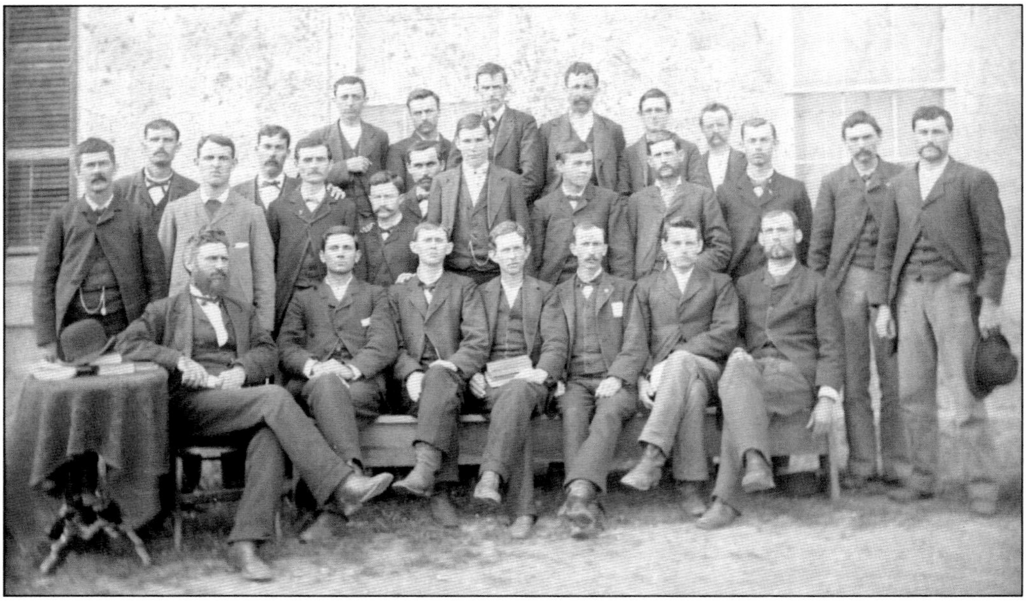

This photograph of the Timothean Society at Trinity University was taken during the 1884–1885 school year. This organization originally functioned as a theology class for pre-ministerial students. It was reorganized in 1891 as a pre-ministerial literary society. The students are pictured with Benjamin McLeskey (seated with arm on table), Trinity University's third president, who served from 1883 to 1885. (Trinity University Special Collections and Archives.)

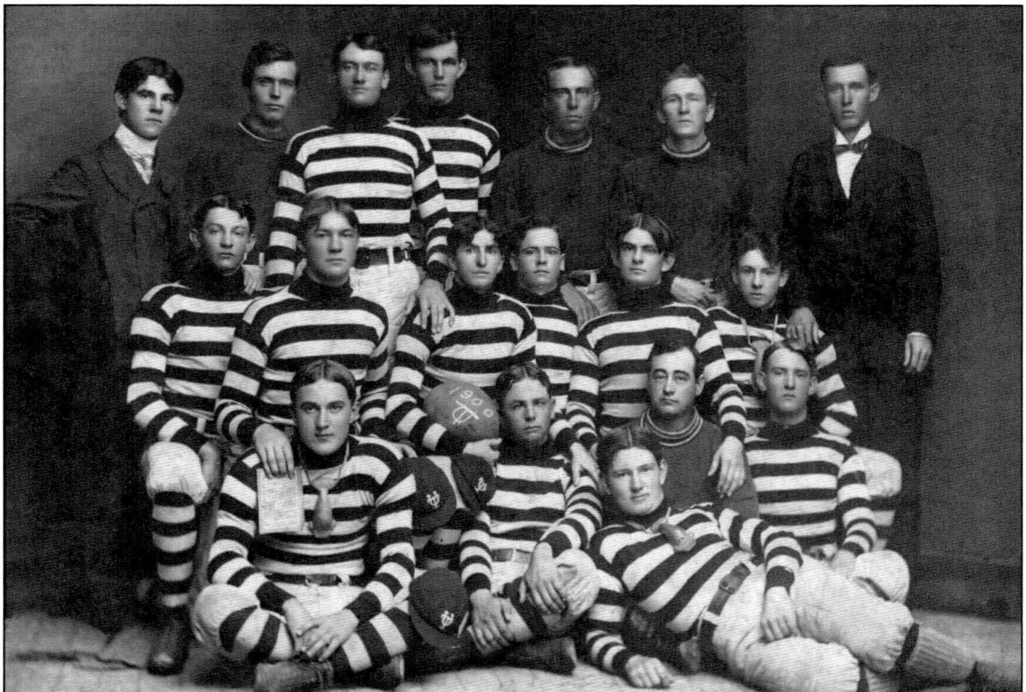

The Trinity University football team poses in 1900. This was the university's first intercollegiate football team; its first game was in Waco against Baylor University. Unfortunately, Trinity was defeated by a score of 17-0. (Trinity University Special Collections and Archives.)

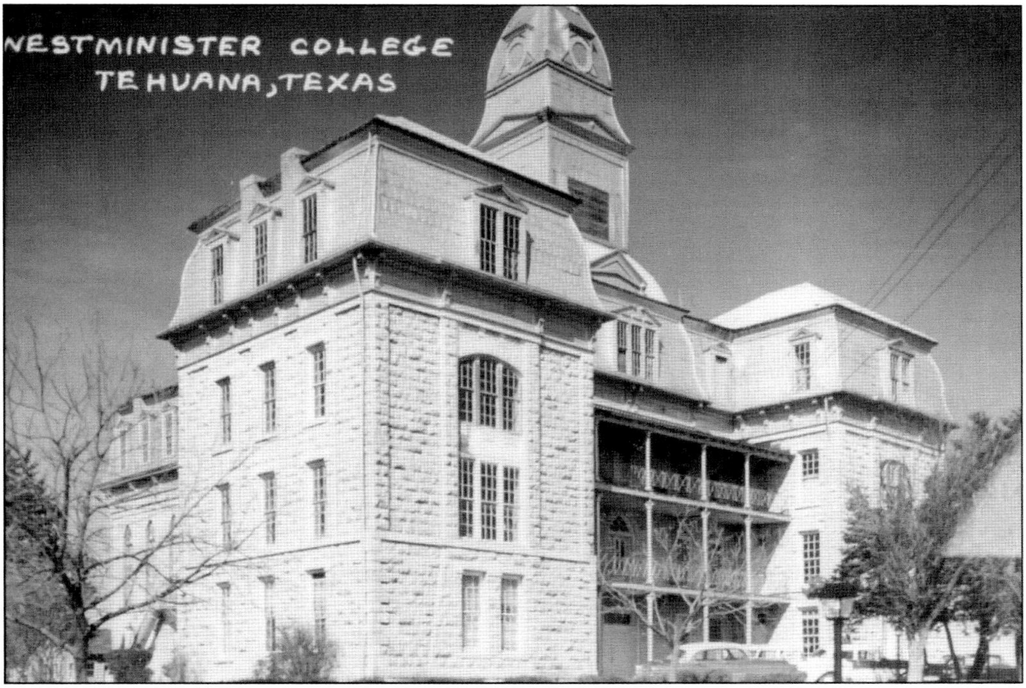

In 1902, Trinity University moved to Waxahachie, and the Tehuacana campus was deeded to the Methodist Protestant Church. Westminster College was successfully operated as a four-year school until 1916, when it became the first officially accredited junior college in Texas. In 1942, the property was given to Southwestern University, which closed the school eight years later. In 1953, it was sold to the Congregational Methodist Church, which established the Westminster College and Bible Institute, offering an associate of arts degree and a four-year curriculum leading to a bachelor of religion degree. In 1969, the college had 95 students, but by 1970, the student body had decreased to 60. With only 35 students in 1971, the college was moved to Florence, Mississippi. Both photographs show the Westminster campus during the 1950s. (Both, Limestone County Historical Museum.)

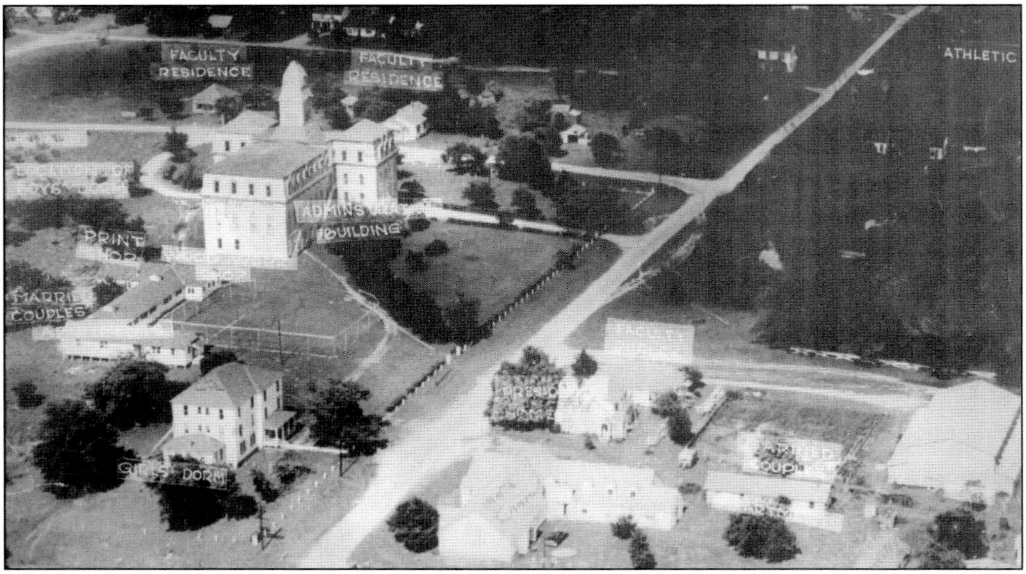

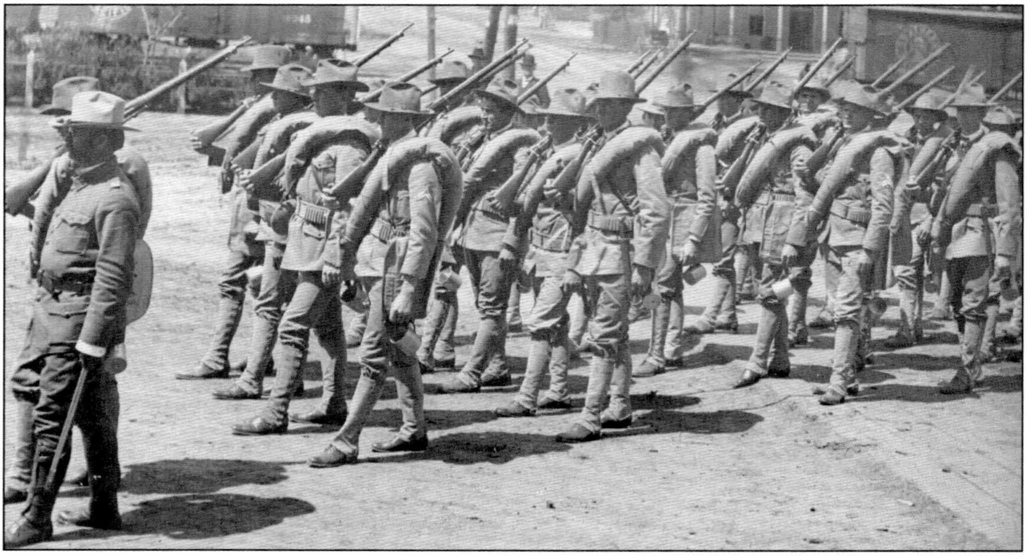

This photograph shows the local unit of the Texas State Militia, the Mexia Minute Men, waiting to board the train for service in the Spanish-American War. The unit was mustered into service on May 12, 1898, as Company L of the 2nd Texas Volunteers and stationed in Florida to defend against a possible Spanish attack from Cuba. The men were mustered out of service on November 9, 1898. (Gibbs Memorial Library.)

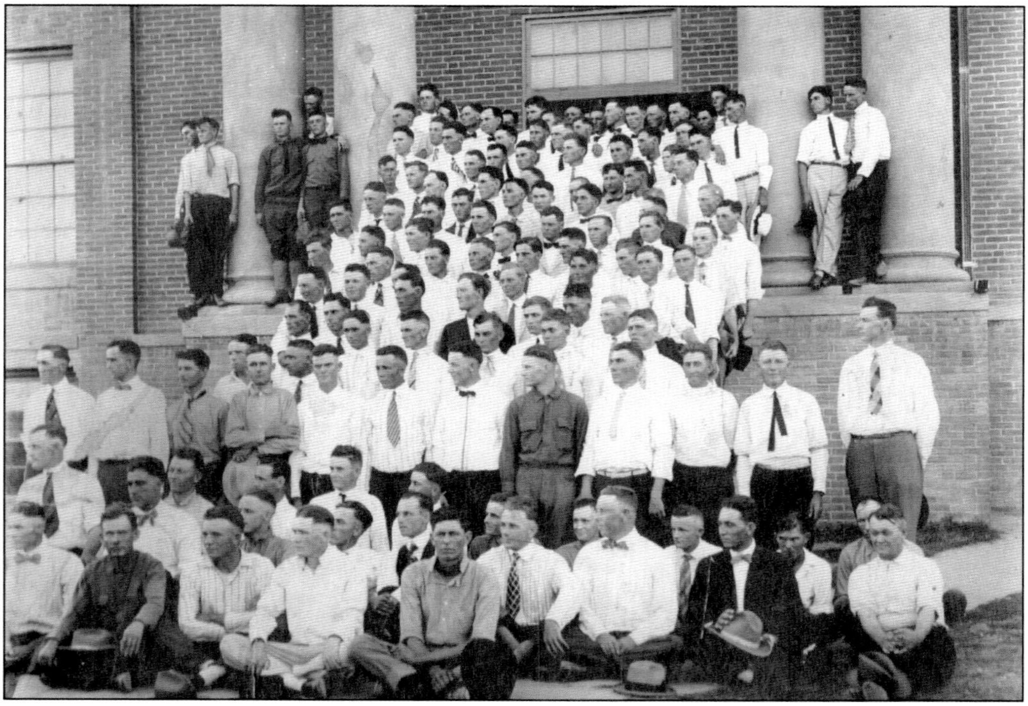

Pictured are the members of Company K on the front steps of the old courthouse. Made up of 140 enlisted men and 3 commissioned officers, largely from Groesbeck and surrounding areas, Company K was assigned to the Sixth Texas Infantry and saw service in Europe during World War I. It was organized in Groesbeck in June 1917 under the commanded of Capt. Scott Reed, a Groesbeck lawyer. (Limestone County Historical Museum.)

Three

Railroad-Era Towns

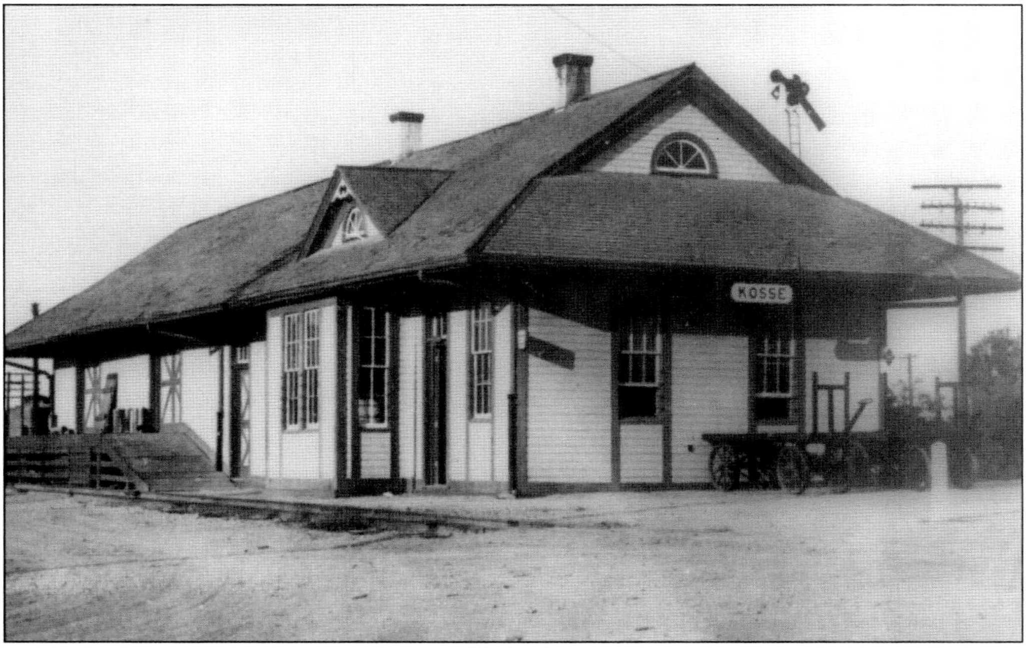

The Houston & Texas Central Railroad reached Limestone County in late 1869 and terminated at a point in the southern part of the county, where the railroad company founded a new town, Kosse. The town was named for Theodore Kosse, a surveyor for the railroad. The Houston & Texas Central Railroad depot in Kosse is shown here. (William Reagan.)

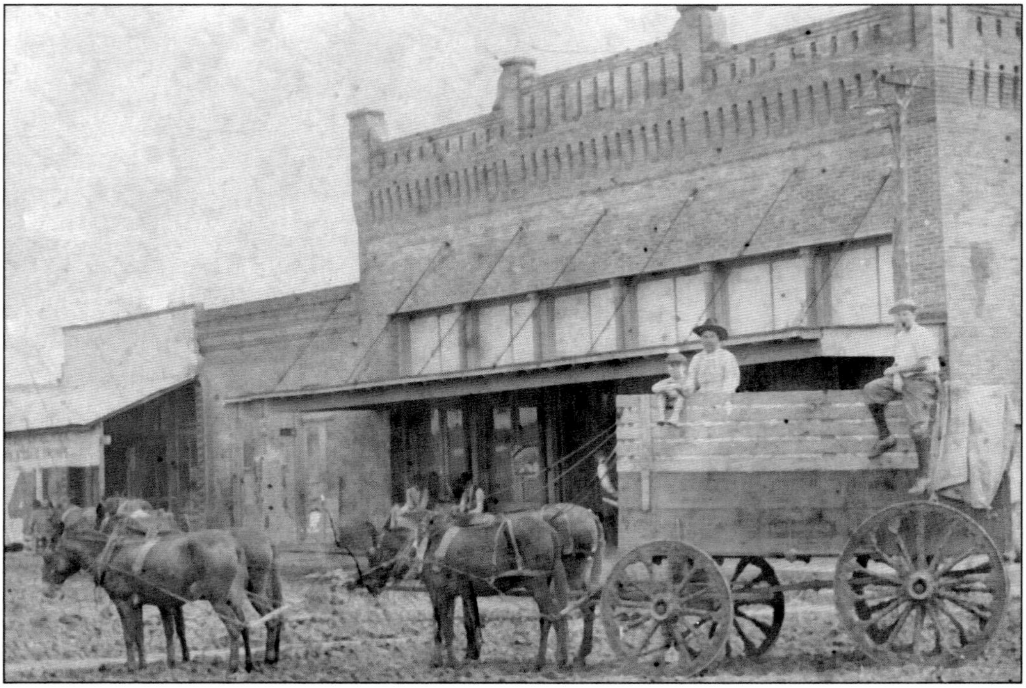

Kosse's city government was established in 1871. By 1880, Kosse had a population of 500 and was home to 39 businesses and 3 churches. In 1884, James O. Jones established the *Kosse Cyclone*, a weekly newspaper that was published until 1943, when it became a supplement of the *Groesbeck Journal*. The first buildings in Kosse were wooden structures, but several brick buildings were erected in the 1870s. Many of the wooden structures burned down; the most destructive fire occurred on December 22, 1895, as a result of which the business blocks were destroyed. Afterward, all buildings were constructed of brick. The early photograph above shows Kosse's muddy Main Street and some of its brick buildings. Below is L.B. Hunt Jr., sitting on the counter in the L.B. Hunt & Son Grocery Store. (Both, Kosse Heritage House.)

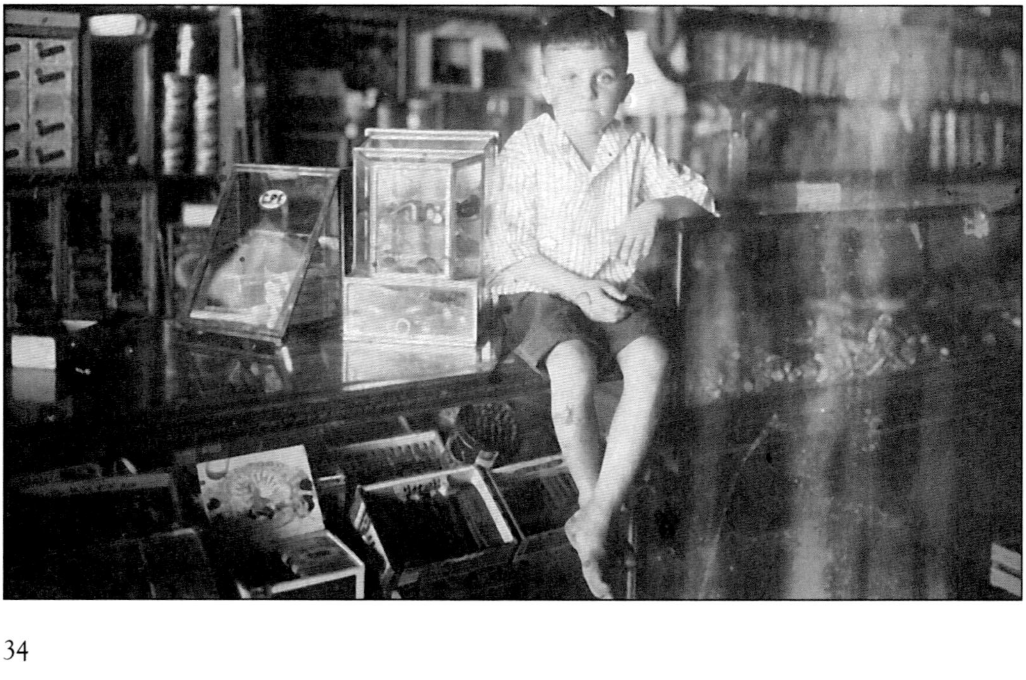

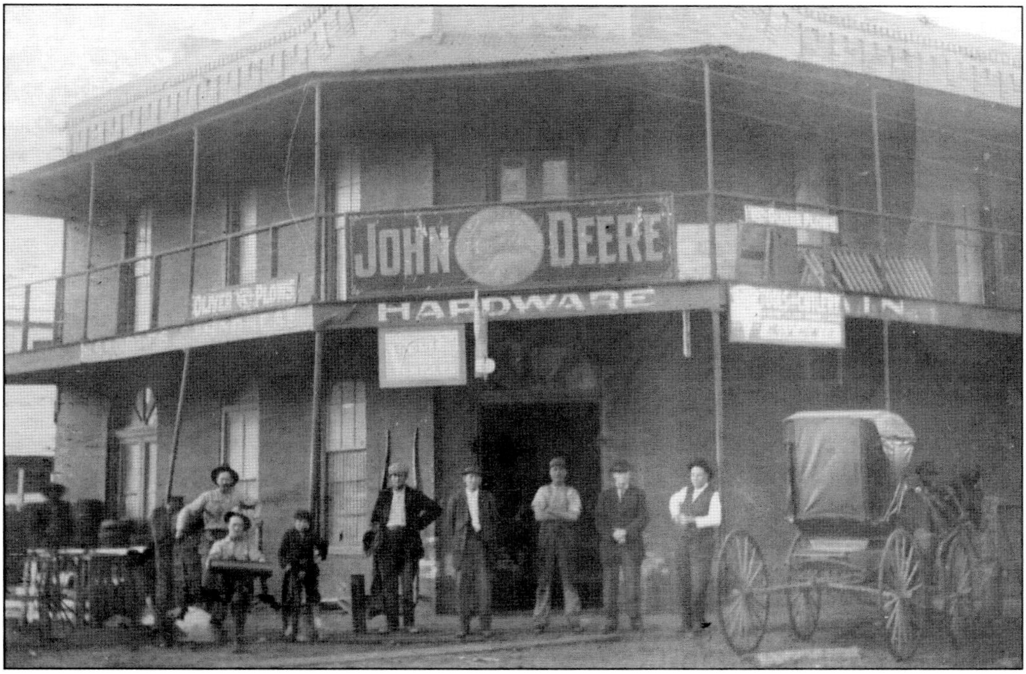

Albert Johnson Jennings and his family settled in the Kosse area in the 1880s. He was a farmer but developed an interest in business. In 1903, he became associated with the Kosse Hardware Company and later became owner. A.J. Jennings is standing on the far left in this photograph of the Kosse Hardware Company. (DeGolyer Library, Southern Methodist University, Ag2005.0001.)

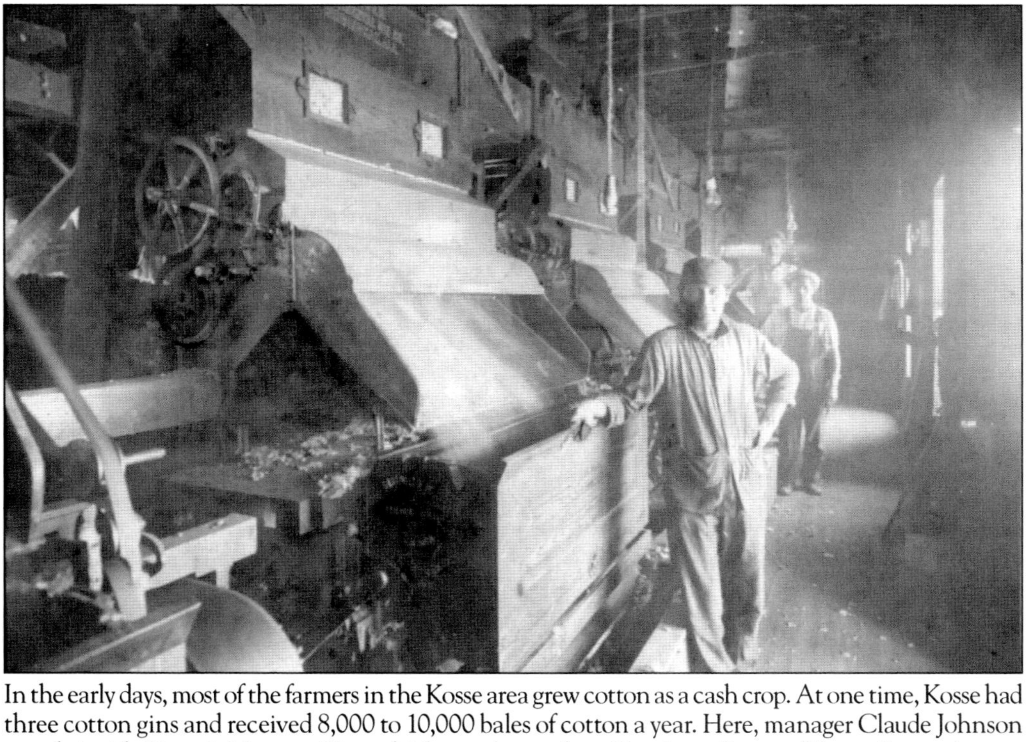

In the early days, most of the farmers in the Kosse area grew cotton as a cash crop. At one time, Kosse had three cotton gins and received 8,000 to 10,000 bales of cotton a year. Here, manager Claude Johnson stands inside Kosse's Munger Gin, which was located on Narcissus Street. (Karen Parten.)

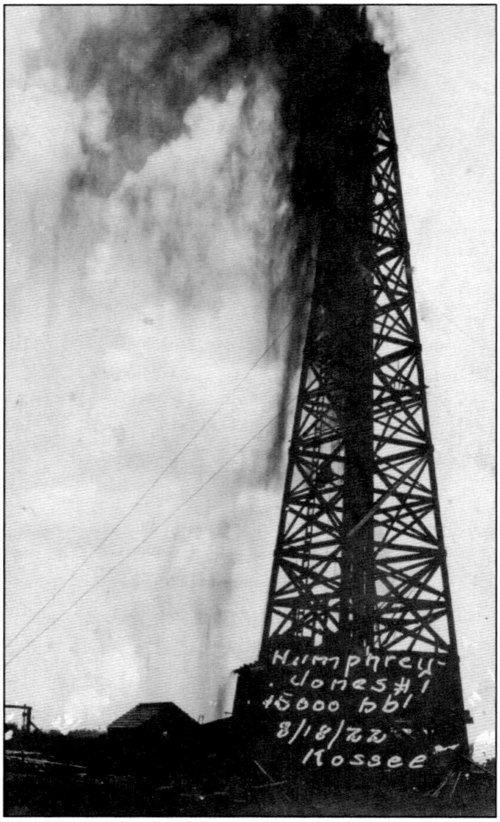

The discovery of oil in 1922 brought prosperity to Kosse. Many buildings were constructed, and several new businesses opened. However, prosperity was short lived. Pictured at left is the Humphreys Jones No. 1 well in Kosse, which was drilled in September 1922. It blew in at 3,800 feet and spewed for 48 hours, producing 50,000 barrels of oil, and then stopped. Over the next two years, 22 wells were drilled in a circle around the Jones well, but each was a dry hole. Below is the Allen Building, which was constructed in 1922 by W.D. Allen. It contained a movie theater, modern gas station, and space for several businesses. (Left, Karen Parten; below, Christine Kelly.)

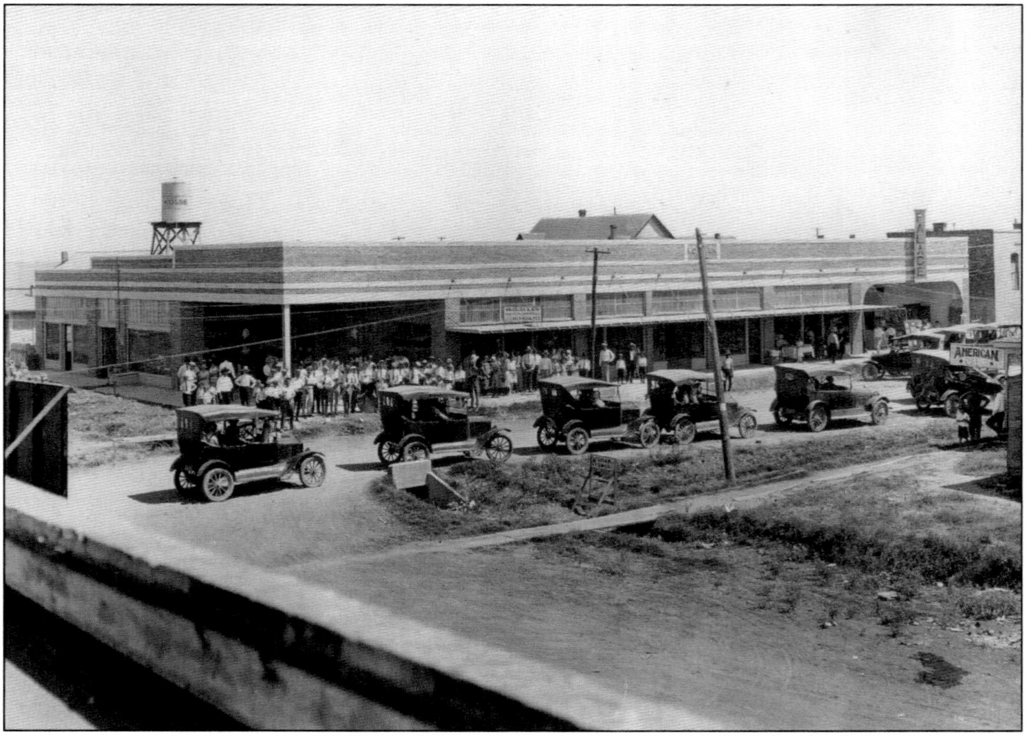

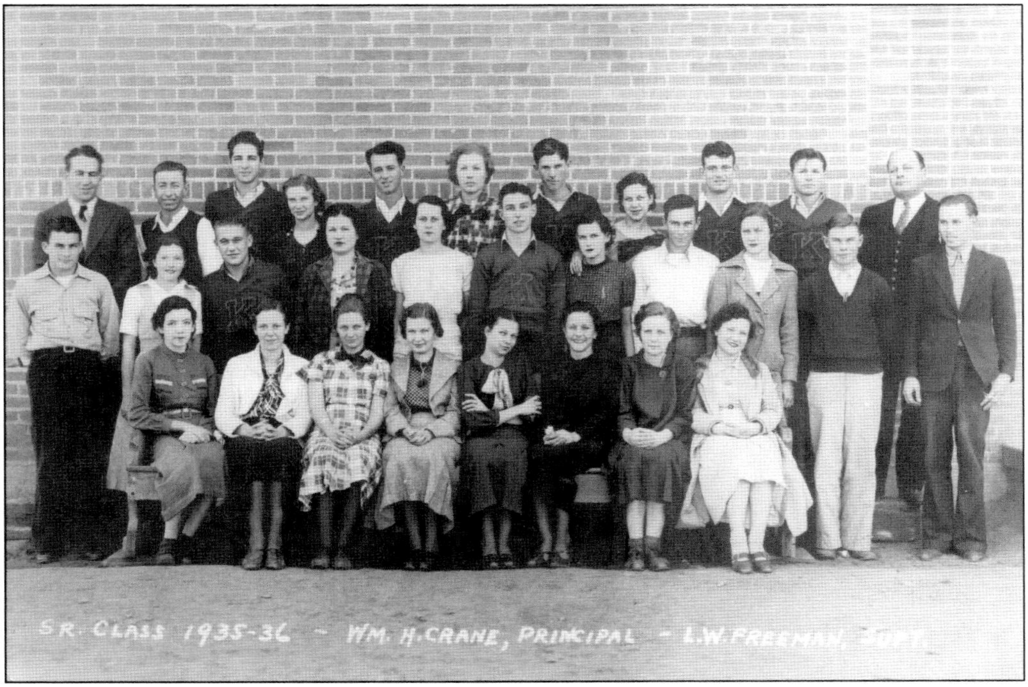

The City of Kosse assumed control of the schools in 1873. This continued until 1907, when the Kosse territory was made into a legal independent school district by a special act of the Texas Legislature. Consolidations with smaller districts increased its size from 10 square miles to 114 square miles. Kosse consolidated with Groesbeck ISD in 1964. Shown above is the Kosse graduating class of 1936. (Kosse Heritage House.)

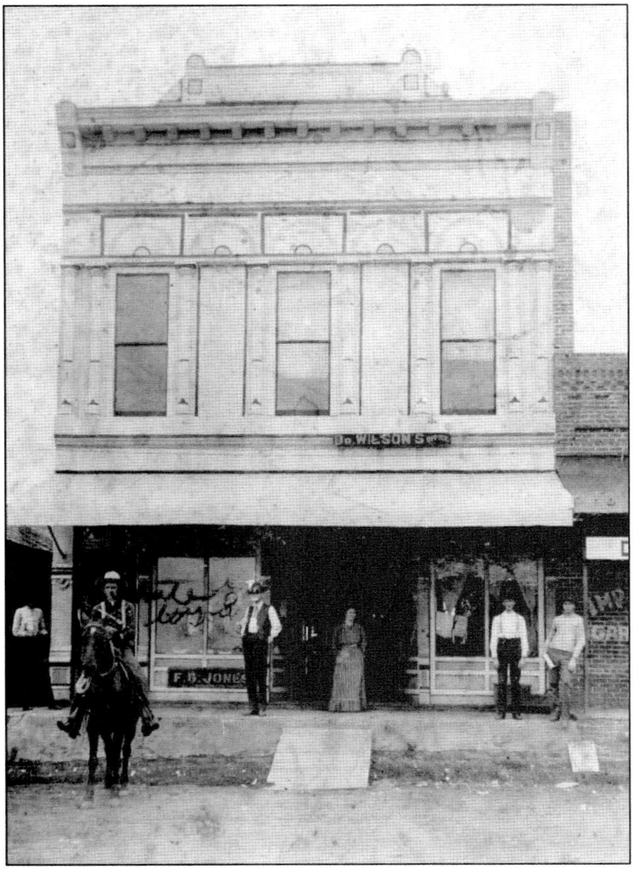

Thornton was established by the Houston & Texas Central Railroad in 1871. By the early 1900s, the town's population was 1,000, and there were 18 brick stores, a bank, a hotel, three churches, two cotton gins, two weekly newspapers, and electric lights. This photograph of the F.G. Jones Building was taken in the late 1880s. Dr. Wilson's office was on the second floor. (G'Ann Smith-Tilley.)

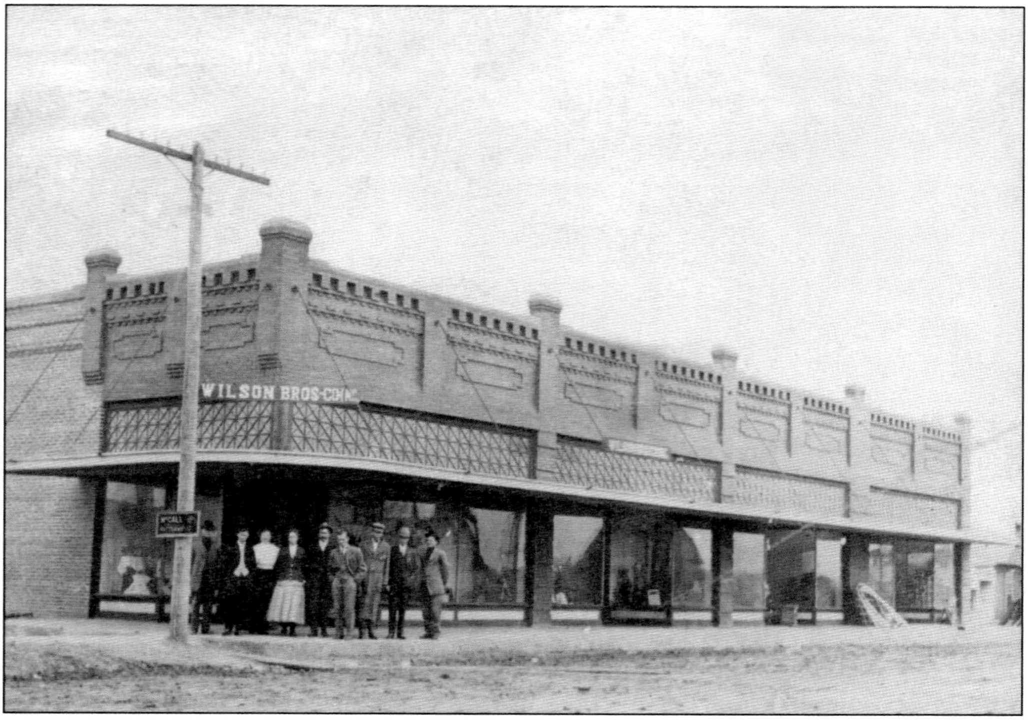

In 1894, J.R. Wilson and Charles Clark opened a general mercantile store in Thornton. Wilson's younger brother, Thomas M. Wilson, succeeded Clark as partner, and another brother, George D. Wilson, was also associated with the business for many years. Wilson Brothers sold clothing, staple foods, hardware, and farm implements and offered various services, such as undertaking. The store closed in 1939. (Limestone County Historical Museum.)

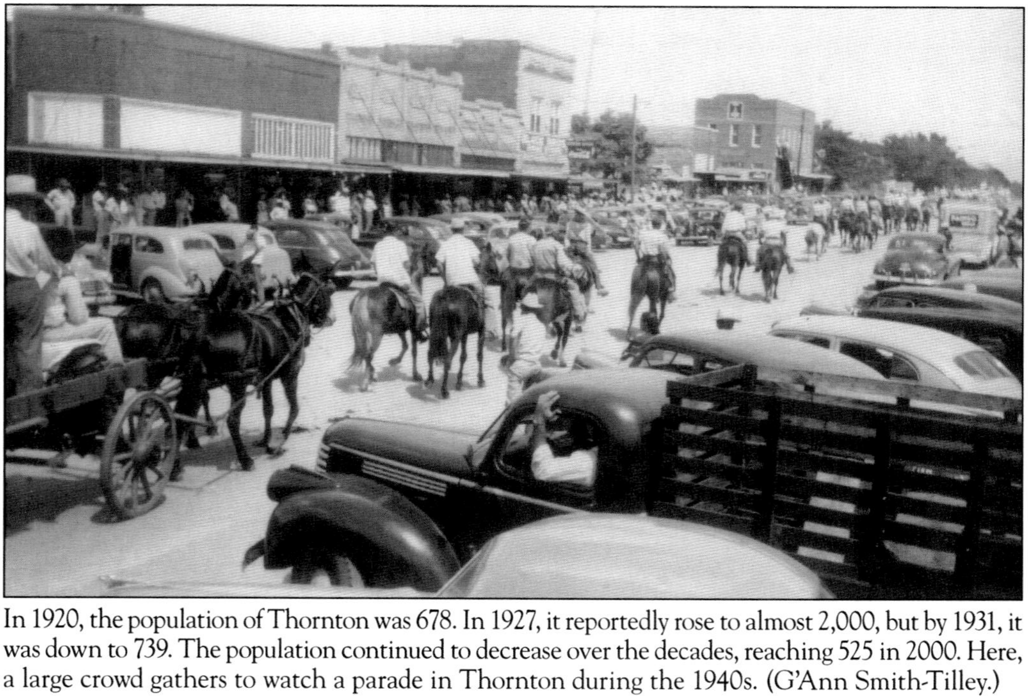

In 1920, the population of Thornton was 678. In 1927, it reportedly rose to almost 2,000, but by 1931, it was down to 739. The population continued to decrease over the decades, reaching 525 in 2000. Here, a large crowd gathers to watch a parade in Thornton during the 1940s. (G'Ann Smith-Tilley.)

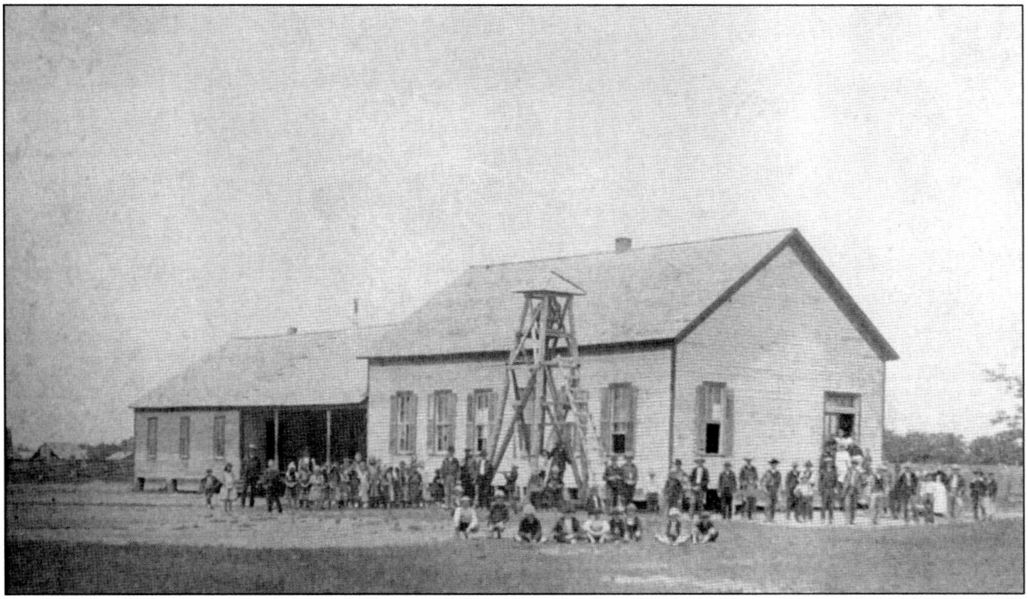

Much of the early life of Thornton centered on the Thornton Male and Female Institute (above), founded in 1877 by Edward Coke Chambers (right) and chartered by the State of Texas as a school of higher learning in 1881. An enrollment of 87 students was reported in 1882. In addition to boarding students, the school provided education for area children. The school prospered and enrollment increased, and in 1884, it merged with the school of Henry P. Davis. This merger led to the creation of the largest school in the county, with an enrollment of 171 students. Of these, 130 students were from outside Limestone County. On August 15, 1889, Edward Chambers sold the school to Davis, who continued to operate it for two more years. (Both, Limestone County Historical Museum.)

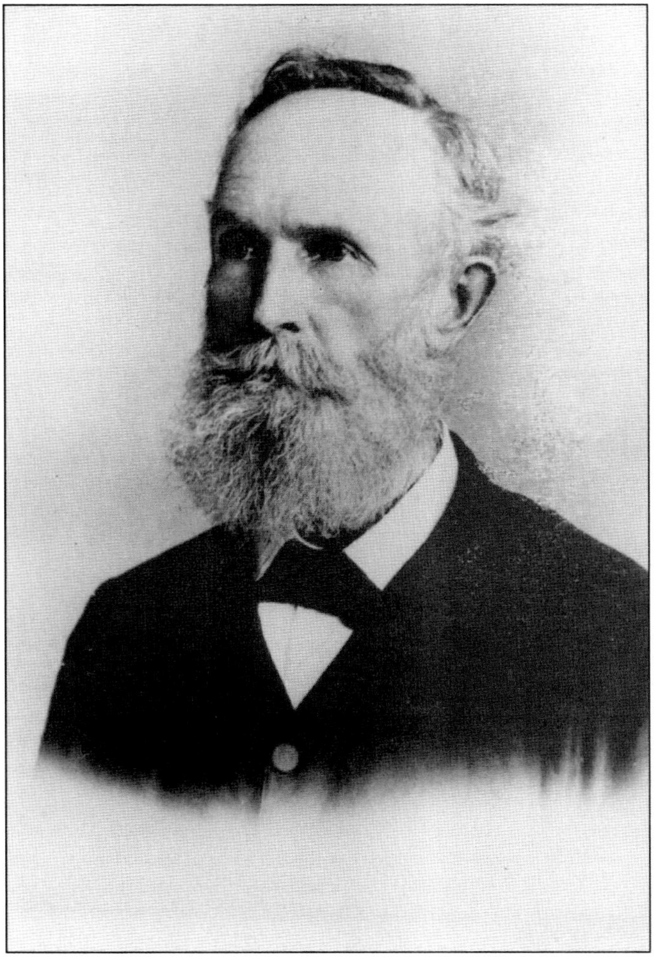

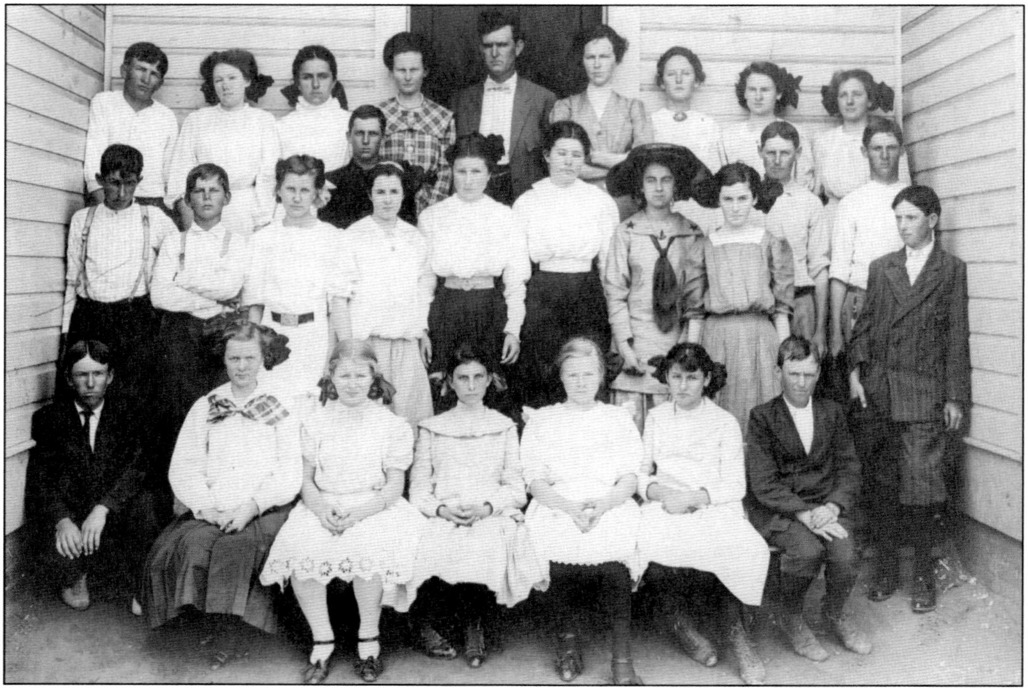

In 1893, Henry P. Davis sold the former Thornton Institute campus to the newly formed Thornton Independent School District. The old school building was used until it was destroyed by a storm in 1903. Construction of a new, wood-framed school building was soon completed. Thornton high school students pose in front of the building in 1910. The school was destroyed by fire in 1920. (Limestone County Historical Museum.)

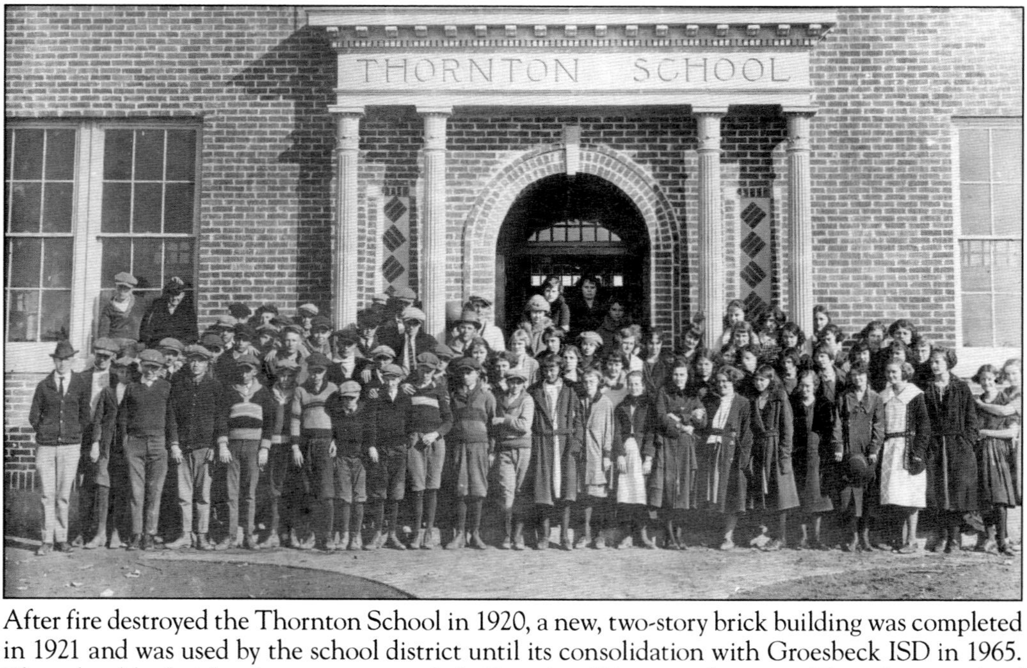

After fire destroyed the Thornton School in 1920, a new, two-story brick building was completed in 1921 and was used by the school district until its consolidation with Groesbeck ISD in 1965. The school had eight classrooms, a study hall, and a 434-seat auditorium. This photograph of Thornton students and teachers was taken in 1921. (Limestone County Historical Museum.)

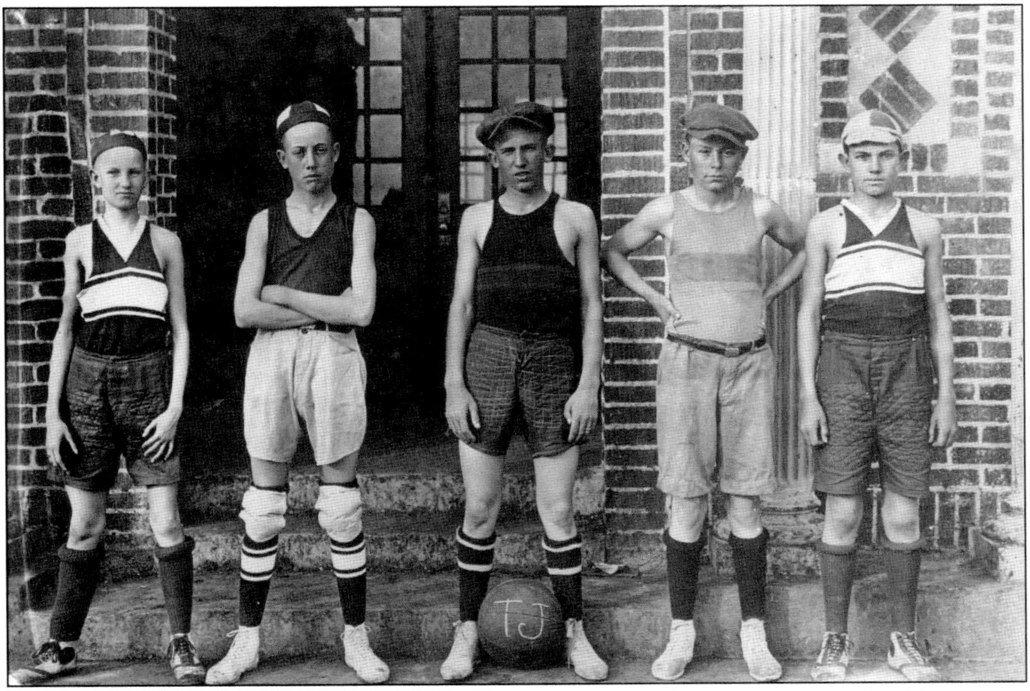

These young Thornton basketball players pose in front of the school building in 1921. Shown are, from left to right, John Earl Lawrence, Culver Smythe, Dick Wimberly, unidentified, and Elgin Cook. Today, the old Thornton School still stands and serves the town's citizens as a community center. (Limestone County Historical Museum.)

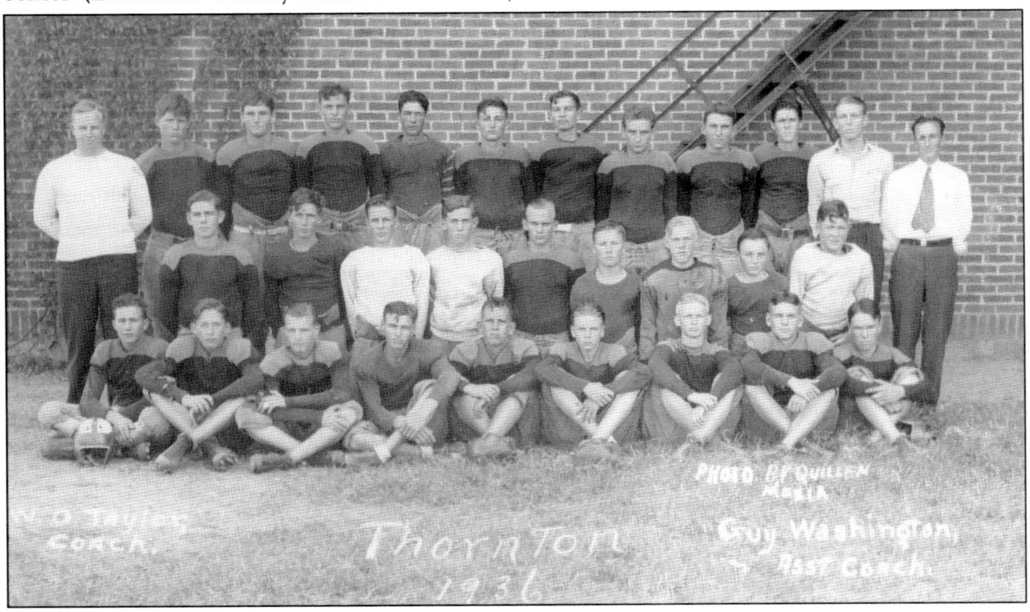

The first Thornton football team was organized in 1923. For the first few years, the Thornton Tigers played six-man football, but around 1928, the first 12-man team took the field. Because of the decline in student population, the Tigers went back to six-man football in 1953. The 1936 Thornton Tigers pose with coach W.O. Taylor (third row, left) and assistant coach Guy Washington (third row, right). (Limestone County Historical Museum.)

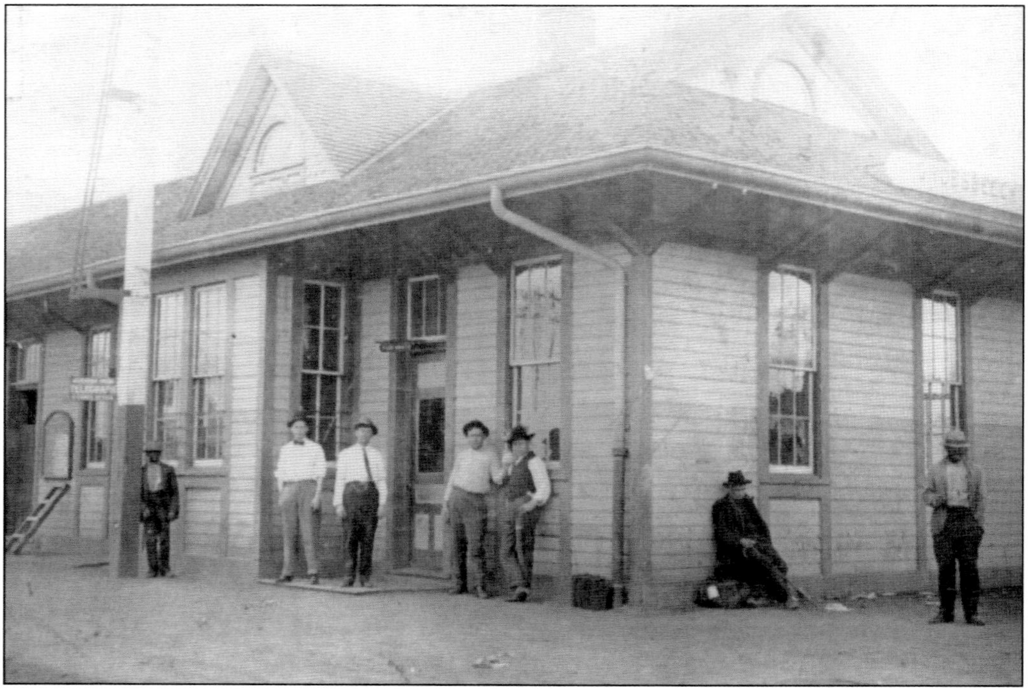

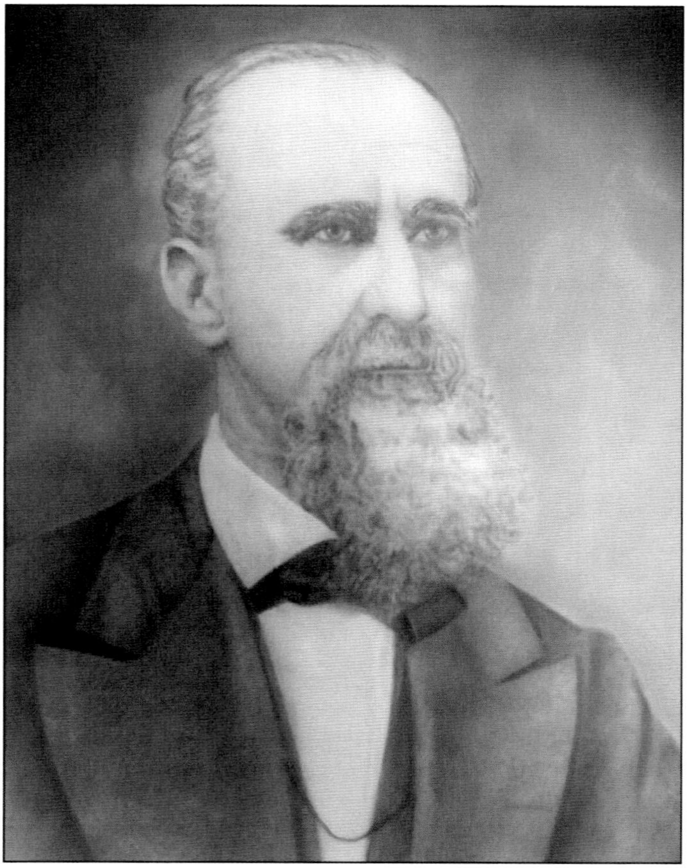

The early photograph above shows the Houston & Texas Central Railroad depot in Groesbeck, a town established by the railroad and dedicated on February 20, 1871. The town was named Groesbeeck, after Abraham Groesbeeck, a director of the railroad and townsite company. On August 25, 1869, Groesbeeck (left) purchased from H.J. Buddington the 984 acres in the Elisha Anglin survey on which the town was laid out. A post office was established on April 12, 1871, and changed the spelling to "Groesbeck." The railroad company continued to use the original spelling for several decades. (Above, Limestone County Historical Museum; left, the City of Groesbeck.)

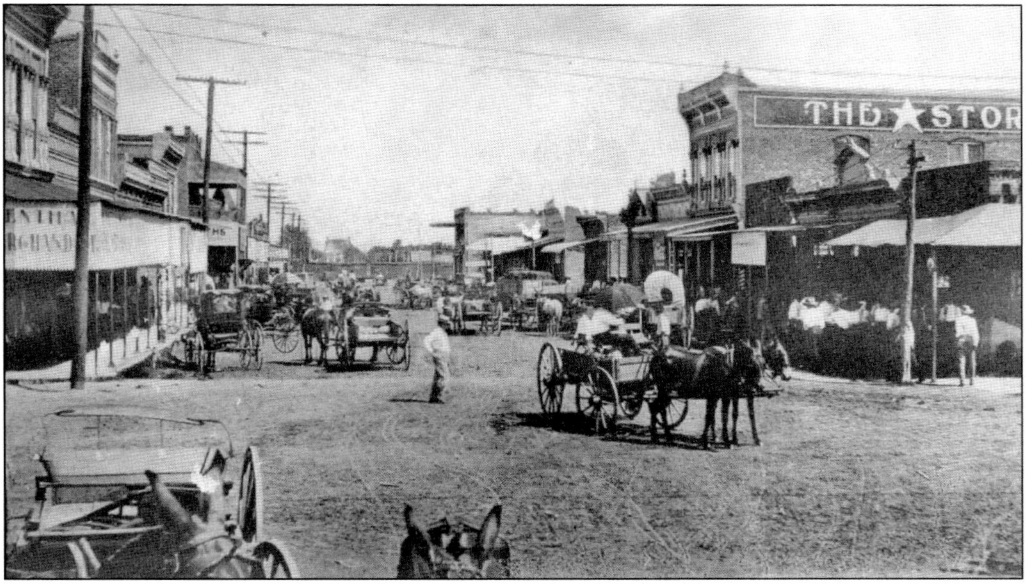

The development of a city government began on April 11, 1871, when Groesbeck was incorporated by an act of the state legislature. Lots quickly sold in Limestone County's newest town. The railroad company had intended for the main streets of Groesbeck to be those on each side of the depot grounds parallel to the tracks. However, most business owners built along Navasota and Ellis Streets. The above photograph, taken in 1911, is of Navasota Street looking east. In the foreground, Navasota is intersected by Ellis Street. Note the train cars on the railroad tracks in the background. The photograph below was taken near the railroad tracks, looking west on Navasota Street. (Above, William Reagan; below, Limestone County Historical Museum.)

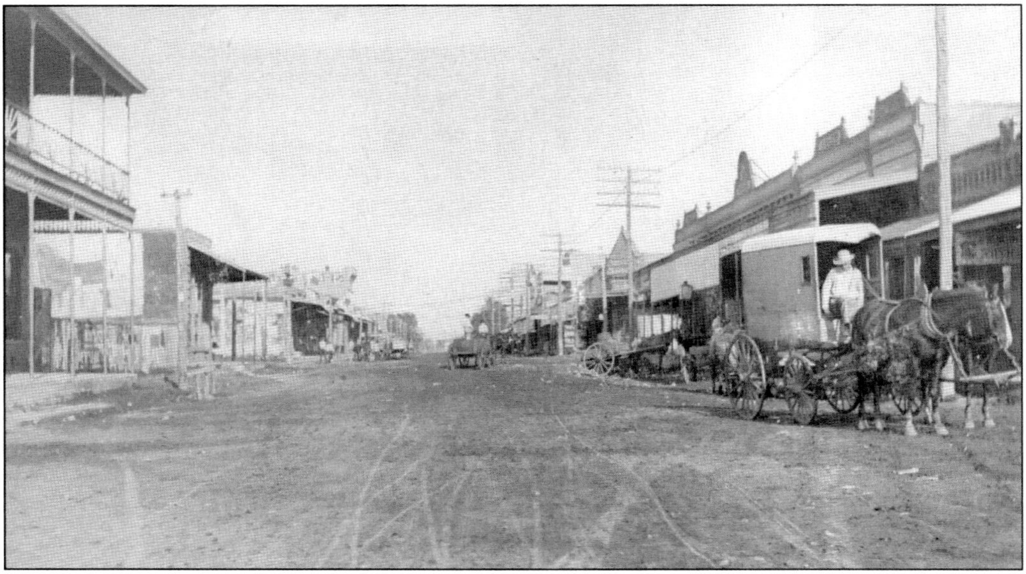

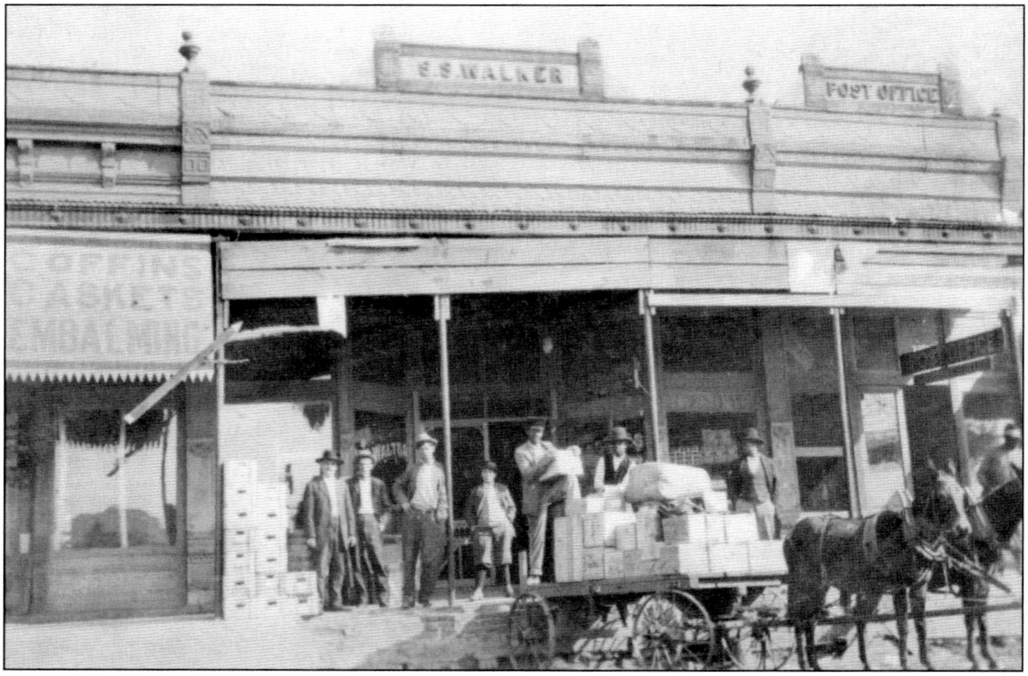

Many businesses have called Groesbeck home over the decades. Dry goods stores and grocery stores were of extreme importance to rural farmers who came to town on Saturdays to purchase supplies for the coming week. Pictured above is the S.S. Walker Grocery Store in 1915. To its right is the post office. In the photograph below is Hicks Grocery Store around 1927. Posing for the camera are Ruth Hicks (left) and Gladys Hicks. Note the large stalks of bananas hanging in the center of the store. (Both, Limestone County Historical Museum.)

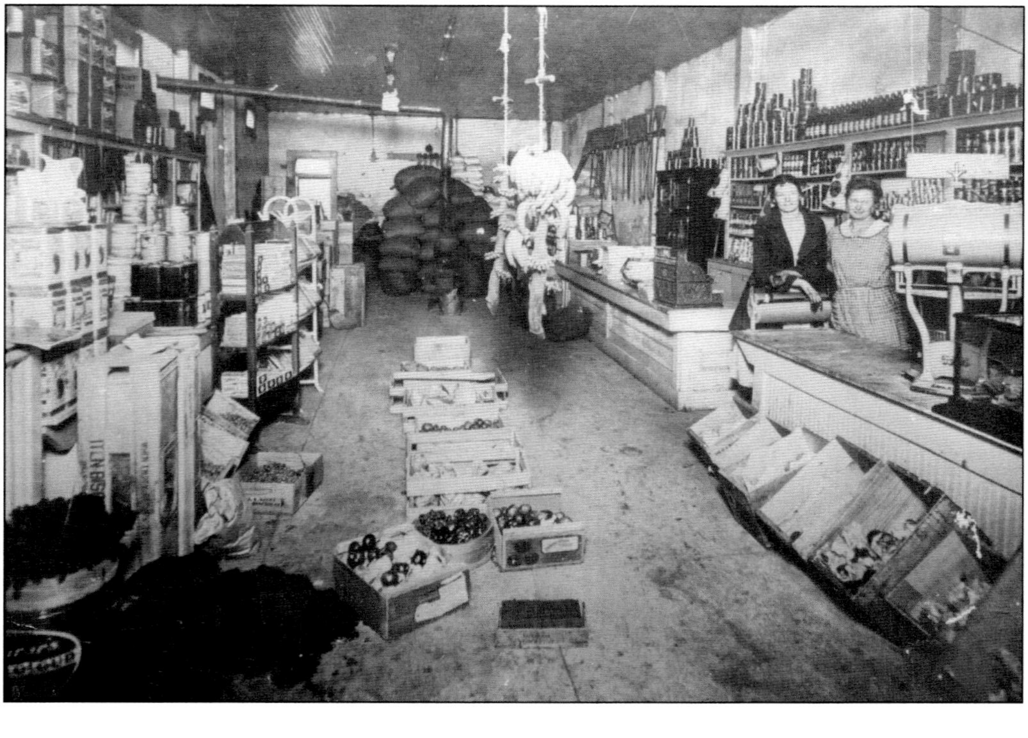

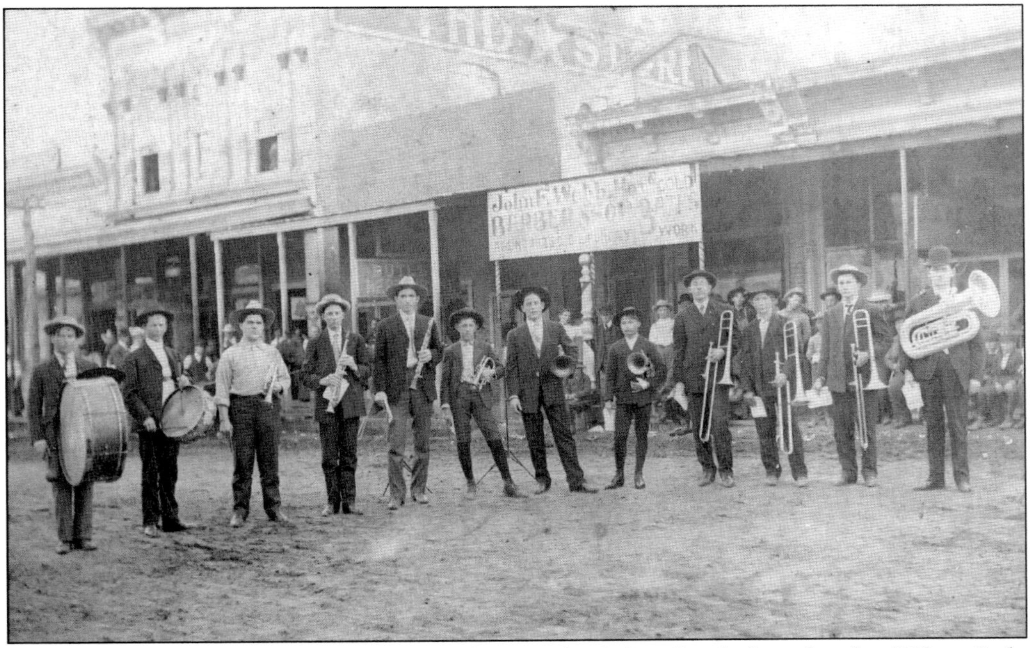

In addition to performing at special events, the Groesbeck City Band often played at Wilson Park, located one mile south of Groesbeck. This photograph was taken in 1912 along the 200 block of West Navasota Street. Signs for the Butler Restaurant and the John E. Webb Barber Shop can be seen in the background. (Limestone County Historical Museum.)

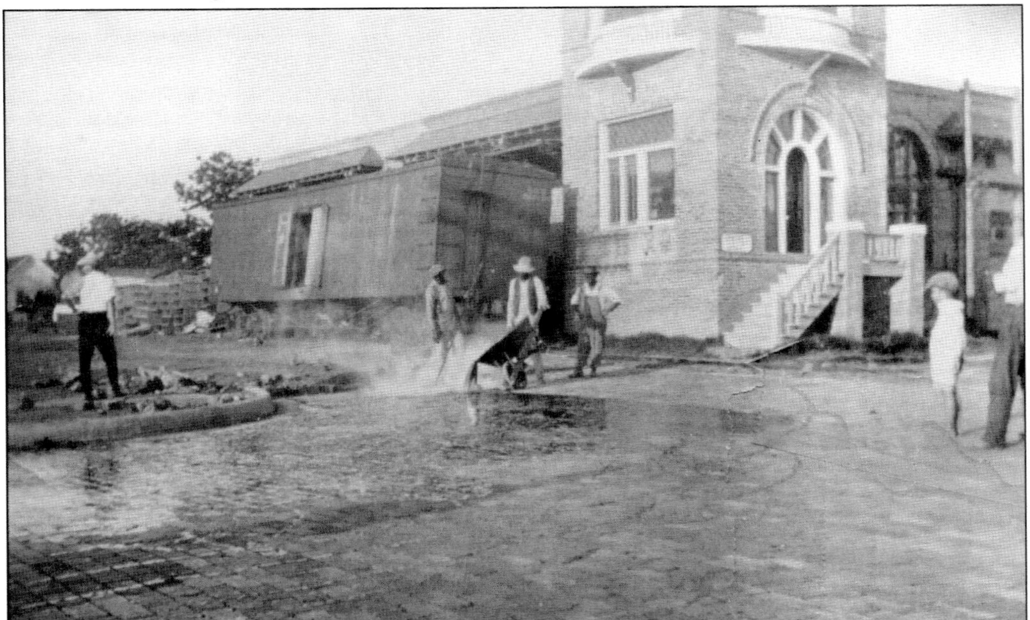

Workers lay bricks on Navasota Street in front of the old ice plant in Groesbeck. All of the downtown streets were paved with bricks during the spring of 1923. The bricks, from the coal-mining and brick-making town of Thurber in Erath County, were larger and harder than ordinary building bricks. The total cost of the project was $15,733.80, a good investment for the city, as the brick streets are still used today. (Limestone County Historical Museum.)

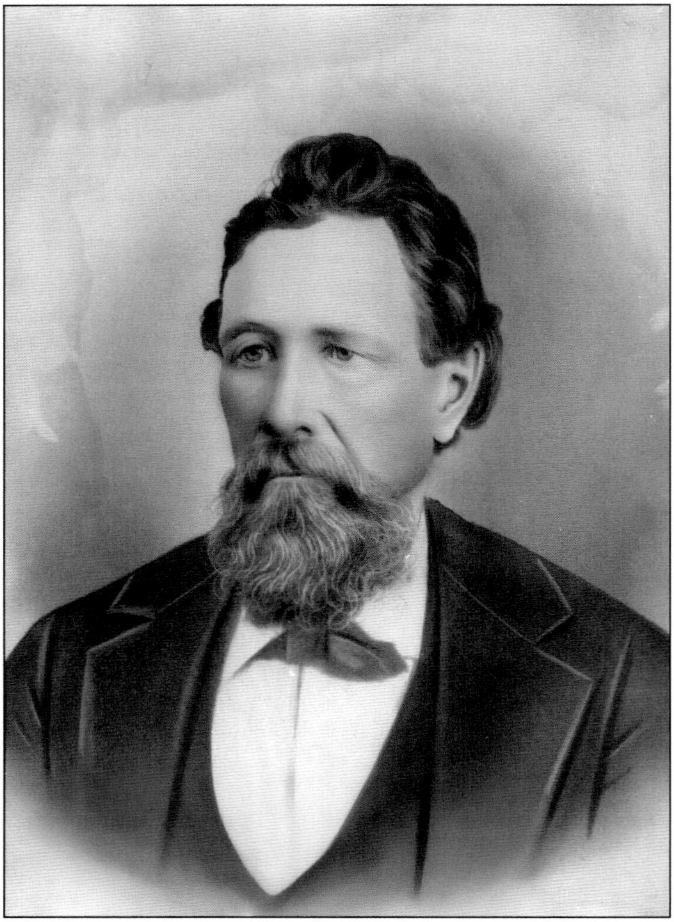

The Cox family served the Groesbeck area with medical services for over 100 years. Pictured at left is Dr. W.T. Cox, who came to Groesbeck in 1872 and served its residents faithfully until his death in 1898. Dr. Wilmer Cox followed in his father's footsteps, and he built the first hospital in Groesbeck in 1923. Dr. Henry Cox worked at the hospital with his father until he died in 1935. Following his brother's death, Dr. Stanley Cox joined his father at the hospital. Dr. Wilmer Cox passed away in 1947. In 1949, Stanley Cox built a large and more modern hospital. Originally a 16-bed hospital, a later addition increased its capacity to 30 beds. Dr. Cox's Hospital (below) closed in 1973 when the South Limestone Hospital opened. (Both, Limestone County Historical Museum.)

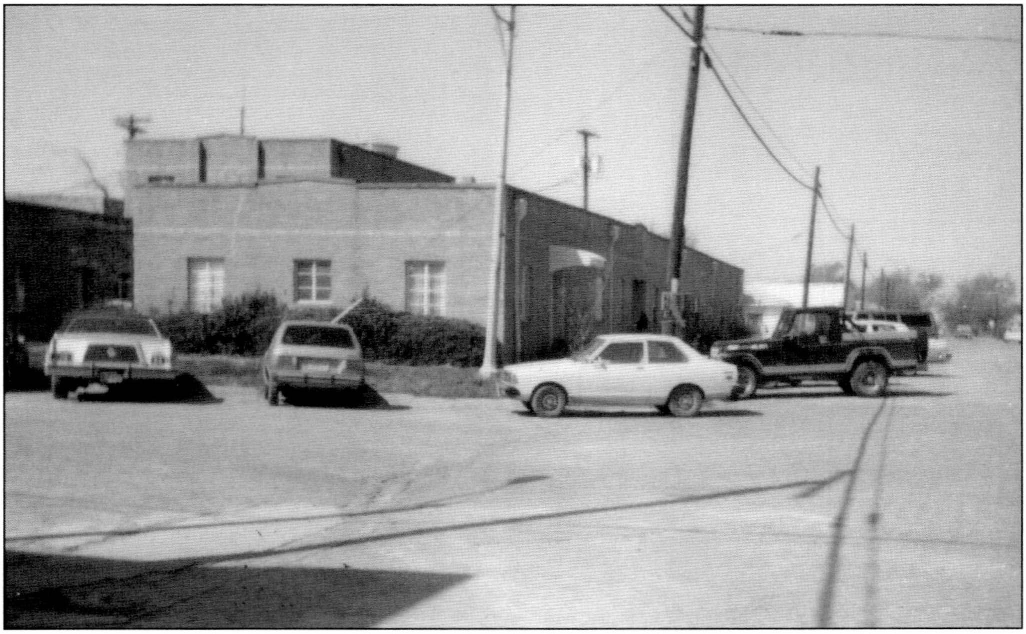

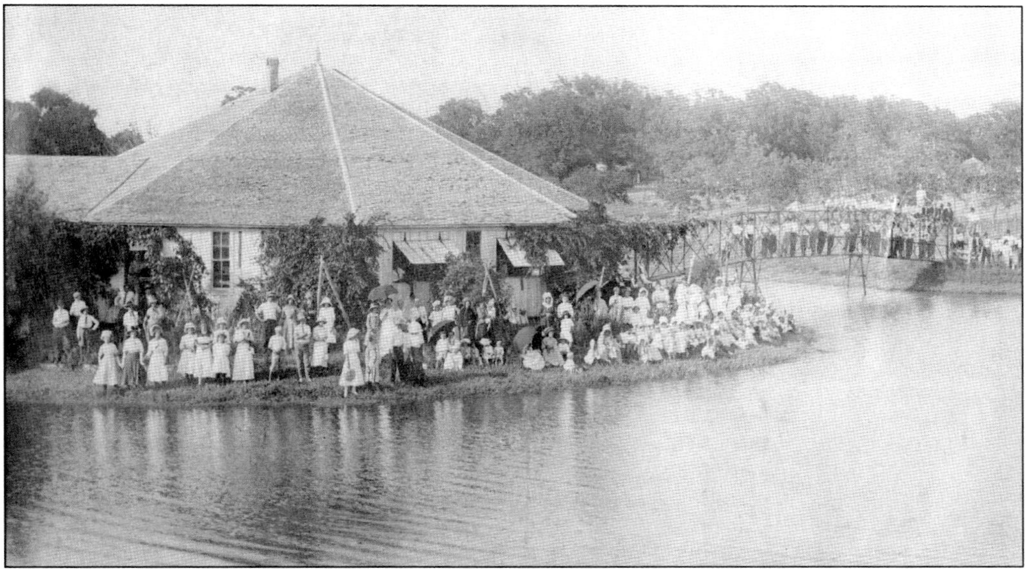

A popular place to be in the early 1900s was Wilson Park, located one mile south of Groesbeck. Built by William Harrison Wilson, the park had a large lake, in the center of which was an island with a pavilion for dancing and roller-skating. The island was connected to the shore by an iron bridge, and a diving board and concrete steps helped facilitate swimming. (Logan Wilson.)

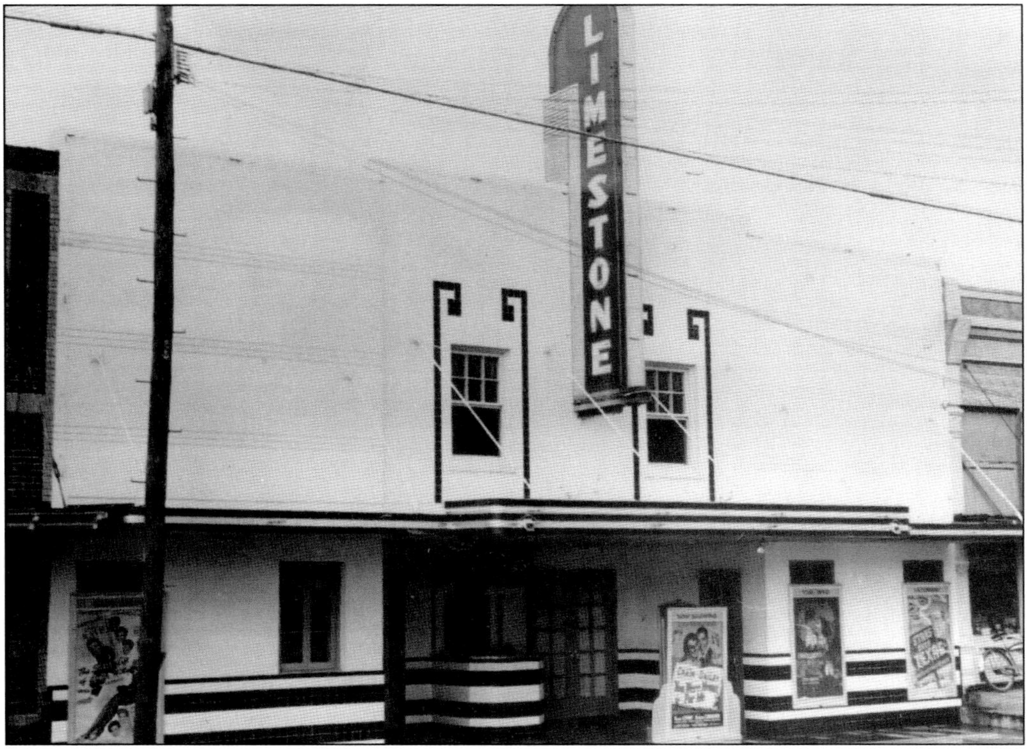

The Limestone Theatre in Groesbeck was located on Navasota Street. It was built in 1937 by Sid Smith, who operated the movie theater until he sold it to Mr. and Mrs. Danny Hardwick in 1973. The theater closed a few years later. Smith also owned the Yale Theatre, which was located directly across the street from the Limestone. (Limestone County Historical Museum.)

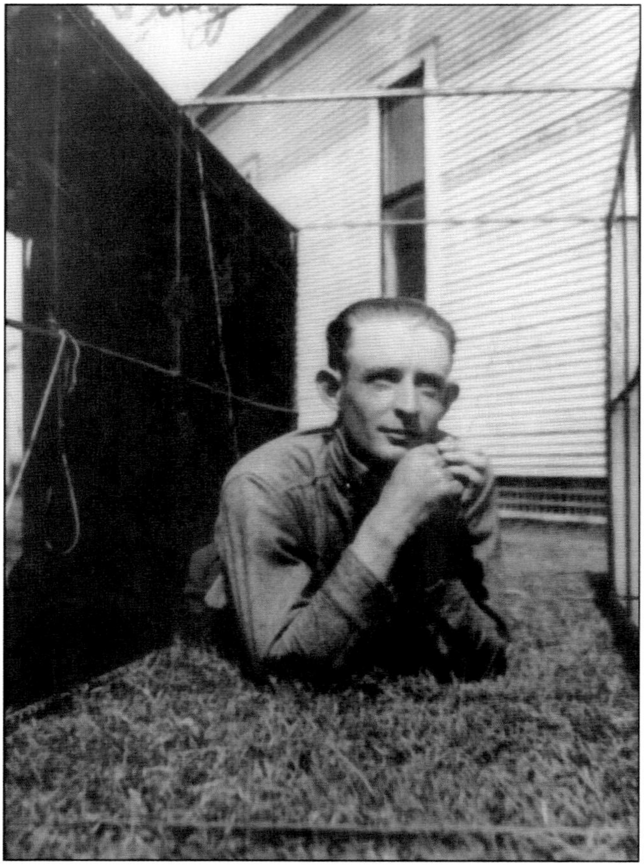

With the increased use of airplanes, the US Weather Bureau established an aerological station in Groesbeck in 1918. Locally, it was called the Kite Station and was one of only five in the country. The temperature, humidity, wind speed, wind direction, and barometric pressure above the earth's surface were measured and studied. This was done by flying huge box kites. An instrument called a meteorograph was mounted in the first kite, and other kites were attached along the flight wire to lift the weight of the wire. At left, W.L. Thompson is pictured making repairs to a kite. Below is the roundhouse, which could rotate downwind to fly the kites. Inside was an electric-driven reel containing several miles of piano wire with a strength of 300 pounds. The Kite Station closed in 1931. (Both, Limestone County Historical Museum.)

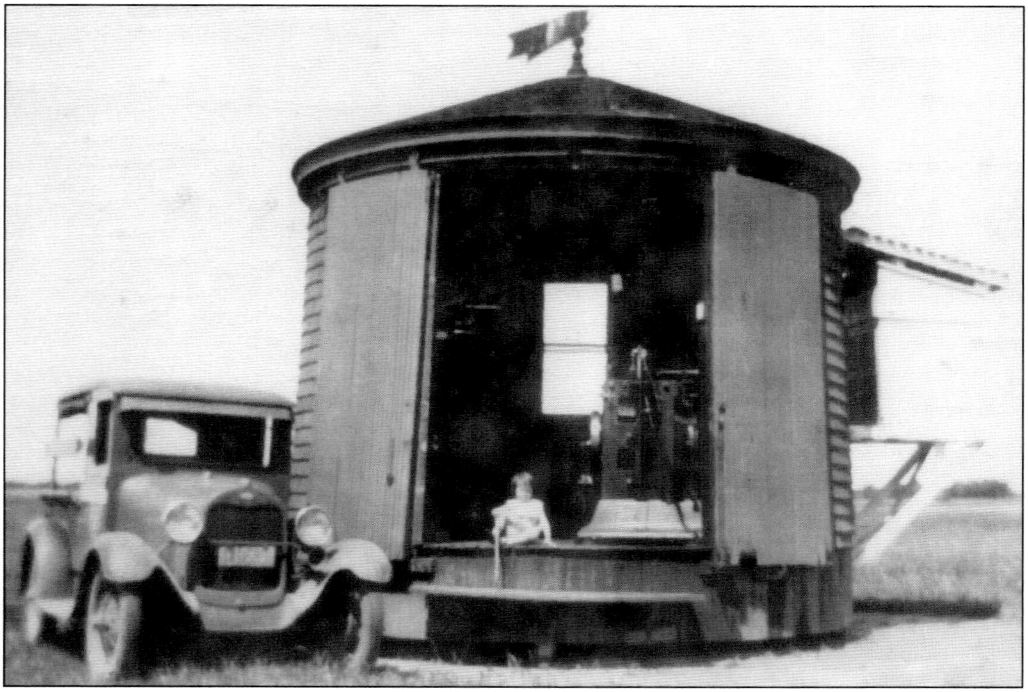

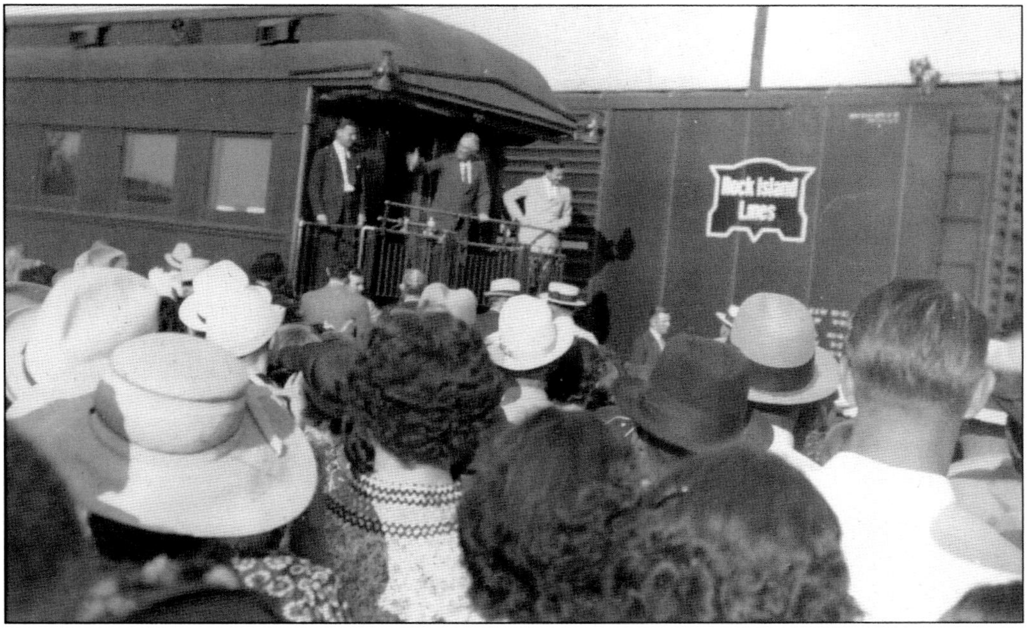

Pres. Franklin D. Roosevelt visited Groesbeck on May 11, 1937 (above). His special train stopped at the Groesbeck depot, where a large crowd greeted him. President Roosevelt speaks to the crowd, and Texas governor Jimmy Allred is on the right. (Frank Seay.)

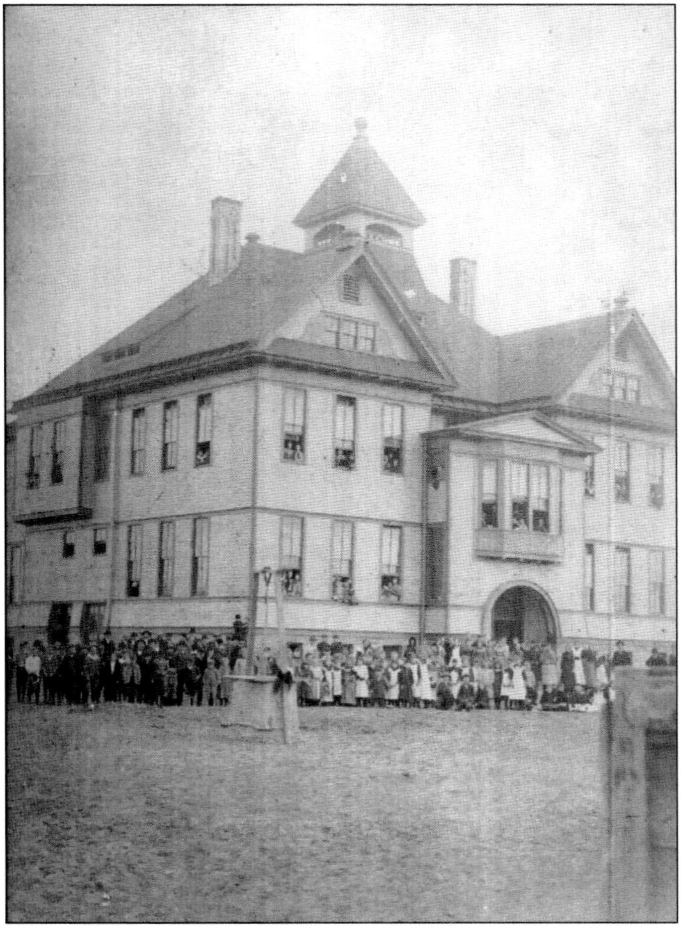

Soon after the Groesbeck Independent School District was created on May 26, 1890, two school buildings were constructed, one for white students and one for black students. In 1896, a new, wooden building was constructed for white students. This second school building served the white students of the district until it was destroyed by fire in 1910. School was in session at the time of the fire, but everyone escaped safely. (Limestone County Historical Museum.)

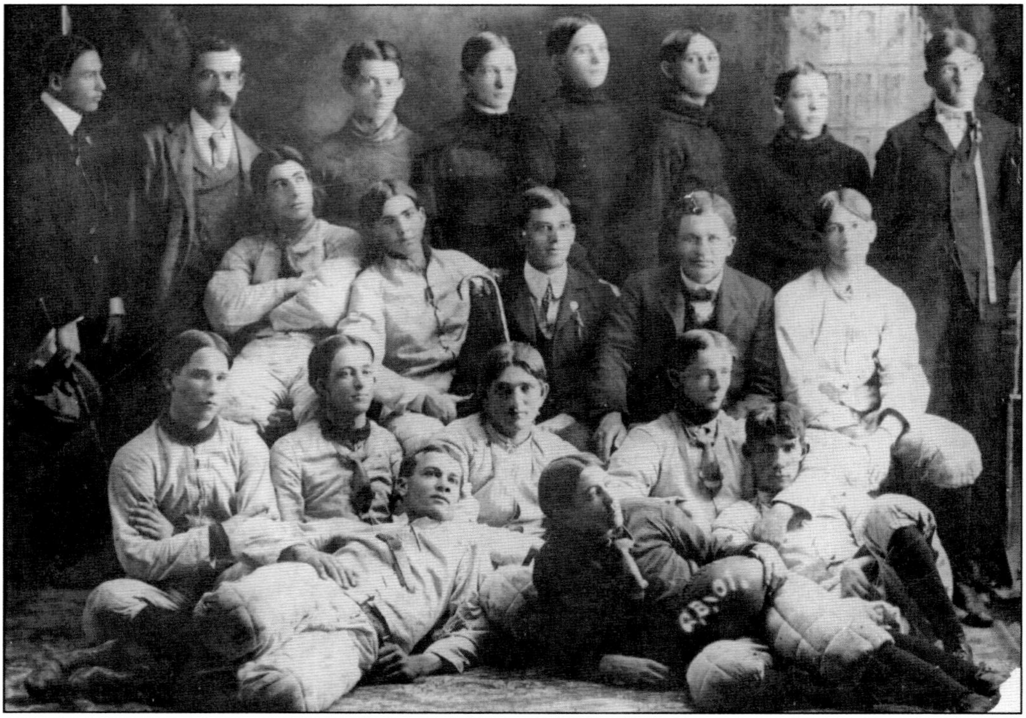

The first Groesbeck football team was organized in 1900. It has been reported by old-timers that this first team lost only one game between 1900 and 1902. According to the first high school yearbook, which was published in 1916, there were no football teams from 1902 until 1915. It was in 1915 that the University Interscholastic League came to Limestone County and when the schools of the county began to compete in academics and athletics at the county level. (Groesbeck School Museum.)

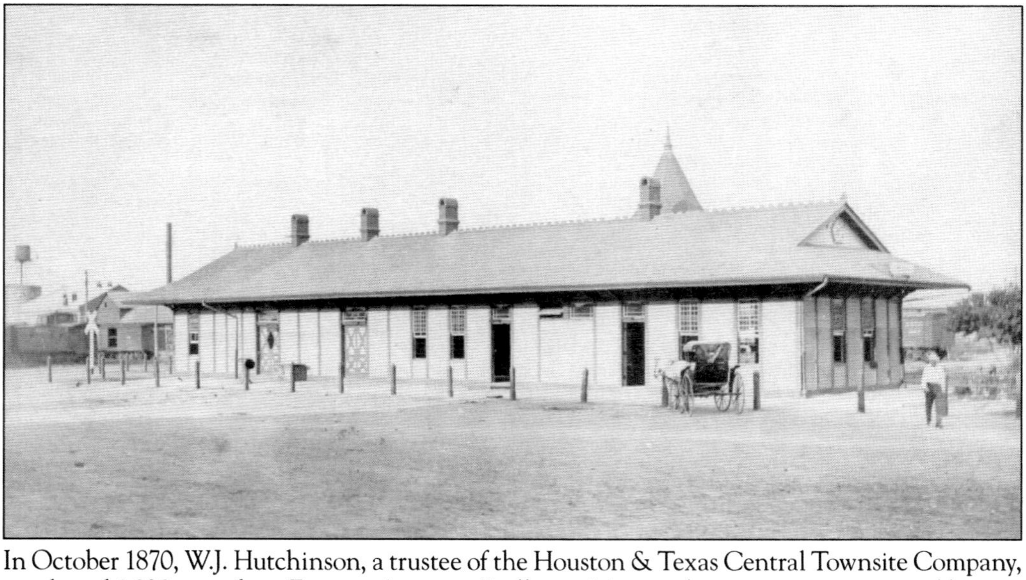

In October 1870, W.J. Hutchinson, a trustee of the Houston & Texas Central Townsite Company, purchased 1,930 acres from Enrique Antonio Guillermo Mexia, who was agent over several leagues of land belonging to him and his sister. A town was laid out and named Mexia in honor of the Mexía family. Shown here is the Houston & Texas Central Railroad depot in Mexia. (William Reagan.)

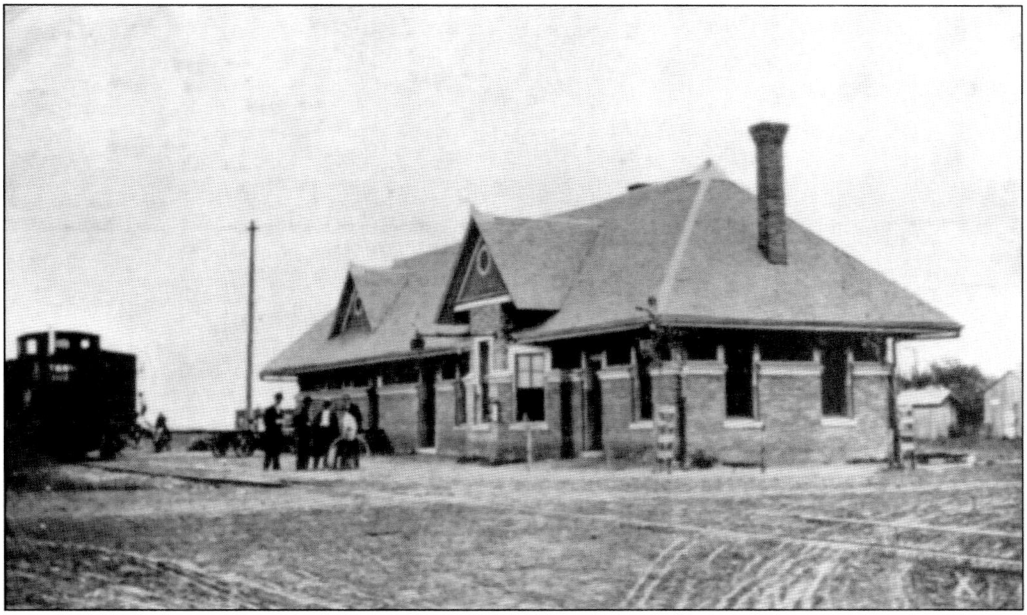

In 1903, the Trinity & Brazos Valley Railroad constructed a line from Cleburne to Mexia and later extended it to Teague in Freestone County. This led to the construction of a second railroad depot in Mexia, shown here around 1910. This railroad line was abandoned in 1942. (William Reagan.)

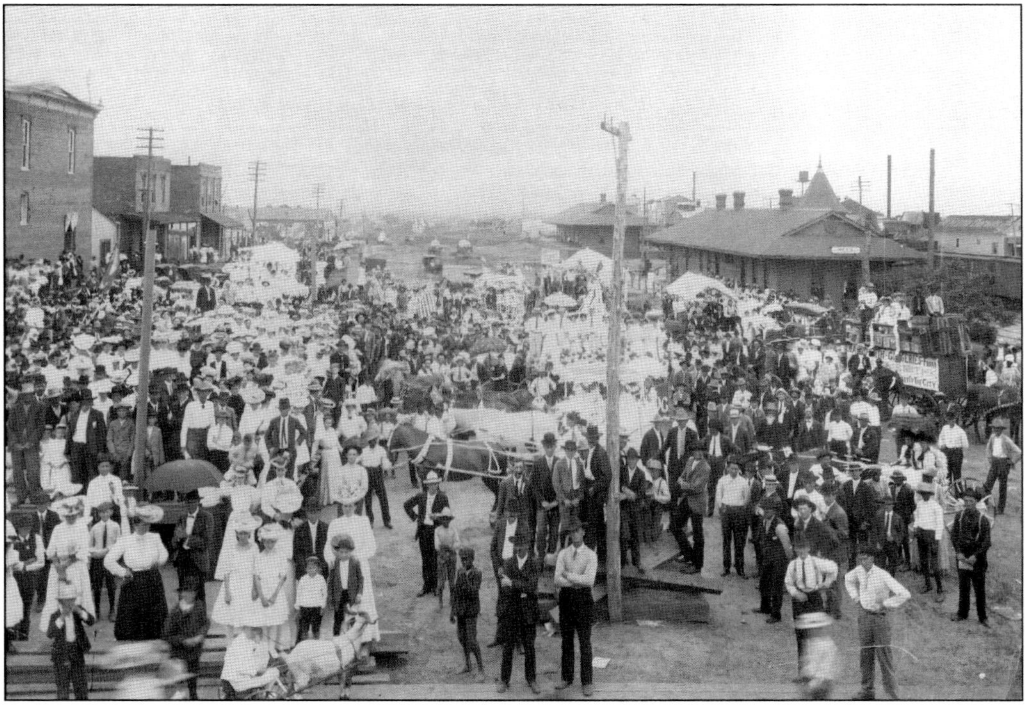

In 1905, a celebration was held in Mexia to mark the completion of a water line from Springfield to Mexia, which provided the residents with running water. In addition to a parade, Hugh Everett and Sid Carroll engaged in a water fight with fire hoses in the middle of Commerce Street. The Houston & Texas Central depot (near right) and the Trinity & Brazos Valley depot (rear, at right) can be seen in this photograph. (Gibbs Memorial Library.)

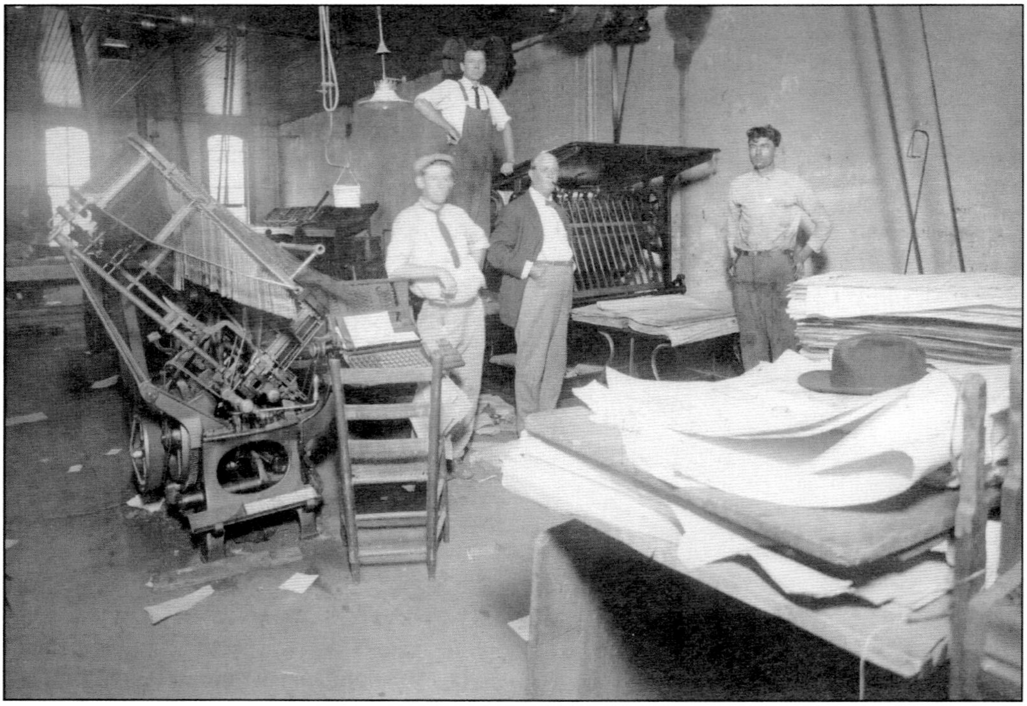

Maj. N.P. Houx arrived in Mexia during the 1880s and established the Houx Printery in a small wooden building, where he conducted his printing business and published the *Weekly Ledger*. In 1899, Houx established the first daily newspaper, the *Mexia Evening News*, currently the *Mexia News*. In this c. 1910 photograph, Major Houx (center) and three of his employees stand by the linotype and press of the *Mexia Evening News*. (Gibbs Memorial Library.)

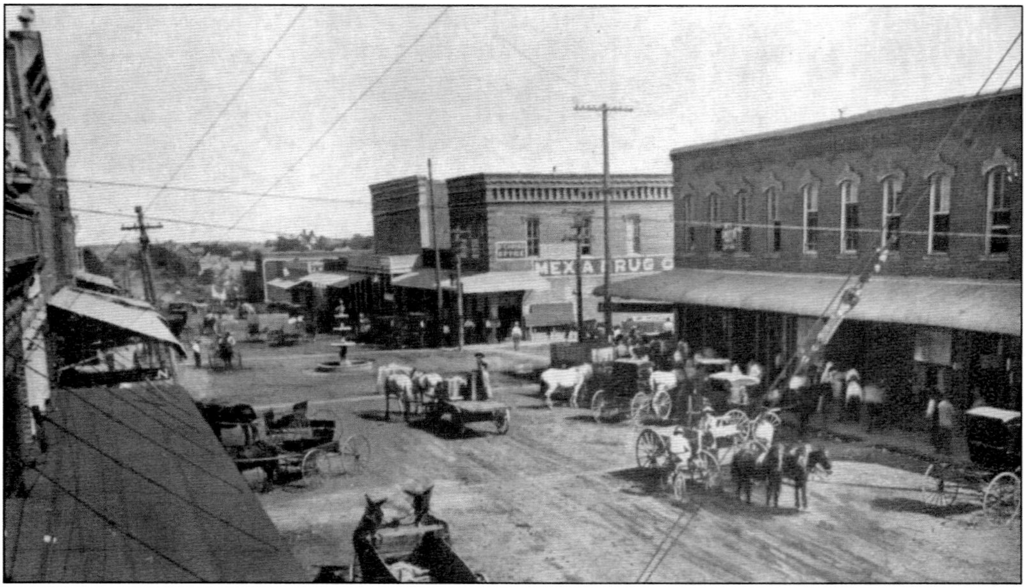

Shown here is the intersection of Sherman and Commerce Streets in the early 1900s. The unpaved streets and the horse-drawn wagons and buggies show what life was like in Mexia before the arrival of the automobile. The fountain in the middle of the intersection was used for watering horses. (William Reagan.)

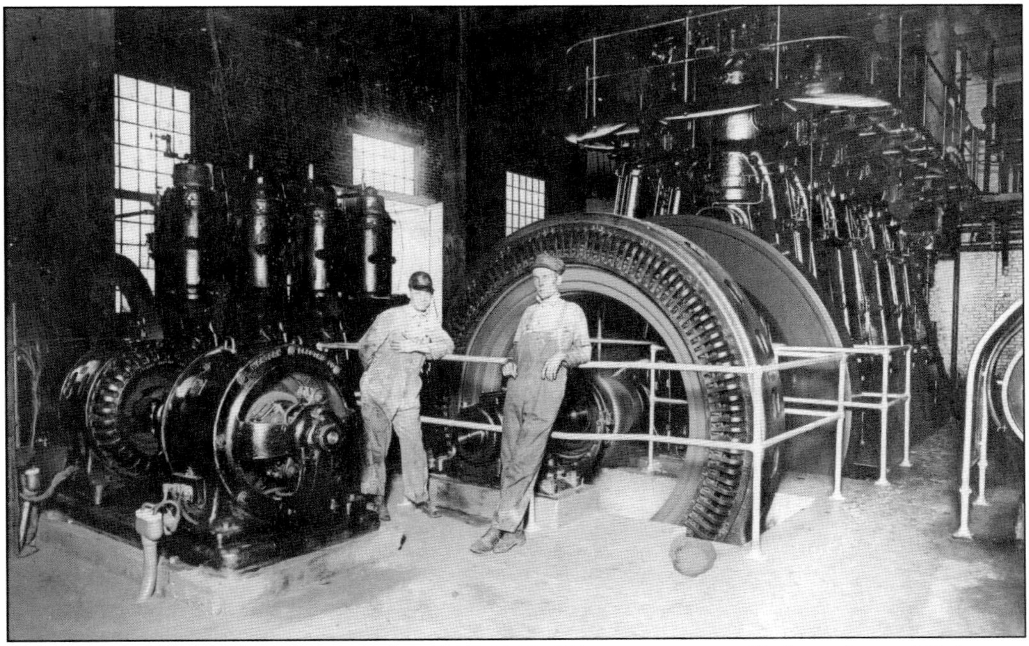

Mexia's first light plant was completed in 1903. Wiring was installed to about 100 homes and all businesses. Almost all homes were wired within a year. Electricity was provided for only a few hours each night. The generator was turned on from dusk to midnight. J.V. Cox (right) and a Mr. Jorden are pictured in front of a large diesel engine that was installed in the light plant in 1923. (Larry Sewell.)

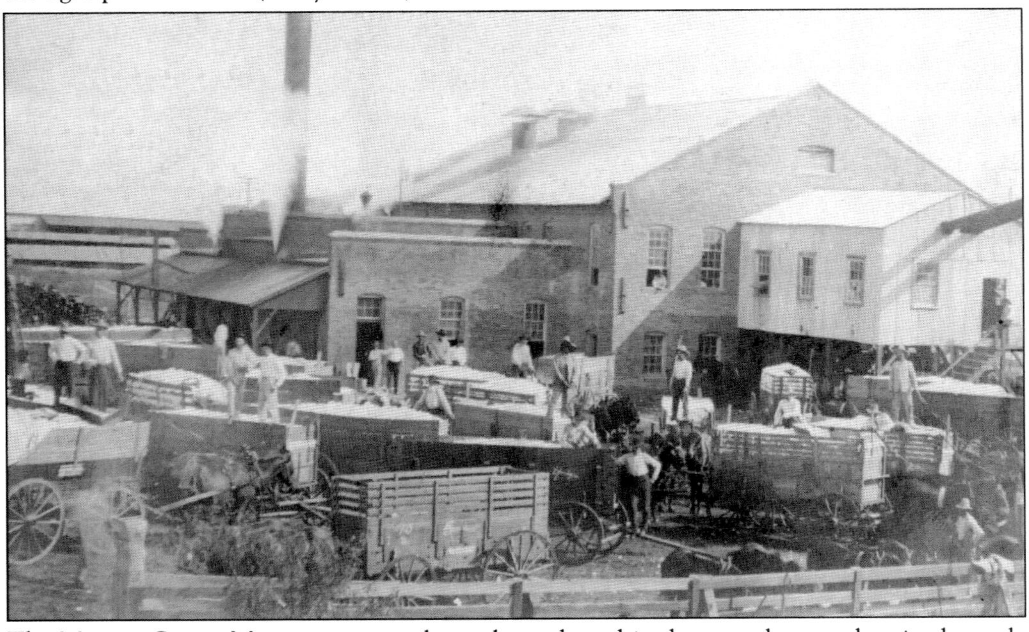

The Munger Gin in Mexia was a very busy place when this photograph was taken in the early 1900s. Robert Munger patented several improvements related to the ginning process, and these were implemented in the ginning industry all across the South as well as in other parts of the world. He operated other gins in the county and established the Munger Improved Cotton Machine Manufacturing Company of Dallas in 1889. (William Reagan.)

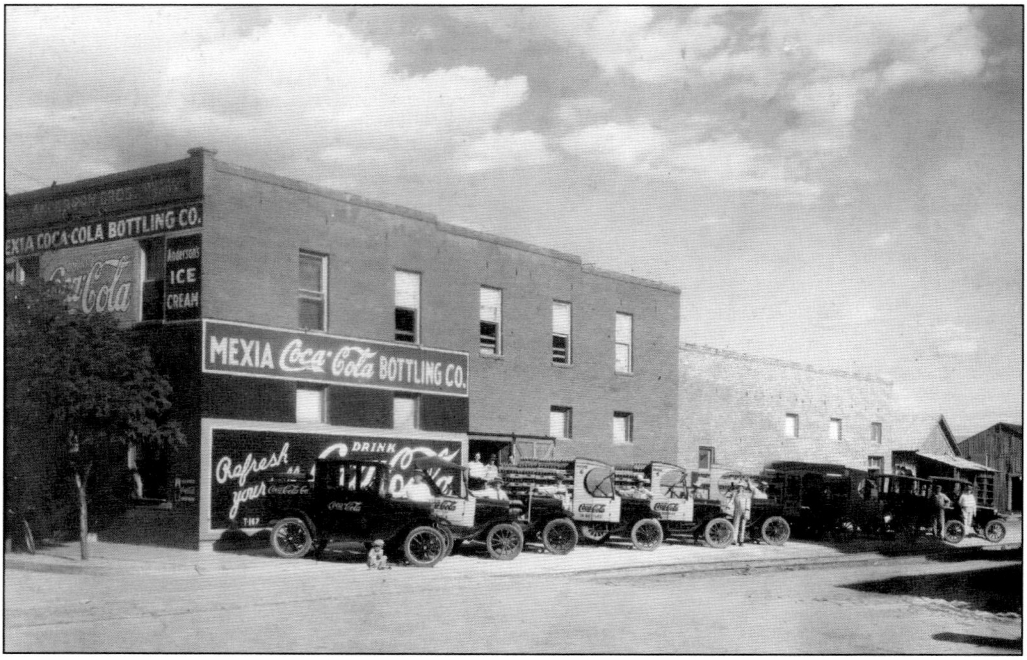

The Mexia Bottling Works was established in 1888. In 1904, it became the Mexia Coca-Cola Bottling Company. Previous owners were M.W. Anderson and his daughter Viola Cartwright. In 1975, the Thomas Browning family purchased the plant and changed its name to the Cen-Tex Coca-Cola Bottling Company. The Coca-Cola plant and its fleet of delivery trucks are pictured in 1924. (Mexia School Museum.)

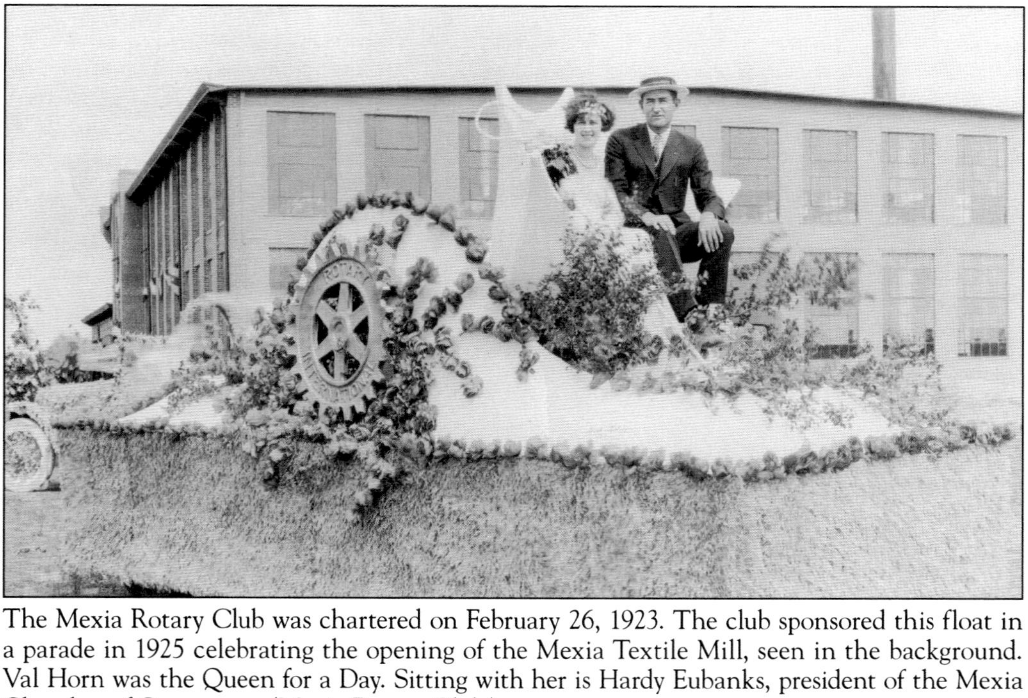

The Mexia Rotary Club was chartered on February 26, 1923. The club sponsored this float in a parade in 1925 celebrating the opening of the Mexia Textile Mill, seen in the background. Val Horn was the Queen for a Day. Sitting with her is Hardy Eubanks, president of the Mexia Chamber of Commerce. (Mexia Rotary Club.)

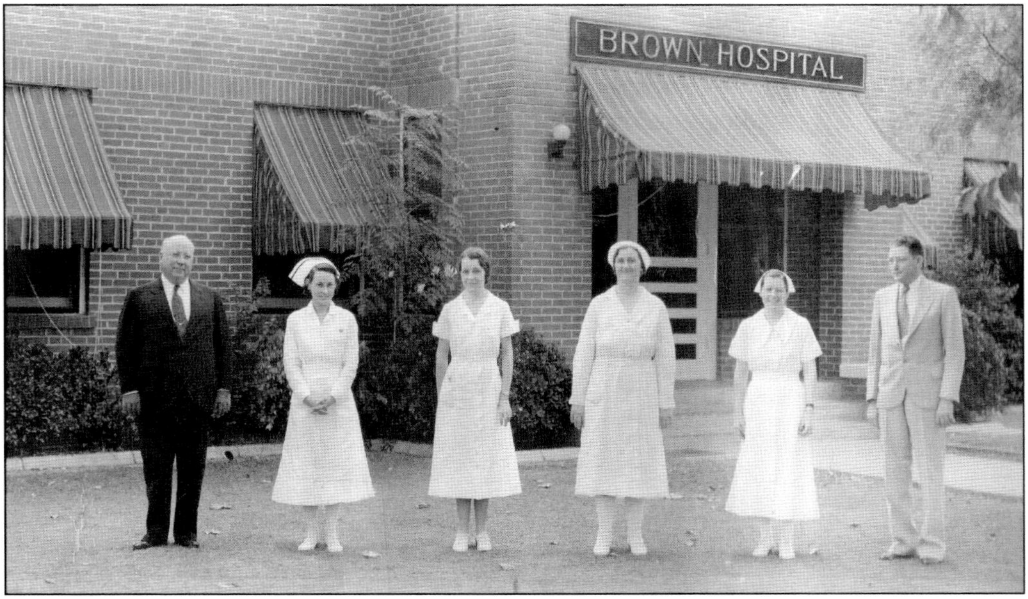

Brown Hospital was built in 1922 by Dr. Marion Brown. It originally had 16 beds for white patients and 4 beds for black patients. The hospital closed on December 31, 1961. Shown here are, from left to right, Dr. Brown, two unidentified nurses, Nurse Hazel Hawpe, an unidentified nurse, and Dr. C.C. Edgar. (Mexia School Museum.)

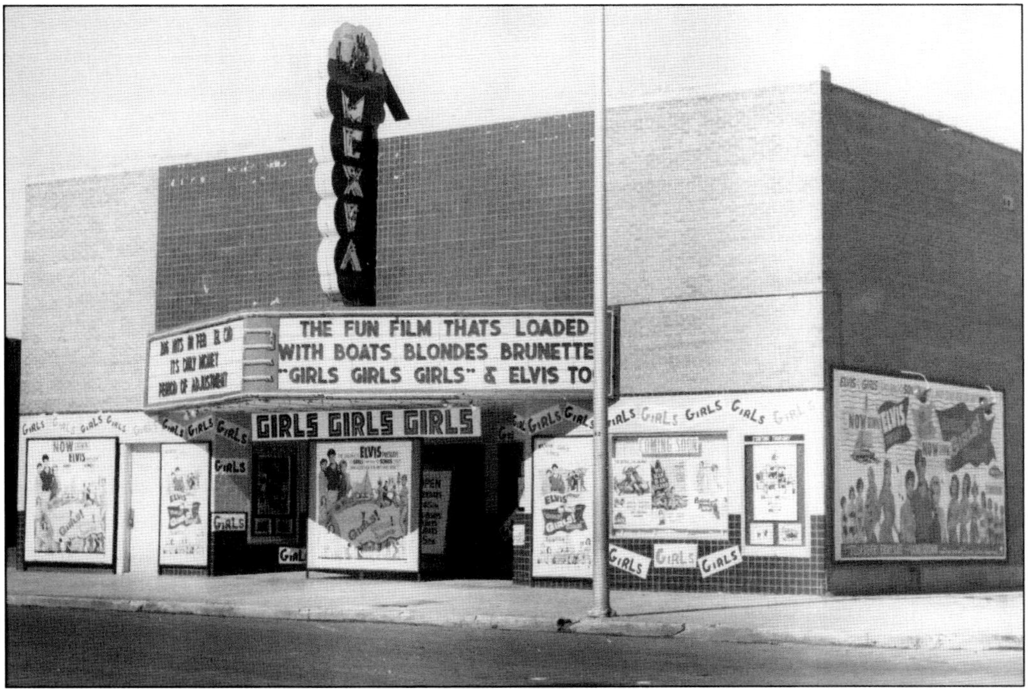

There have been several movie theaters in Mexia over the years. Originally owned and operated by Maurice Easterling, the Mexia Theater opened in 1949. The projectors were installed and maintained for many years by Orville Timberlake. In this 1962 photograph, the theater is covered with advertisements for the Elvis Presley movie *Girls! Girls! Girls!* The Mexia Theater closed in the 1980s. (Oklahoma Historical Society.)

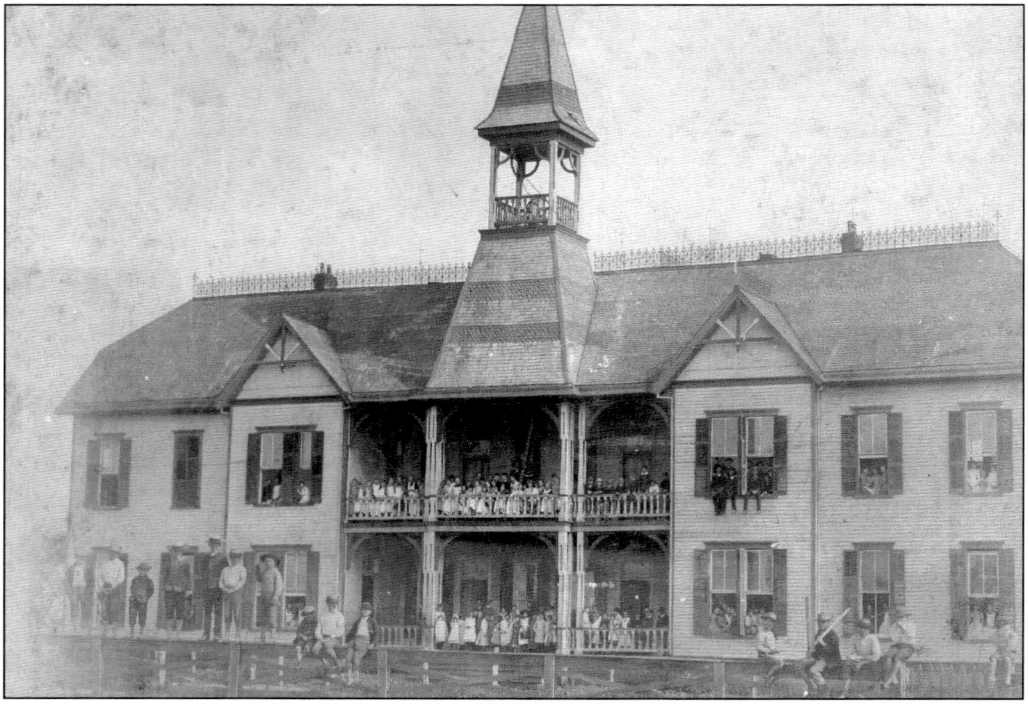

Mexia's public school system was established in April 1883. The city council agreed to act as a committee to choose the location of a school building, selecting property belonging to the railroad on Sumpter Street. The lot was purchased, and bonds in the amount of $10,000 were issued for the construction of a school. Pictured above is the first school building, which opened in September 1884. It had two stories, with five classrooms on the first floor and two small rooms and an auditorium on the second floor. There were five teachers, and Gen. John Creed Moore was appointed the first superintendent. This school was destroyed by fire in 1904. The below photograph is of an early Mexia elementary classroom. (Both, Mexia School Museum.)

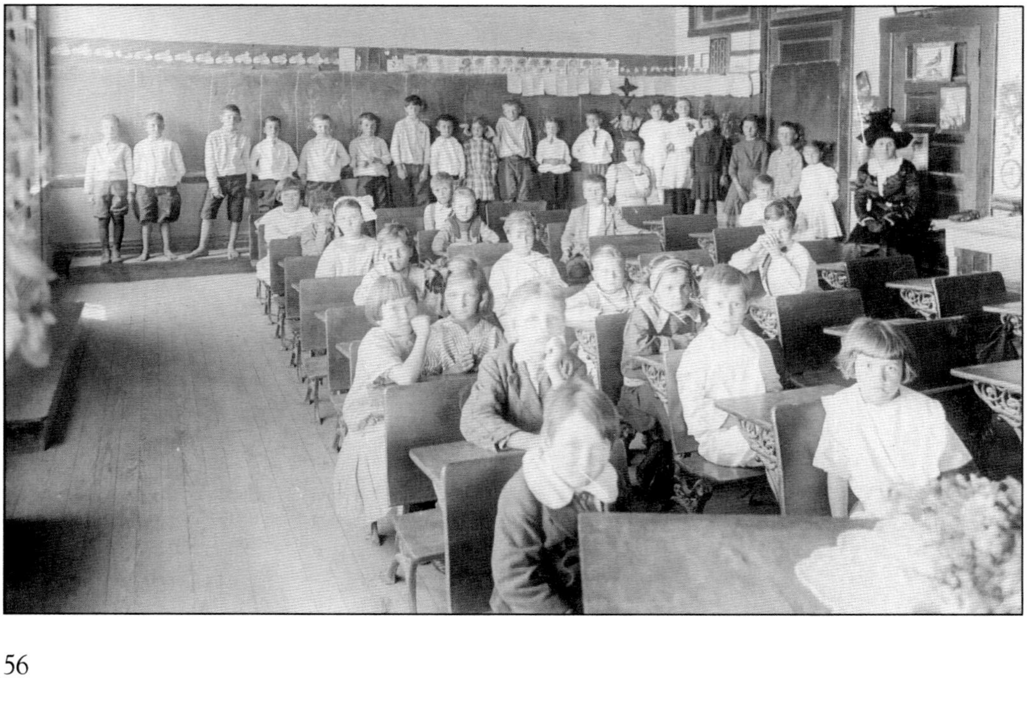

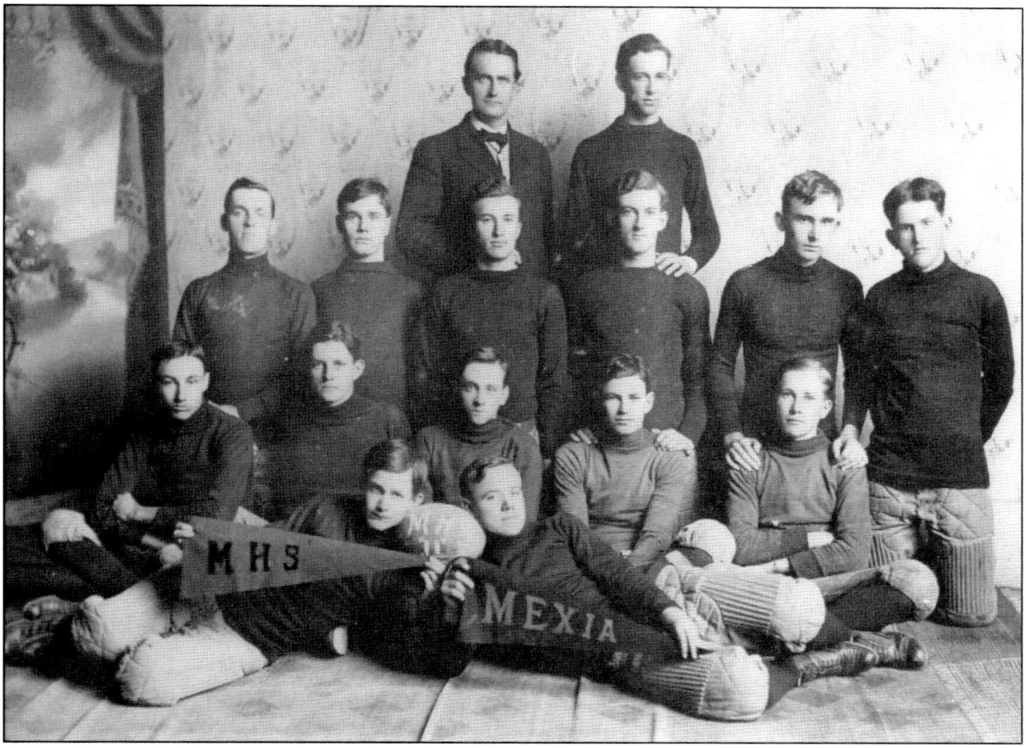

Mexia High School's first organized football team is shown above in 1911. Posing for the team photograph are, from left to right, (first row) Marvin Steen and W.H. Wallace Jr.; (second row) Wendell Ryan, W.B. Rennolds, Wright Kincheloe, Ab Steele, and Douglas Cogdell; (third row) ? McReynolds, Sid Hurley, Howard Dailey, Oscar Denning, Vincent Gantz, and Loman Cox; (fourth row) coach A.G. Koenig and C.P. McKenzie. That year, the team played Corsicana, Blooming Grove, and Hubbard. Below is a photograph of the Mexia Blackcats in 1928. (Both, Gibbs Memorial Library.)

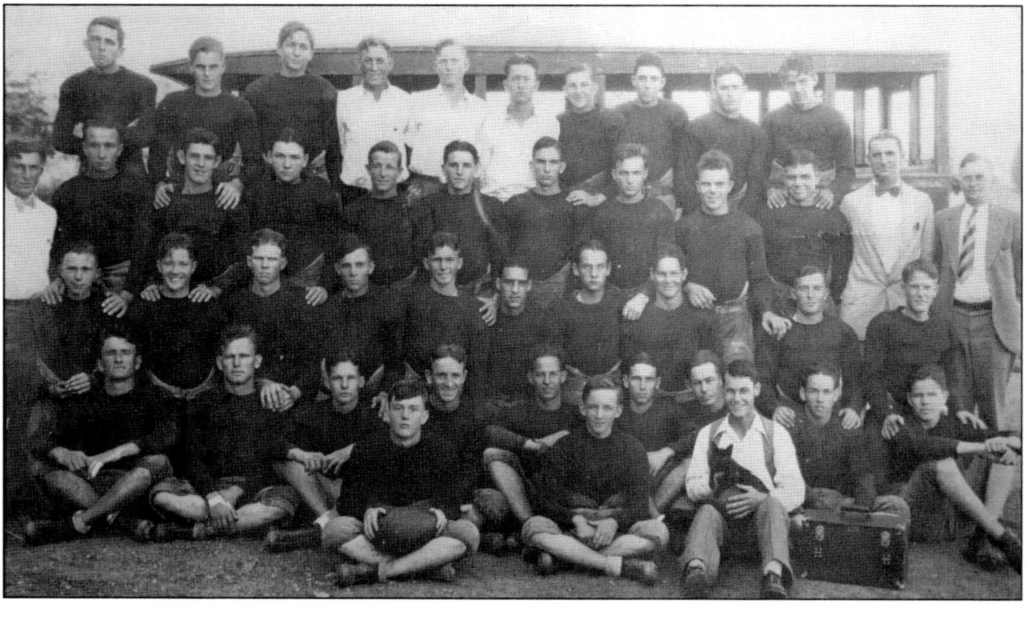

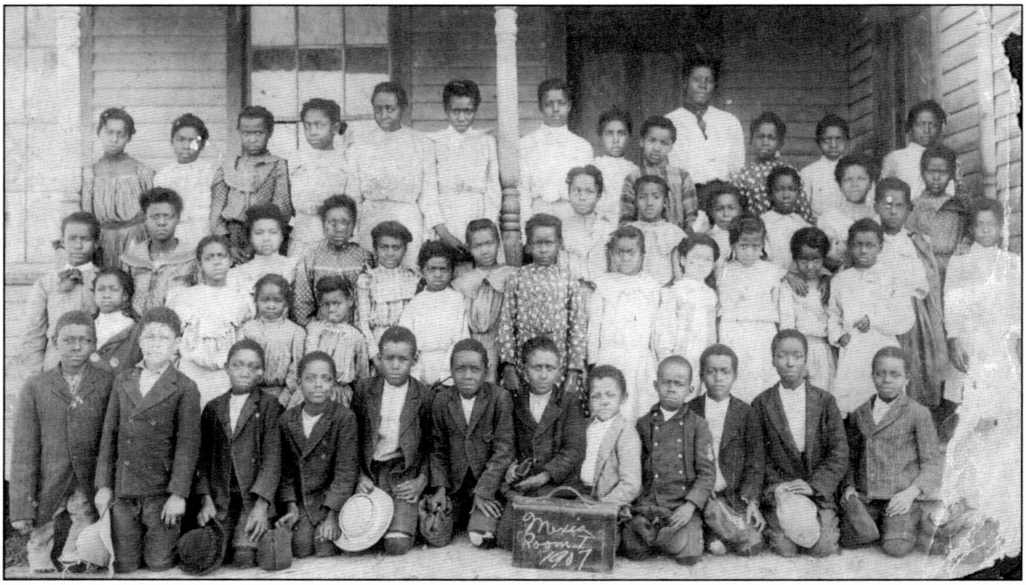

The first public school for African American students was established in 1883. The wood-frame building had two rooms. It was located on the corner of North Herman and East Sumpter Streets and had entrances facing each street. A smaller building was later moved behind the school for elementary students. This school was destroyed by fire around 1915. African American students pose at the school in 1907. (Mexia School Museum.)

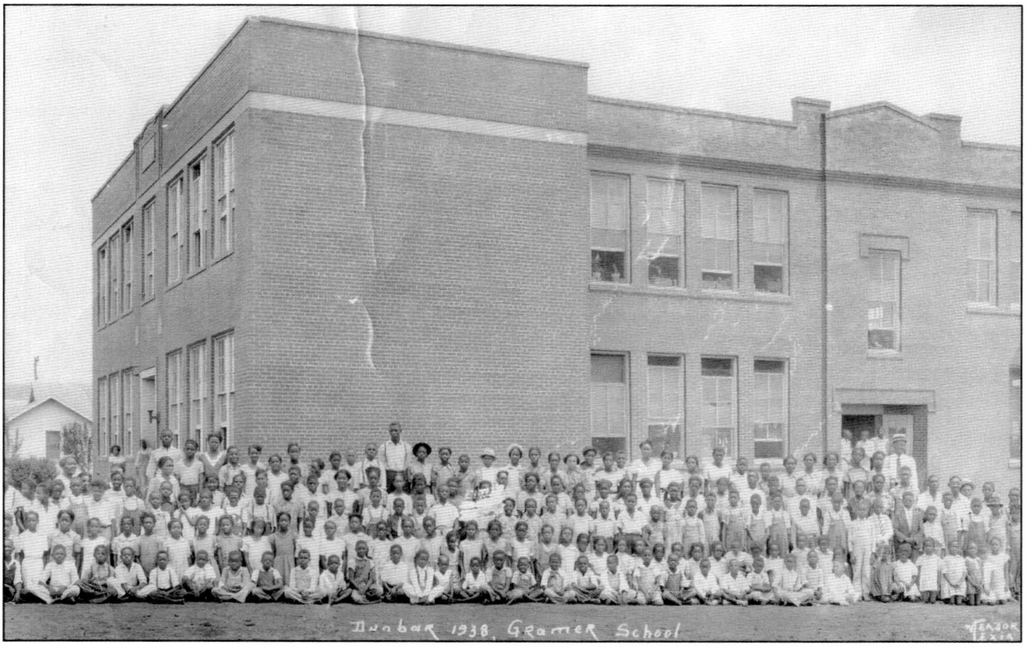

In 1915, a two-story, brick school building was constructed for African American students in Mexia. It was named Dunbar School and was located on the 500 block of West Main Street. It was condemned in 1948, and the new Dunbar School was constructed. Used until Mexia's schools were integrated in 1968, the building was demolished in 1973. Pictured in front of the original building are Dunbar elementary students and teachers in 1938. (Mexia School Museum.)

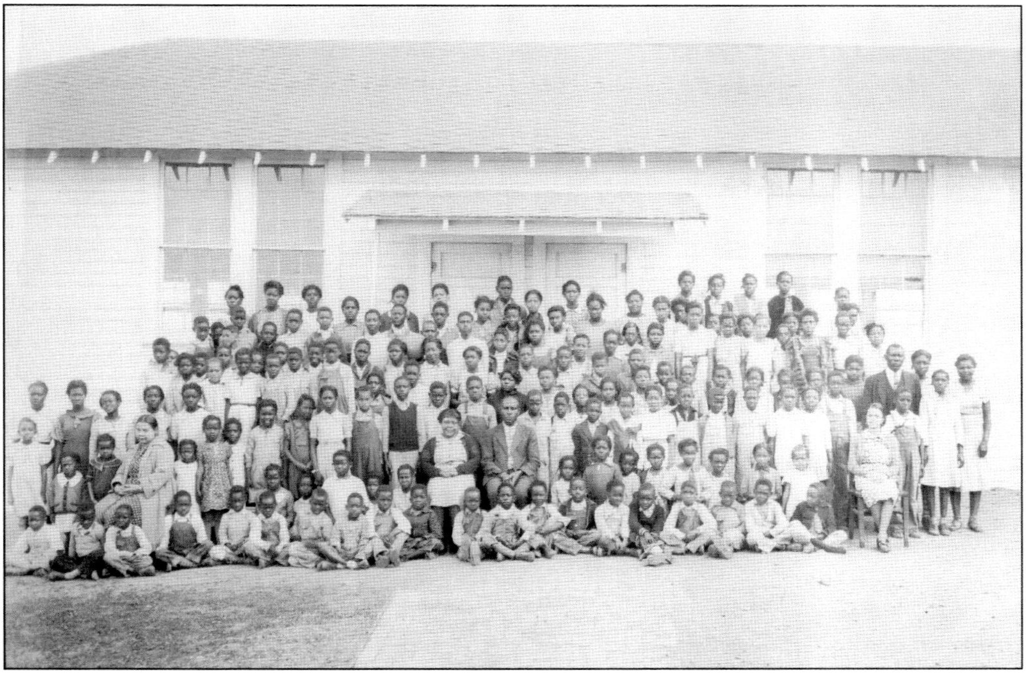

Around 1895, a school was established in East Mexia for African American students living east of the tracks. School was held in various locations until the 1920s, when two wood-frame buildings were moved to the corner of Main and Presley Streets. Named for Fredrick Douglass, the Douglass School eventually housed only elementary grades. A new building was constructed in the late 1950s. Pictured are Douglass students in 1935. (Mexia School Museum.)

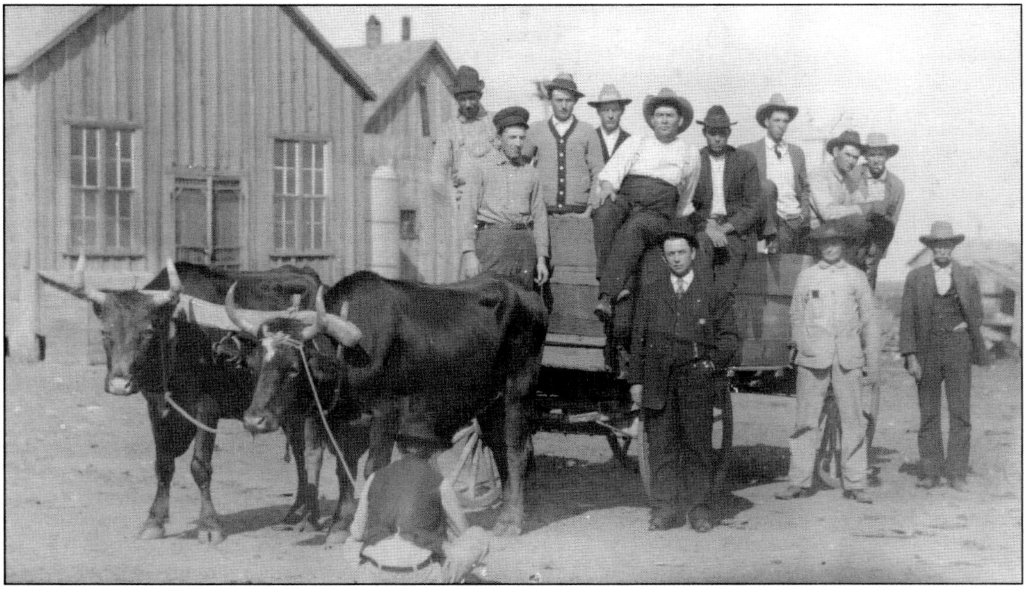

Coolidge was established in 1903 by the Trinity & Brazos Valley Railroad when it built a line from Hubbard to Mexia. The town was named for Thomas Jefferson Coolidge, a stockholder in the railroad. A post office was established in 1903, and the town was incorporated on April 19, 1905. This 1905 photograph shows several Coolidge residents posing with an ox-drawn wagon. (Incommons Bank of Coolidge.)

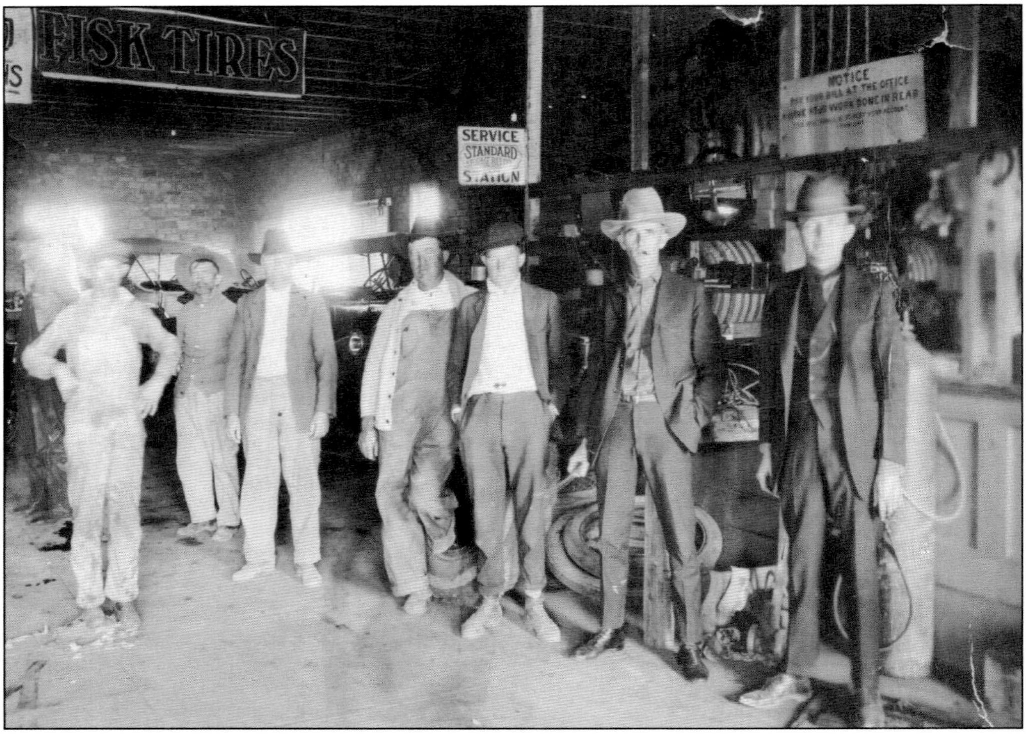

Pictured above is the Coolidge Ford dealership in 1921. The men are, from left to right, Zack Williamson, John Hawkins, Henry Harris, Marvin Bolen, Jake Robbins, Peyton Still, and Jack Driver. Below is a 1920s photograph of the Coolidge Fire Department. Shown are, from left to right, (first row) Loyle Daniels, Milburn Copland, Carl Hill, Paul Jones, Fred Bryan, John H. Nelson, Jim Alex Robbins, Earl Freeman, Tracy East, and Bill Strickland; (second row) Owen R. Cotton, Edgar Brigance, Dewitt Grooms, Carl B. McClain, Joe W. Hancock, Asa Lamb, Hennie Miller, Jay Robbins, Ray Robbins, and John Pearson. (Both, Incommons Bank of Coolidge.)

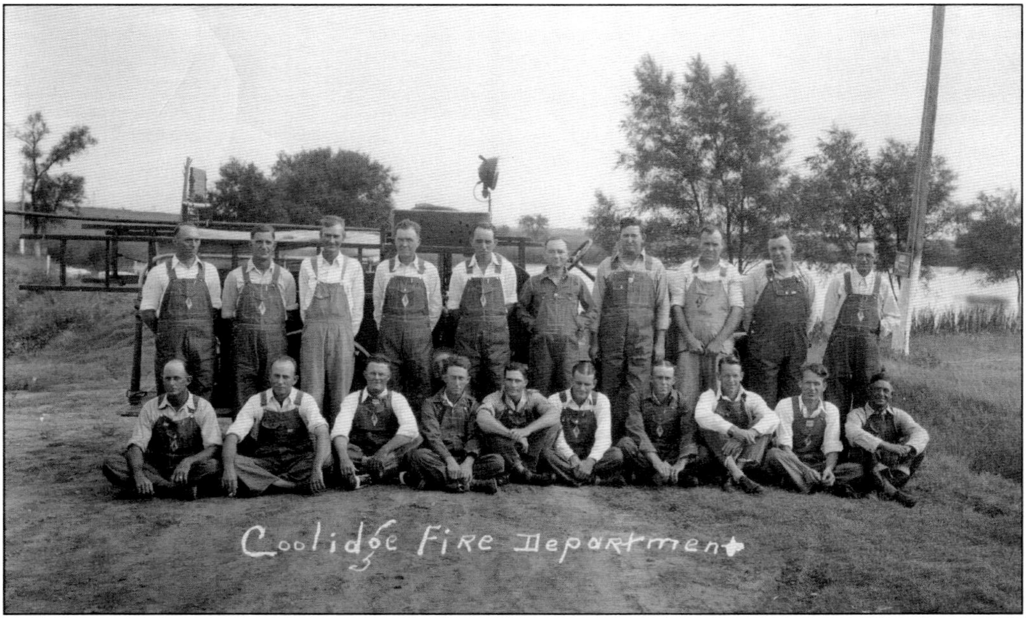

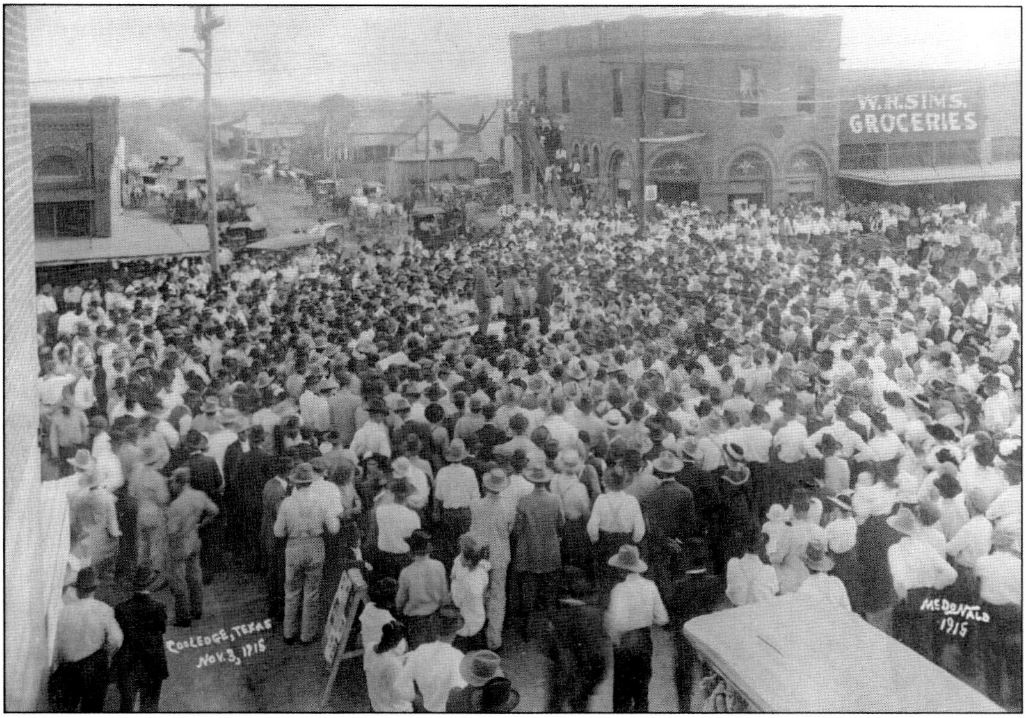

The main street of Coolidge was not only the major thoroughfare of the city, but was also used as a gathering place for weekend drawings and a meeting place to deliver important news. In this photograph, taken on November 3, 1915, Coolidge voters pack the downtown streets to hear the results of the November 2 election. (City of Coolidge.)

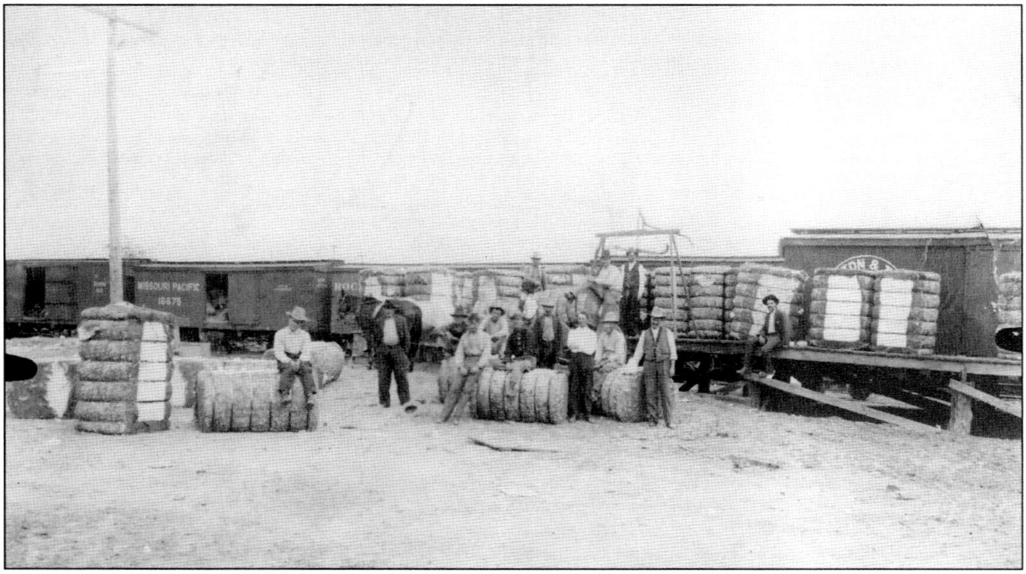

Personville, in southeastern Limestone County, was established in 1854 by B.D. Person. The town became a stop on the Nelleva Cut-Off, which was built by the Houston & Texas Central Railroad in 1906. The cotton dock at Personville is shown here in 1910. Here, cotton bales were loaded onto railcars and shipped to market. The Nelleva Cut-Off was abandoned by the railroad in 1934 after it began losing money. (Bob Crider.)

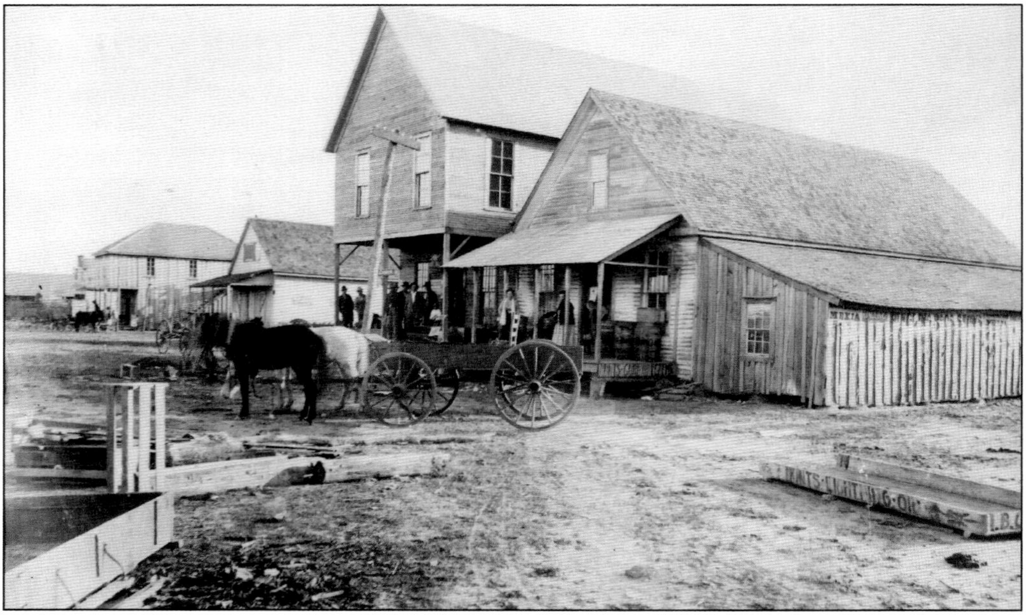

In 1855, Personville had only two residences, a blacksmith shop, and a saloon. Within two years, the community had eight residences, three dry goods stores, two groceries, a blacksmith shop, a bowling alley, and a cotton gin. In 1882, John Frank Boyd taught school and established the Boyd Drug and General Merchandise Company. He was also the unofficial undertaker. R.P. Merrill opened a dry goods store in the early 1880s that was reported to have an extremely large stock for that time. By 1914, the town had a population estimated at 200. A.B. Crider's mercantile store occupies the two buildings in the foreground in the photograph above, taken in 1910. In the photograph below, taken the same year, is the blacksmith shop of Josh Crider. (Both, Bob Crider.)

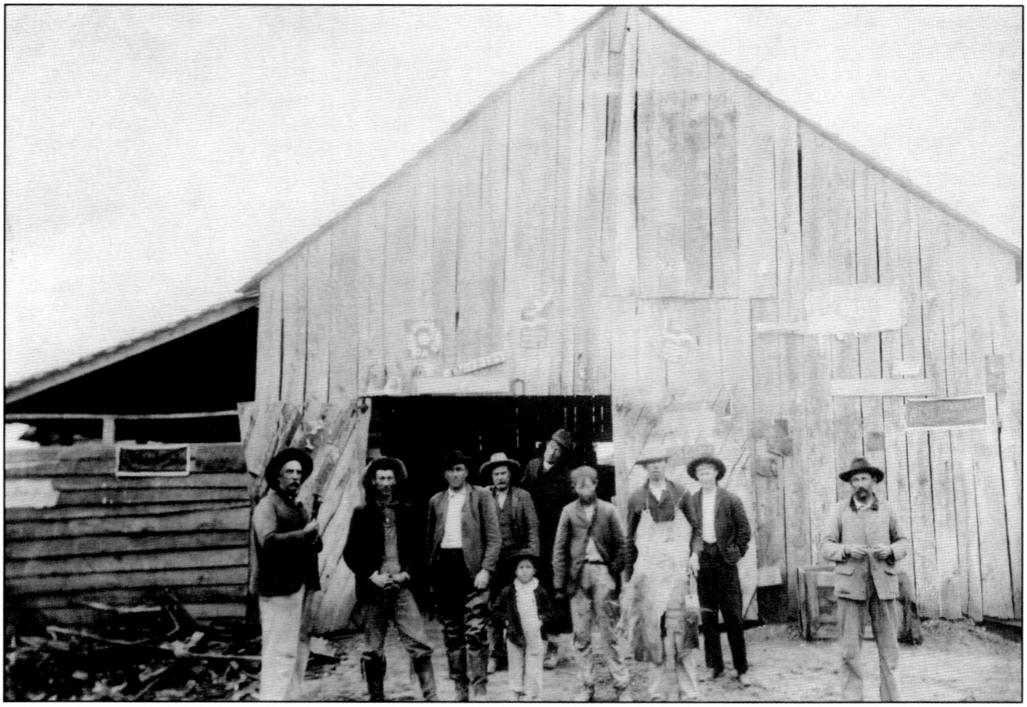

Four

Farming Communities

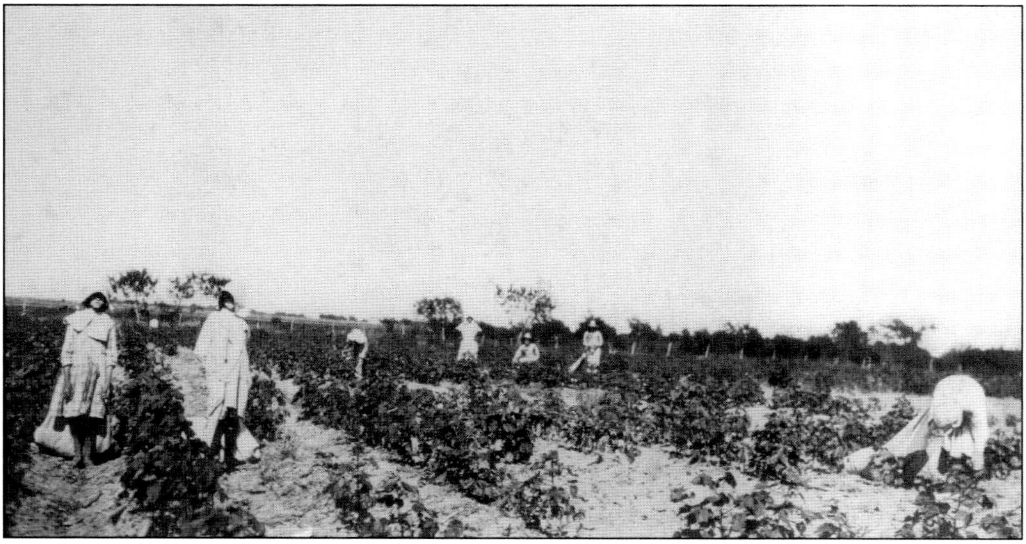

The coming of the railroads to Limestone County accelerated the production of cotton. Many family farms growing cotton as the cash crop sprang up. Communities developed in all parts of the county, each with a school, one or two churches, one or two stores, a blacksmith shop, and at least one cotton gin. Here, members of the Quint Rasco family pick cotton near Thornton. (Limestone County Historical Museum.)

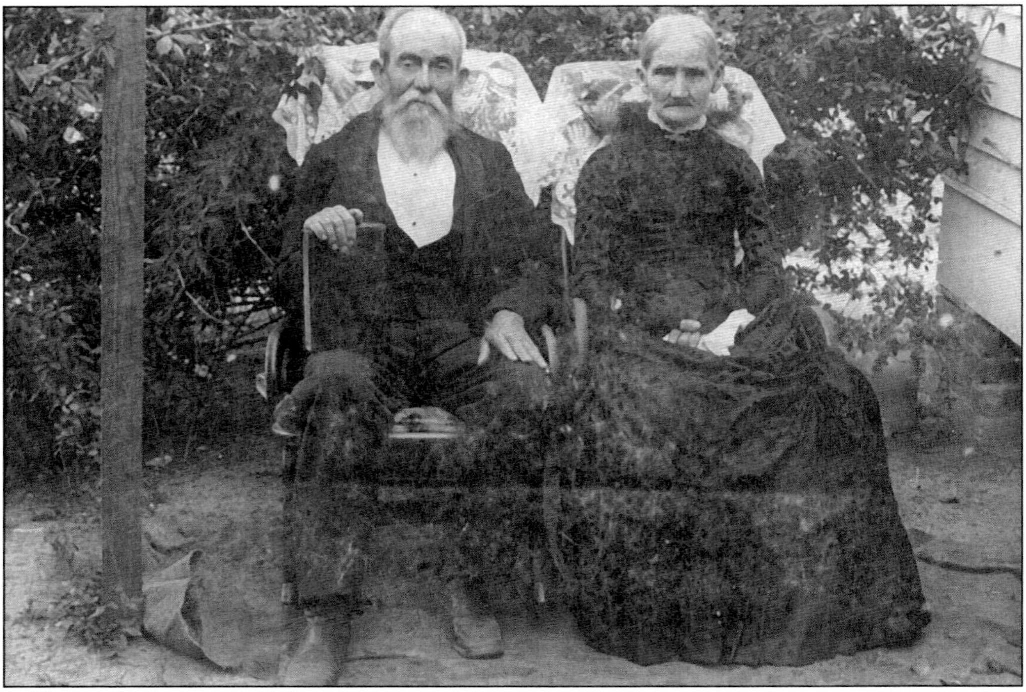

Pictured above are James and Narita Jane Kennedy Armour. In 1859, they moved their family to Tehuacana in Limestone County. They lived there for three years, during which time James contributed to the establishment of the first school. James then purchased land west of Tehuacana. He began to improve it when the Civil War began. He enlisted in the Confederate army, serving in the Western Division. He laid out the town of Armour on his land in 1882. At its peak, Armour had several businesses, two steam-powered gristmills, a school, two churches, and a population of 100. The community quickly disappeared after 1903 when the railroad established the town of Coolidge one mile north. Pictured below are members of the Armour chapter of the Eastern Star and family members on May 4, 1902, the chapter's second anniversary. (Both, Limestone County Historical Museum.)

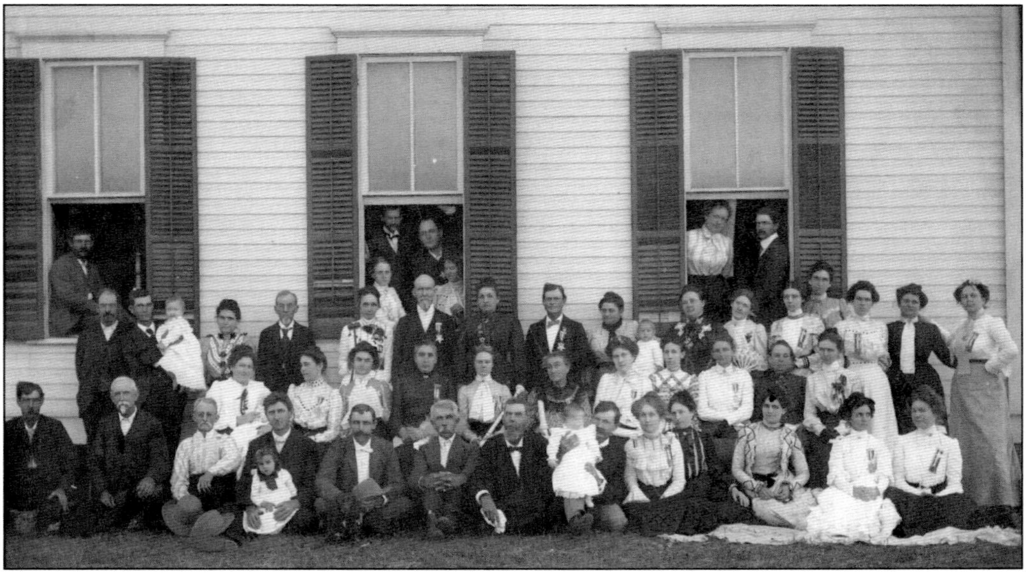

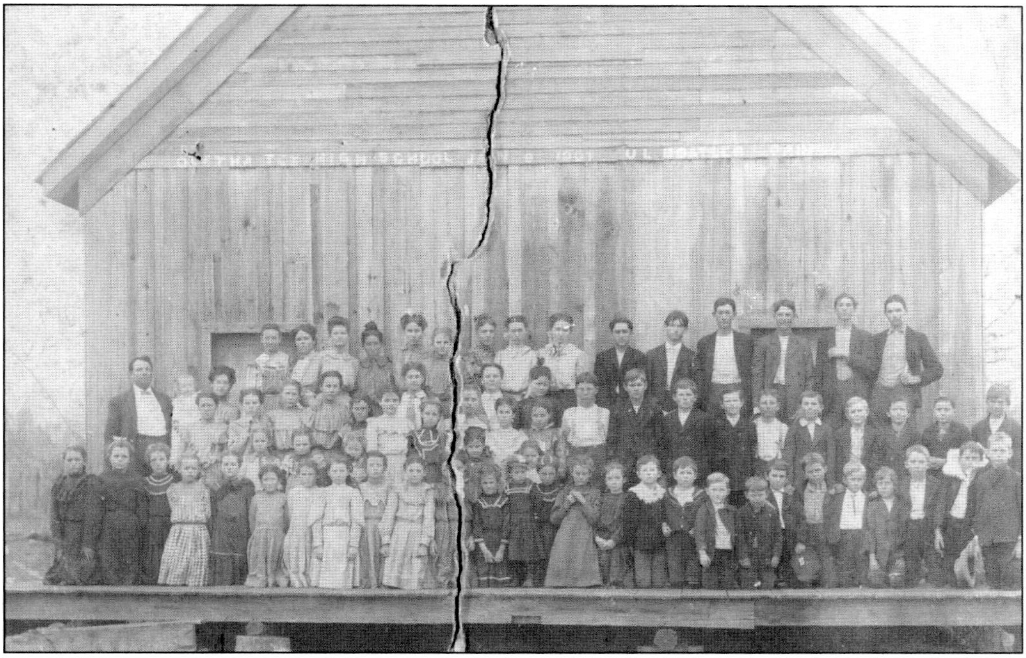

Under the community system created by the Texas School Law of 1876, a school could be created by the county judge at the request of a group of parents. The School Law of 1884 mandated that community schools change to a district system. Limestone County was exempt, but most county schools gradually adopted the district system. Pictured above is a community school at Oletha in 1907. In 1911, the Oletha community was within the Center Point Common School District, which later consolidated with Independence, Mount Joy, and Union school districts to form the Oletha Consolidated School District. Below is an early photograph of the Rocky Point School during the late 1800s. Rocky Point Common School District was created in 1896 and consolidated with the Box Church district in 1931. (Above; William Reagan; below, Faye Dunn.)

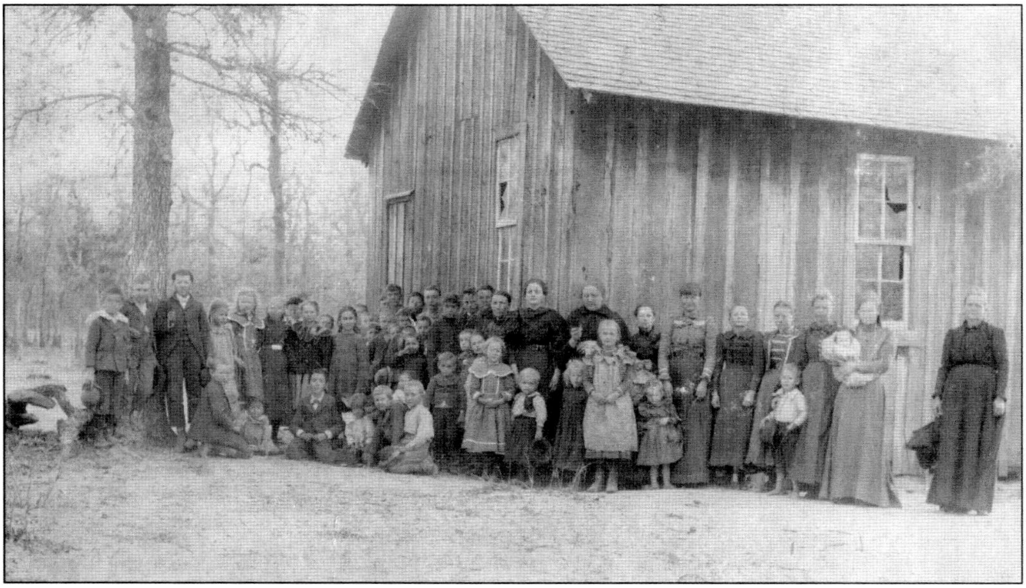

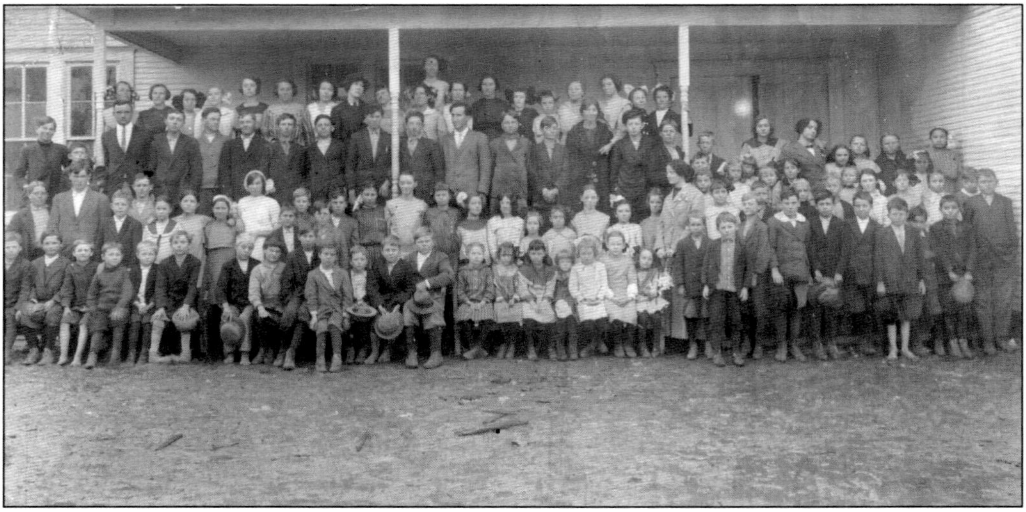

Box Church was settled by the McClellan, Rasco, Herod, and Hyden families in 1857. It was named for a church established in the community in the 1890s. The Box Church School District was created in 1902. It consolidated with Rocky Point School District in 1931, forming the Box Church Consolidated School District. It then consolidated with Groesbeck in 1950. Shown here is the Box Church School in 1913. (Limestone County Historical Museum.)

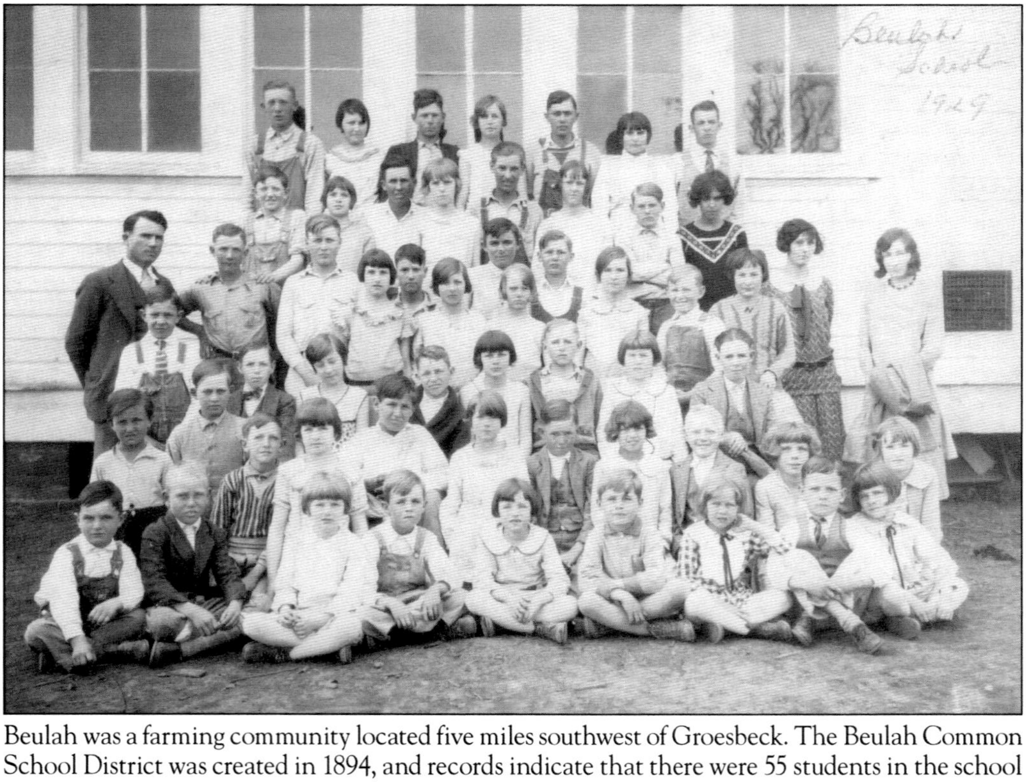

Beulah was a farming community located five miles southwest of Groesbeck. The Beulah Common School District was created in 1894, and records indicate that there were 55 students in the school in 1896. Only the school and several houses made up the community in the 1940s. The Beulah School District consolidated with Groesbeck ISD in 1949. Here, Beulah School students and a teacher pose in 1929. (Limestone County Historical Museum.)

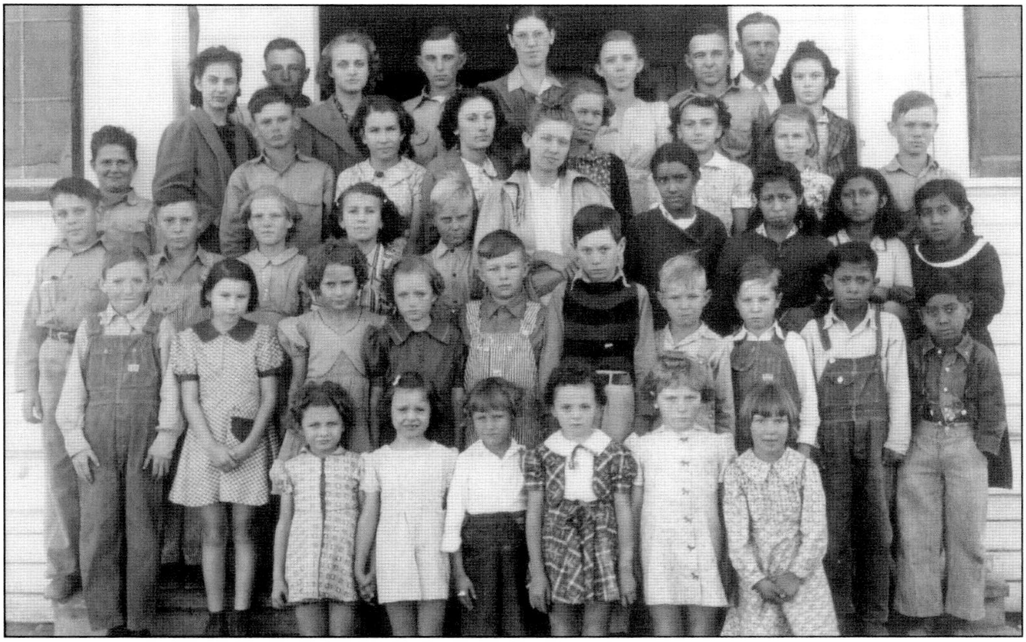

Frosa was named for Jose Frosa, one of the early settlers of the area. A post office was established in 1877, after farmers had moved from the nearby sandy areas to the blackland prairie that surrounded the community. The Frosa School District was created on May 14, 1900. In 1952, the district consolidated with Groesbeck ISD. Shown here are the students of the Frosa School in 1938. (Mildred Monk.)

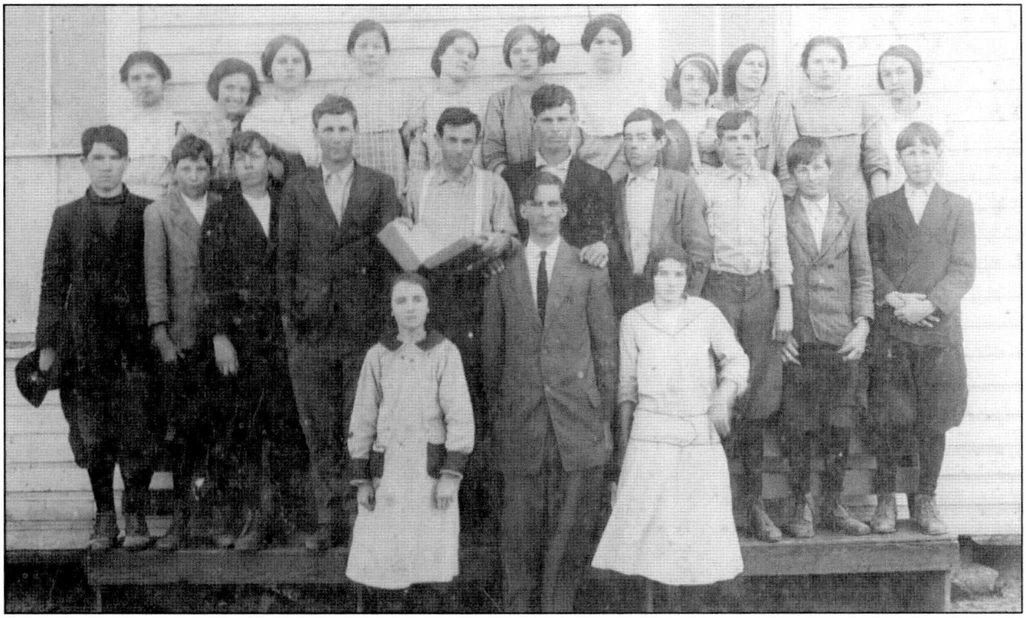

The Independence Common School District was created on September 13, 1897. By 1935, it had consolidated with Mount Joy, Union, and Center Point school districts to form the Oletha Consolidated School District, which in turn merged with Groesbeck ISD in 1962. Here, Independence High School students pose with their teacher, L.D. Sanders (first row, center), in 1913. (Limestone County Historical Museum.)

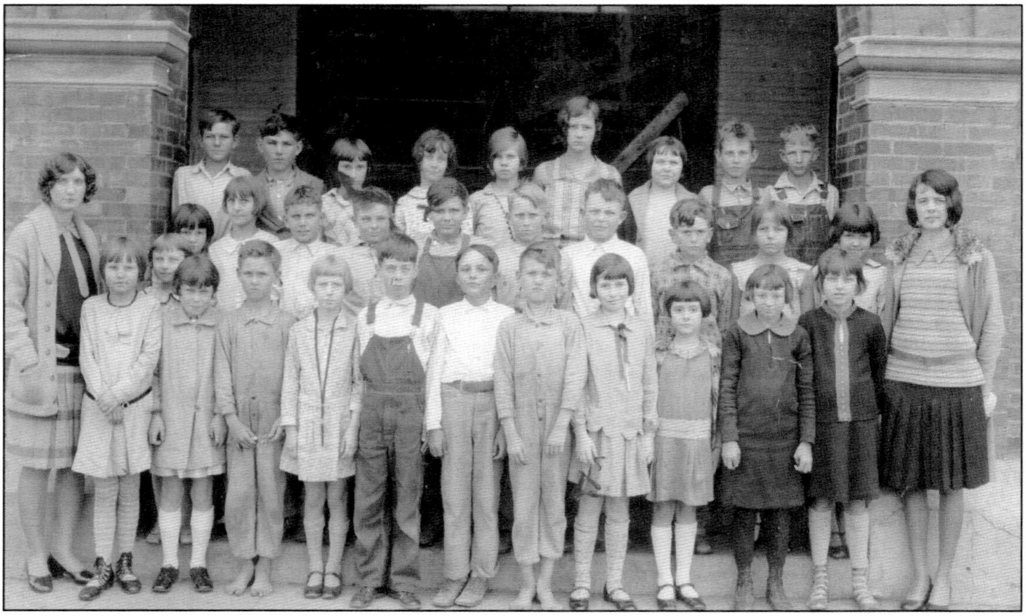

People settled in the Ben Hur community after Joseph Nussbaum began selling small tracts of land to farmers. A.T. Derden named the community in honor of Lew Wallace's book *Ben Hur.* A post office was established in 1895, and the Ben Hur School District was established on December 14 of that same year. It consolidated with Mart ISD in 1957. Students of the Ben Hur School pose with their teachers for a photograph in 1933. (Limestone County Historical Museum.)

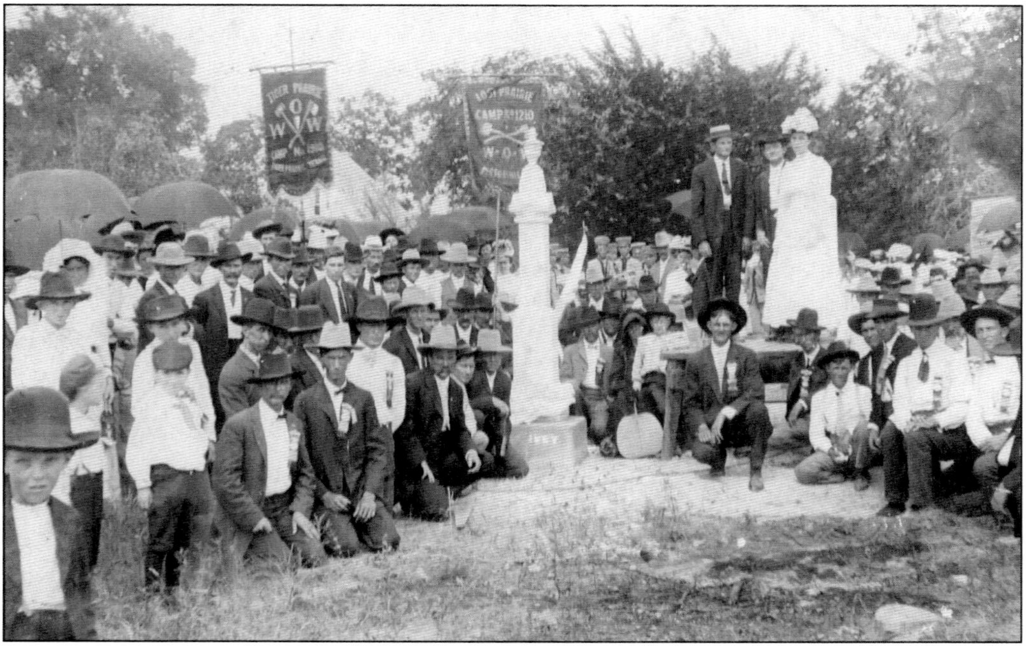

Settled in the early 1850s, Lost Prairie was one of the earliest communities in the region. The Lost Prairie Church, established in 1853, is the oldest church in Limestone County. It and the cemetery are the only evidence of this community's existence. This 1889 photograph shows members of the Tiger Prairie and Lost Prairie Woodmen of the World camps dedicating a Woodmen of the World marker in the cemetery. (Bob Crider.)

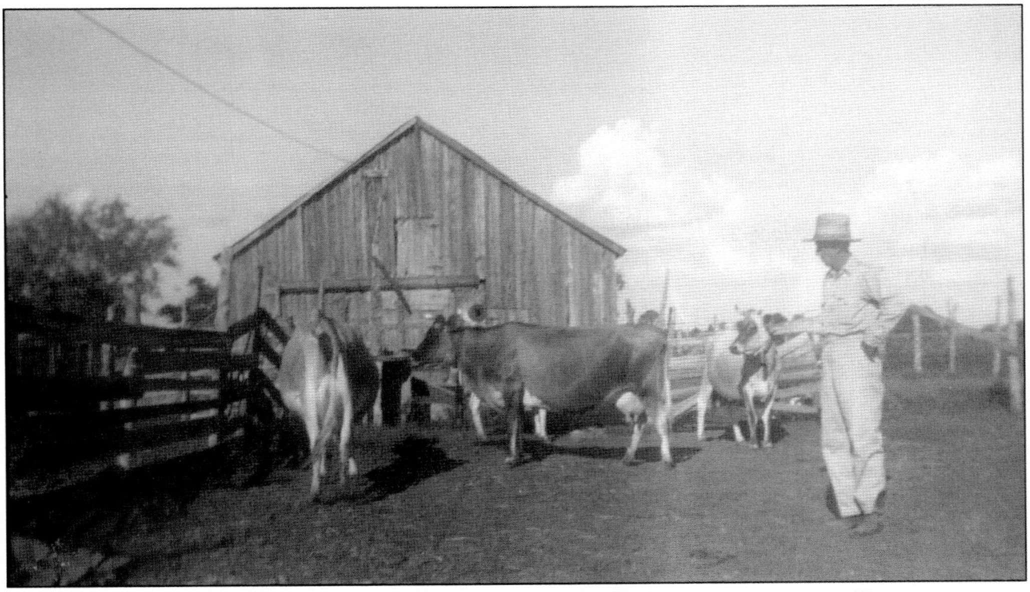

L.D. York is shown with his dairy herd on his farm in the Kickapoo community. Dairy cows were very important to farming families in Limestone County, providing the milk, cream, and butter that housewives used to prepare meals for their families. Milking cows and churning butter were daily chores often assigned to younger children. (Louis York.)

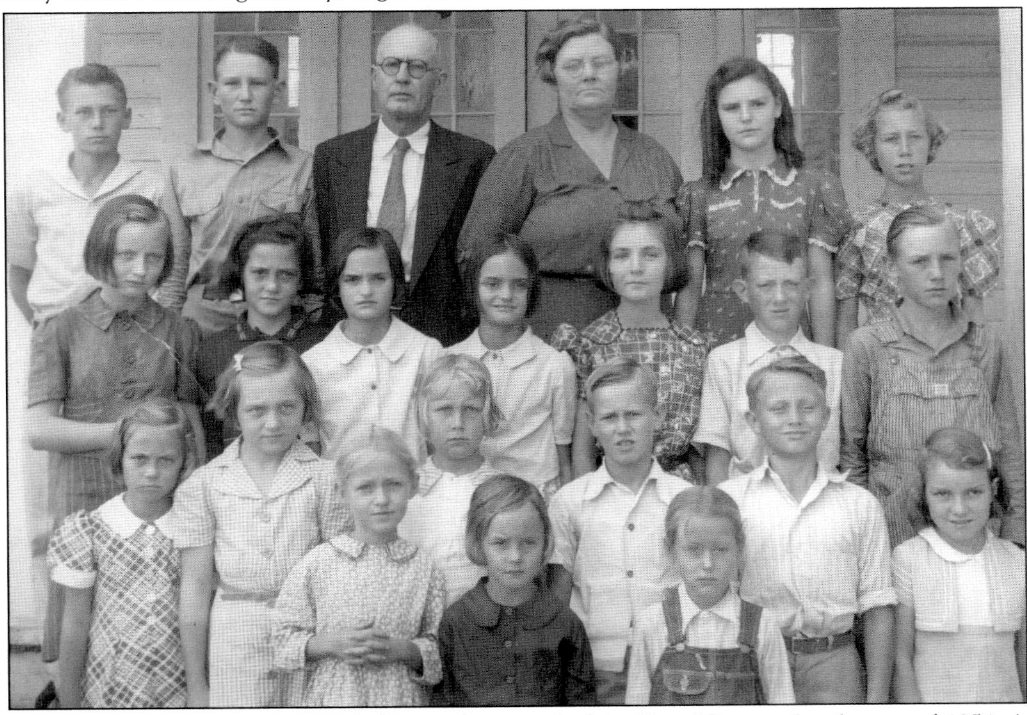

The Odds community was founded upon the arrival of the David Barron family around 1854. A post office was established in 1899, and the Locust Grove School District was formed that same year to serve the children of Odds and the surrounding area. It consolidated with the Groesbeck Independent School District in 1949. The students and teachers of the Locust Grove School at Odds pose in 1939. (Bobbie Muhlinghause.)

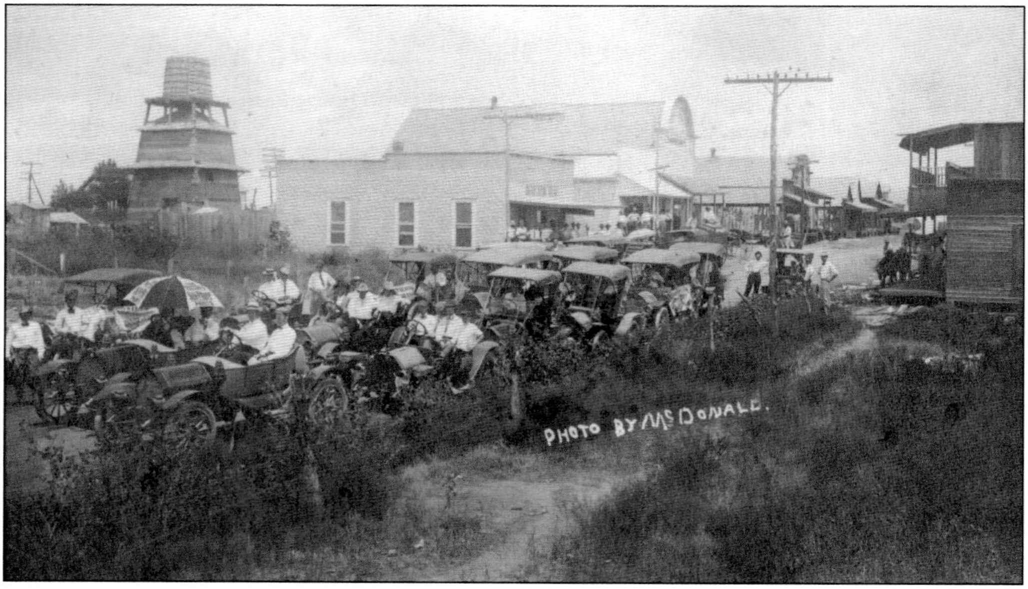

Prairie Hill was named for the rise in elevation between Christmas Creek and the Navasota River. By 1896, it had a population of 200, five churches, a blacksmith shop, a school, two hotels, a general store, a gristmill, two cotton gins, daily mail service, and a Masonic lodge. A group of trade hunters are pictured in Prairie Hill on July 12, 1912. Note the water tower on the left. (Bill Bond.)

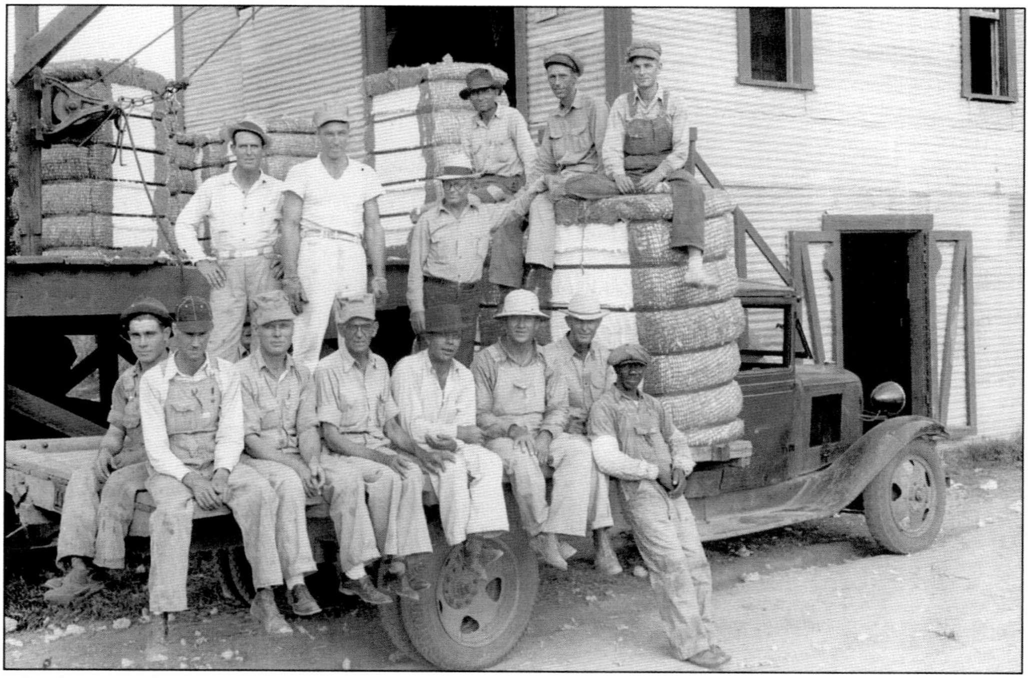

The first people to settle in the Prairie Hill vicinity were attracted to the black loamy soil. Cotton became the major cash crop. Shown posing at the Prairie Hill cotton gin around 1930 are, from left to right, (first row) Shorty McHargue, John Henry Kirkpatrick, Jessie McMinn, Lee Dyer, Stell Waldrop, E.H. Kuehl, Wilbur McFarland, and Henry Miles; (second row) Joe Chapin, Otis Bass, John Lowery (owner), Wes Thornton, Guy Parten, and Bob Stafford. (June Archer.)

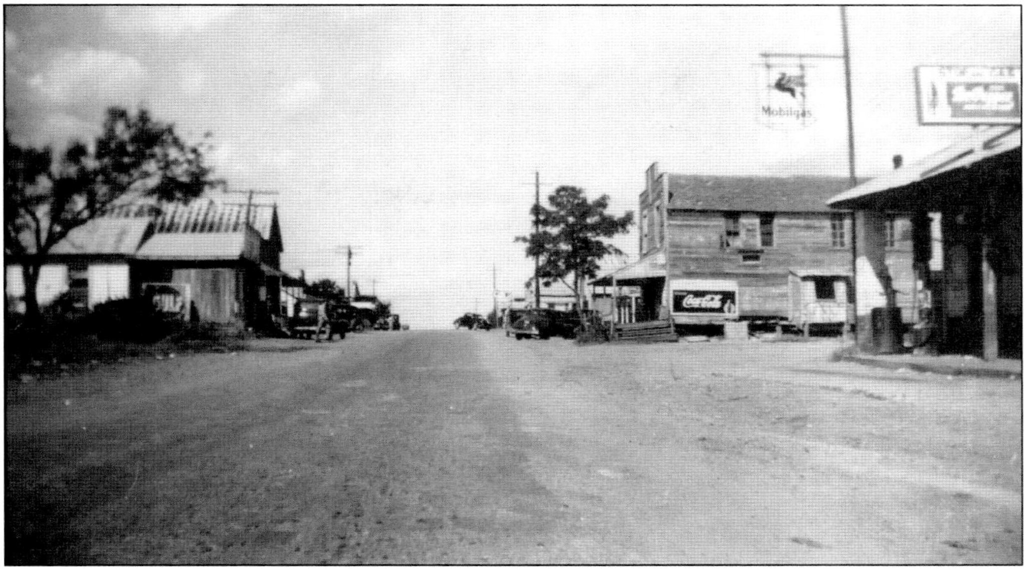

The population of Prairie Hill dropped to 152 by 1904 but began to grow during the late 1920s. By 1933, the population reached 500 but began to decline following World War II. Today, Prairie Hill has a population of about 150. These two photographs show downtown Prairie Hill during the 1930s. The above photograph was taken looking east along Highway 84. On the right side of the highway is the Mobil service station, and the building with the Coca-Cola sign is the drugstore. On the left are the Gulf service station and Runnels Grocery & General Mercantile. Below, Fred Runnels is pictured on the steps of his grocery store. The small building in the background is the Prairie Hill Telephone Exchange. (Both, June Archer.)

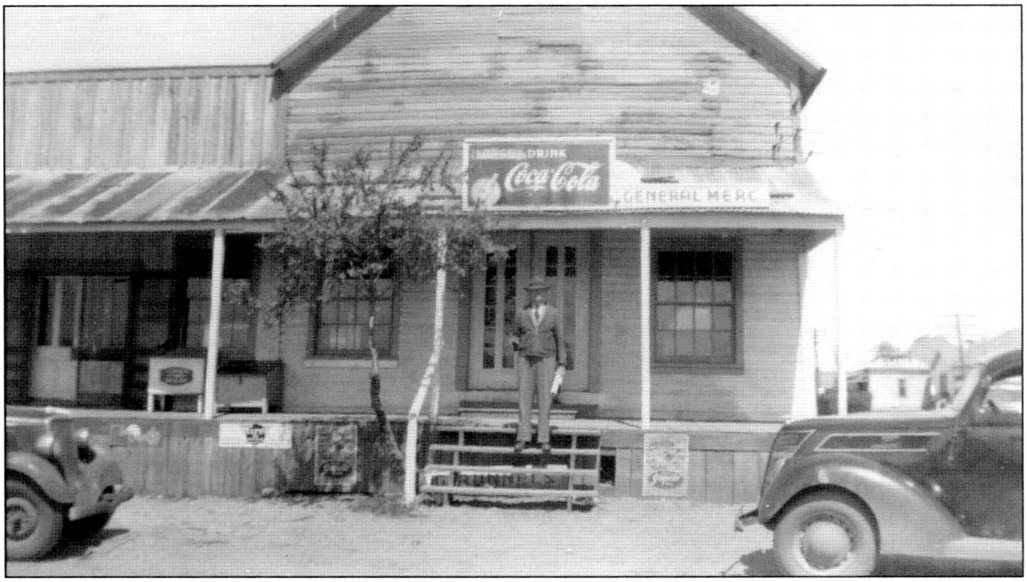

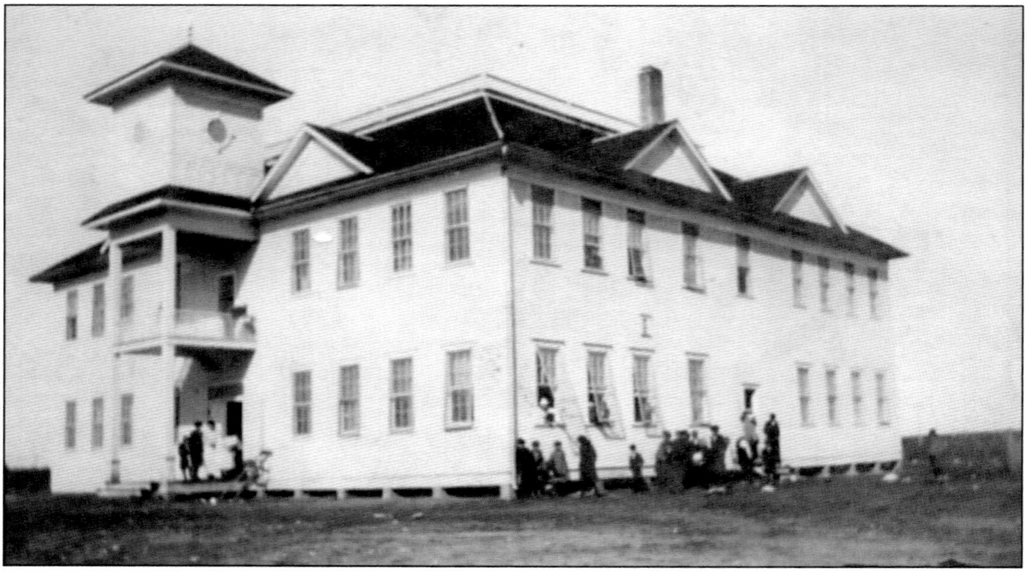

The Prairie Hill School District was created on June 14, 1894. Schools before 1894 operated as community schools. The first school was established in 1884. The first school building was destroyed by a tornado, and a new school was constructed in 1892. It was razed in 1913, and a larger school building, shown here, was constructed. It burned down during the 1919–1920 school term. (June Archer.)

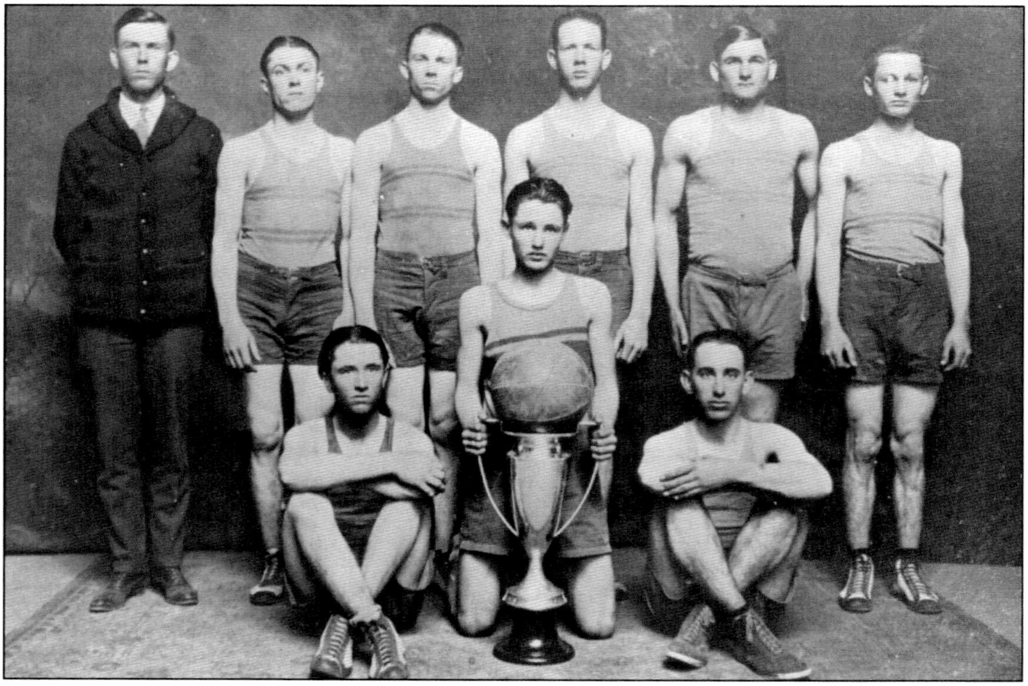

Limestone County schools joined the University Interscholastic League in 1915 and competed against each other in literary and athletic events. Pictured is the 1925 Prairie Hill Owls basketball team, winners of the district championship. The members of the team are, from left to right, (first row) Connor Spivey, Dean Lowe, and Aubrey Dellinger; (second row) coach Clint Bars, R.C. Johnson, Dwain Scott, E.J. Christian, Akie Maynard, and Kenneth Lowe. (June Archer.)

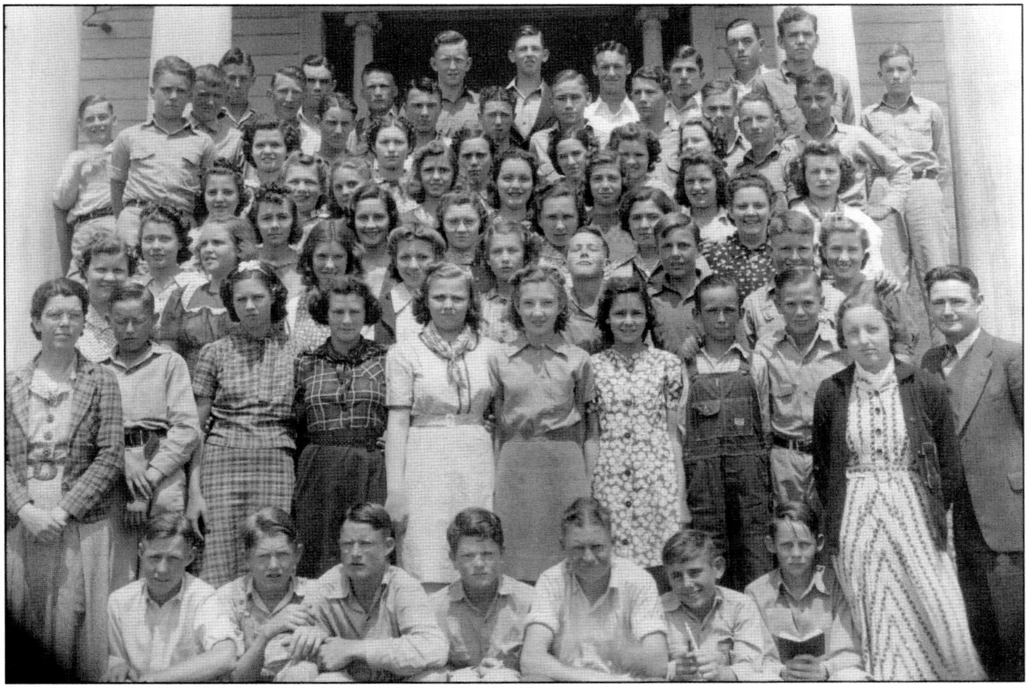

A new brick school building was constructed in Prairie Hill in 1920. In 1939, it burned down, and high school students finished the year at the Baptist church. In this photograph, the high school students of 1939–1940 stand on the front steps of the church. The last Prairie Hill school building was constructed on the Coolidge–Prairie Hill Highway. The Prairie Hill School District consolidated with Coolidge in 1963. (June Archer.)

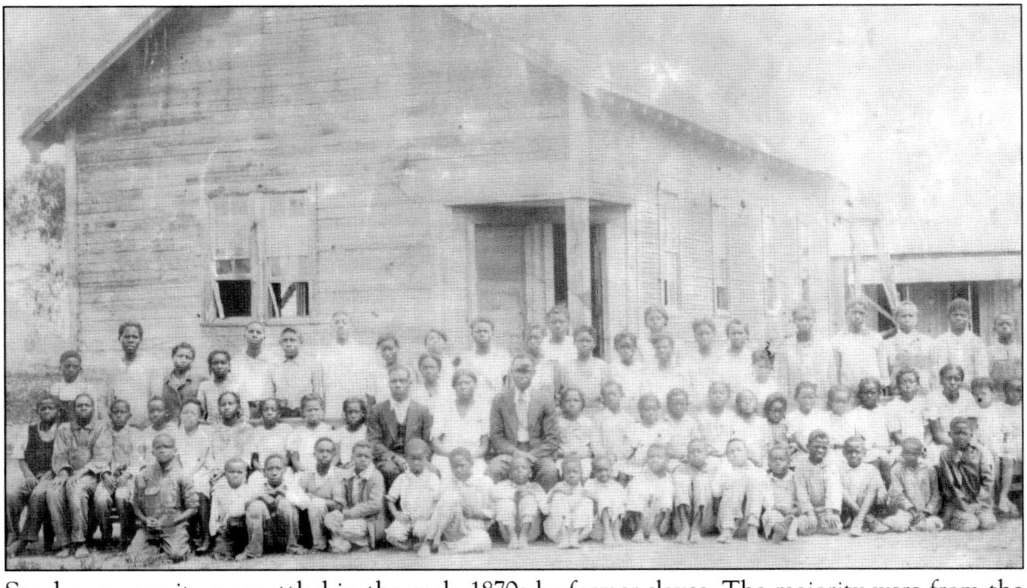

Sandy community was settled in the early 1870s by former slaves. The majority were from the plantation of Capt. R.S. Barber. The settlers immediately formed Sandy Methodist Church and began the process of establishing a means to educate the children of the community. This photograph from the early 1900s shows students in front of the church building where classes were held. (Katharyn Gray.)

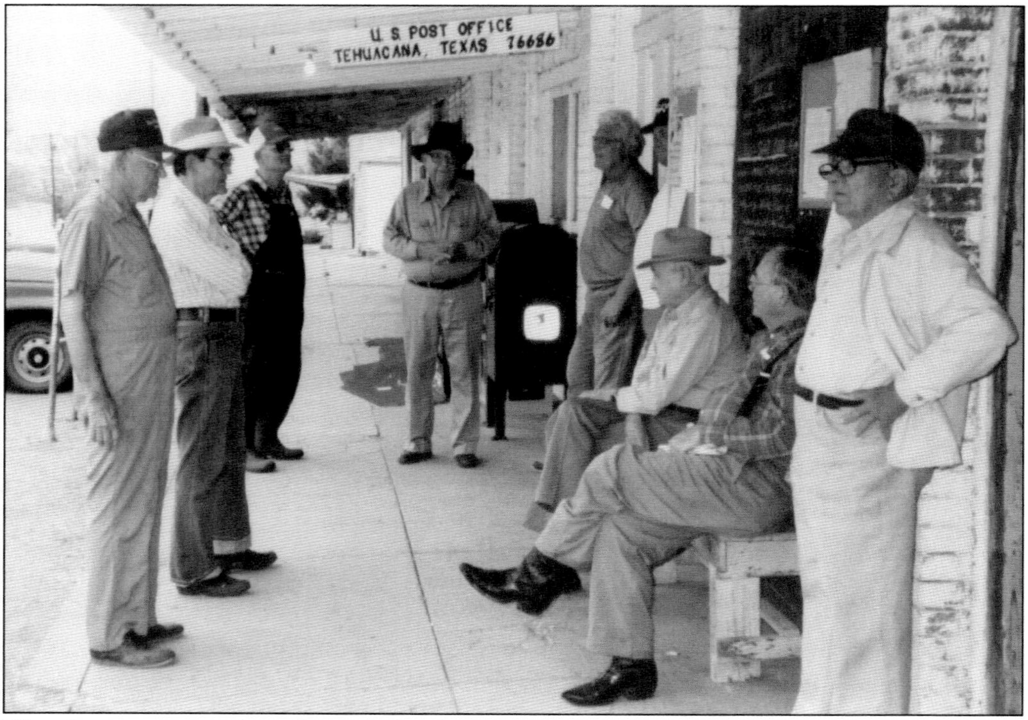

The place to visit and catch up on local gossip in Tehuacana was the post office. A group of gentlemen are shown gathered there in the mid-1980s. The men are, from left to right, J.T. Bounds, W.B. Hammond, Claude Monk, Noel Vinson, David McCartney, Freddie McDade, Robert Lowery, Ray Fessler, and Wallace Needham. (Claude Monk.)

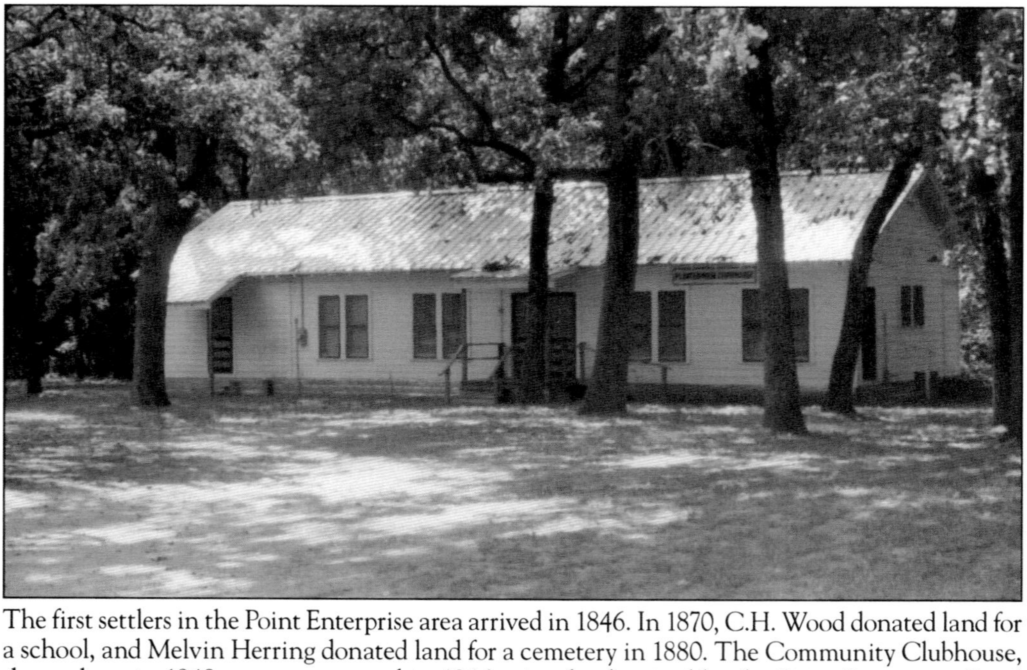

The first settlers in the Point Enterprise area arrived in 1846. In 1870, C.H. Wood donated land for a school, and Melvin Herring donated land for a cemetery in 1880. The Community Clubhouse, shown here in 1948, was constructed in 1946 using funds raised by the Point Enterprise Good Will Club, which was organized in 1937. (Helen Matthews.)

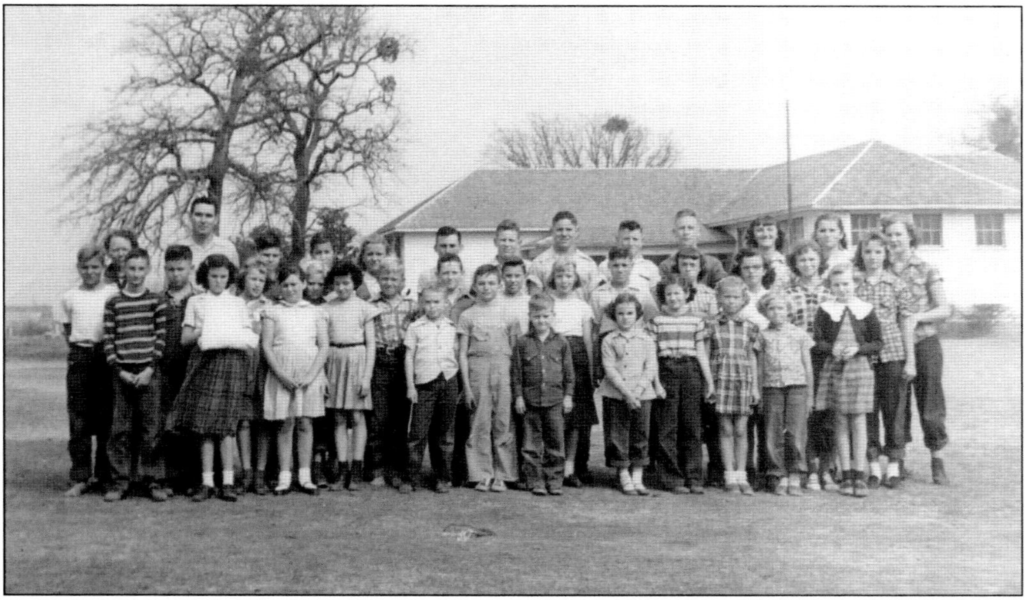

The first school building at Point Enterprise was a one-room schoolhouse built in 1870. The school district was created on March 10, 1894. In 1896, the first school was replaced with a two-room building. A five-room school building was erected in 1917, and an auditorium was added in 1924. The Point Enterprise School District consolidated with Mexia in 1965. The above photograph shows the students of Point Enterprise in 1954. Below is the Point Enterprise Little Rhythm Band in 1940. Shown posing are, from left to right, (first row) Maxine Russell, Jerry Neil Kerzee, Sudie Mary Lightsey, unidentified, and Leon Hall; (second row) Jerry Gardner, Gene Dyson, Joe Schuster, Cora Lee Holt, Bobby Reddock, and Henry Lee Russell; (third row) a Mrs. Franklin, two unidentified, Juanita Williams, C.H. Van Dyke, Jimmy Joe Williams, Lewis Lightsey, Marie Fore, and a Mrs. McGee. (Both, Helen Matthews.)

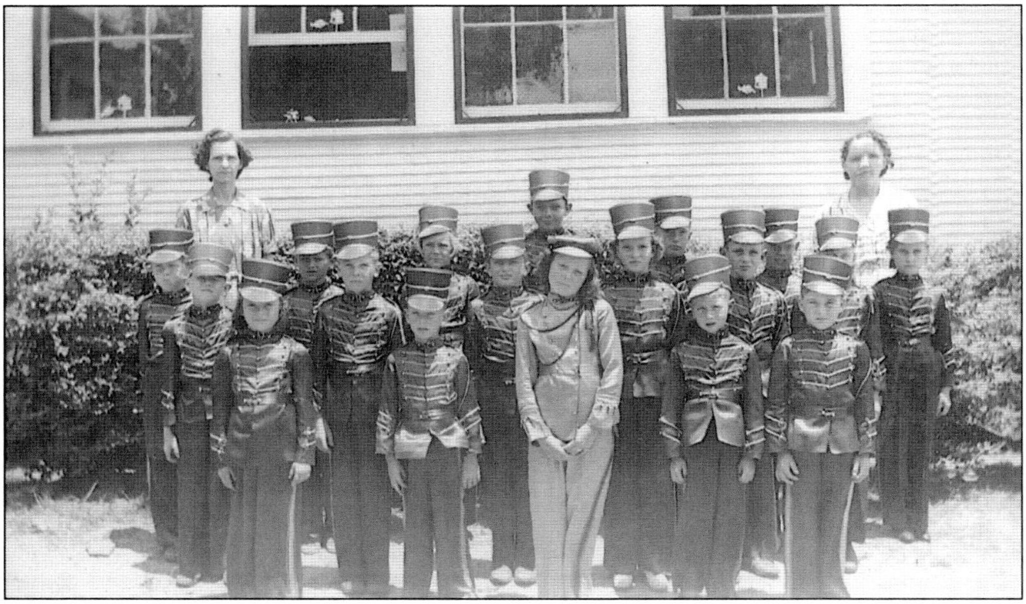

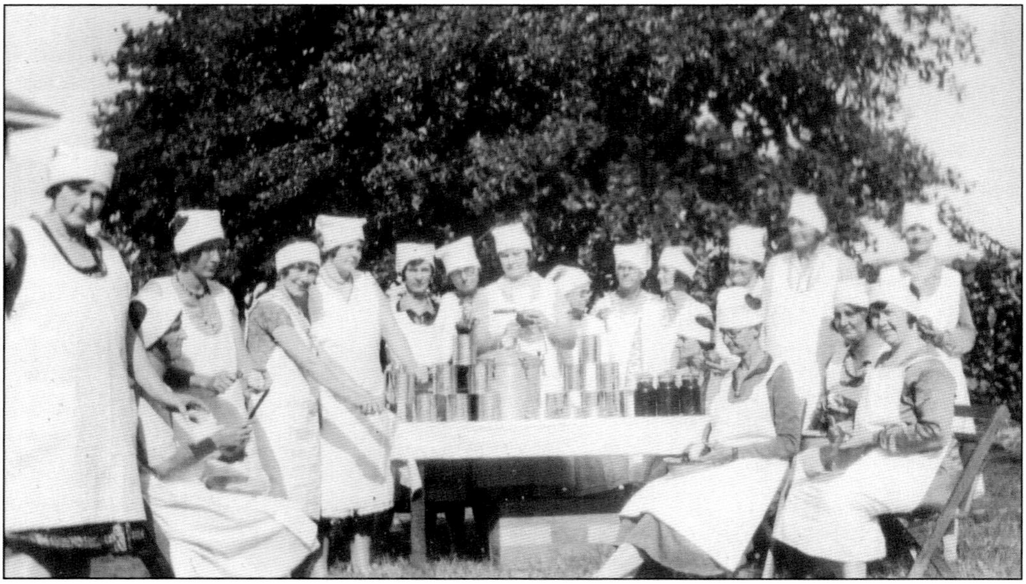

The Point Enterprise Home Demonstration Club was organized around 1920 and was very active until it disbanded in 1963. Ladies of the community met to learn and improve domestic skills. Members are shown here in the 1930s presenting the results of their home canning skills. (Helen Matthews.)

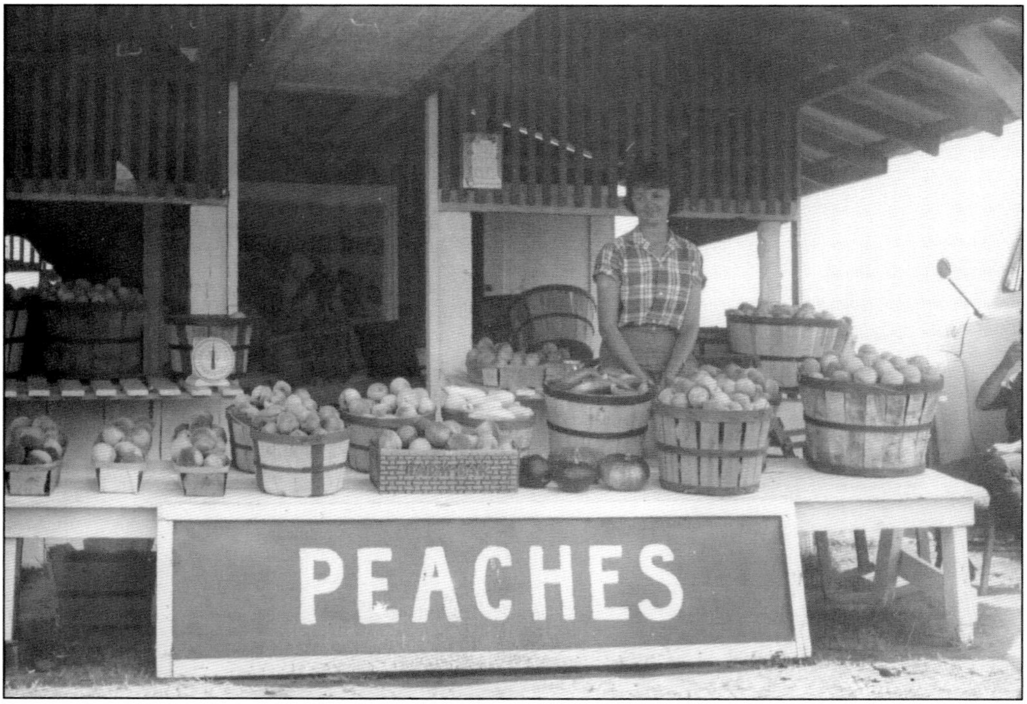

Point Enterprise has grown fruit for over a century and is well known for peaches. During the 1950s, owners of fruit orchards were E.E. Lightsey, Bill Hudson, Clyde Speights, Felix Speights, Alvin Winkler, Mike Schuster, P.B. Cate, Loman Cox, Ray McGee, Charlie Hinchliffe, L.A. Lightsey, I.L. Capers, Farmer Franks, and Gary McKinney. Helen Schuster is seen here at her father's peach stand in the mid-1960s. (Helen Matthews.)

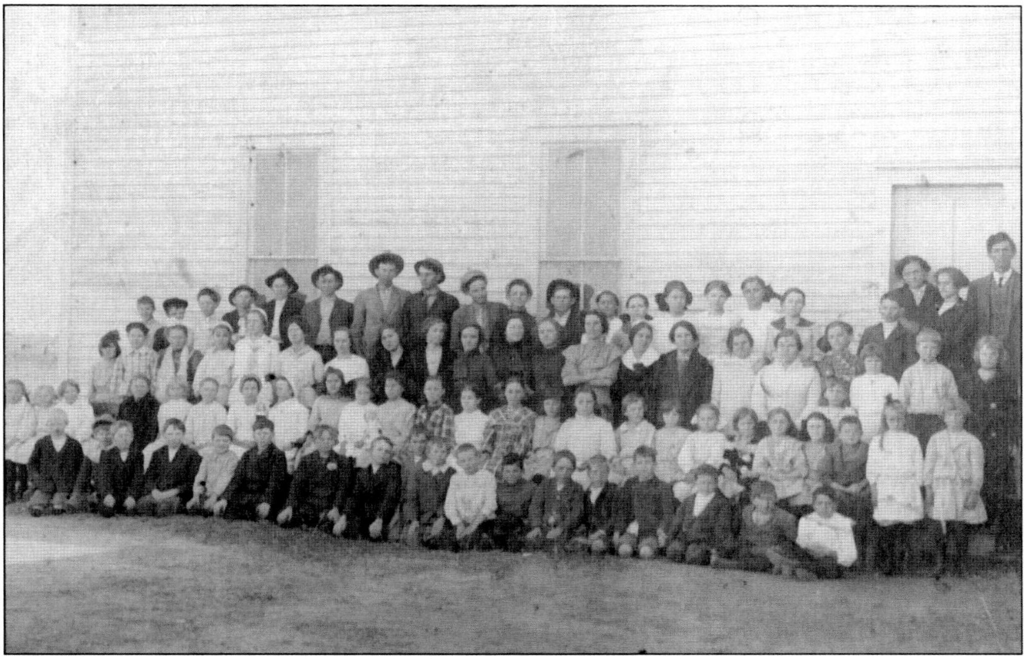

The community of Shiloh, named for the Civil War battle, was settled immediately following the war. Gideon Jordan was the postmaster, and John F. Allison founded the first school. The Shiloh School District was created on March 10, 1894. The Shiloh School and its students and teachers are shown here around 1912. (Larry Sewell.)

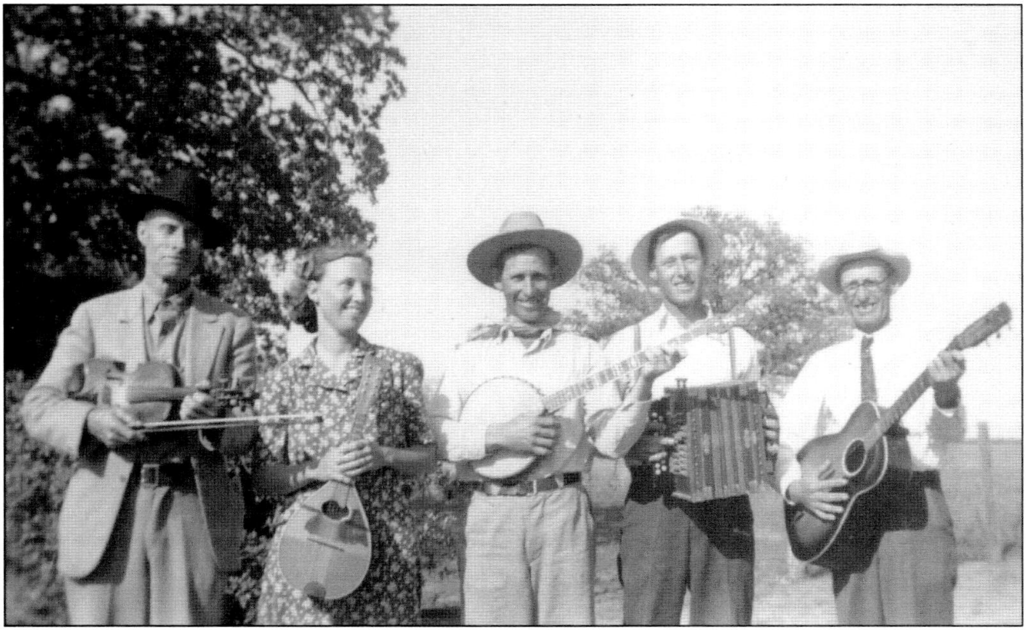

Rural farm families in Limestone County worked hard and appreciated the time they had to socialize with their neighbors. Many people could play a musical instrument and often provided the music at dances and other gatherings. Moses Henson and his children often played at church socials, box suppers, political gatherings, and dances. Shown here are, from left to right, Moses, Vera, Johnie, Silvanous, and Wallace Henson. (William Reagan.)

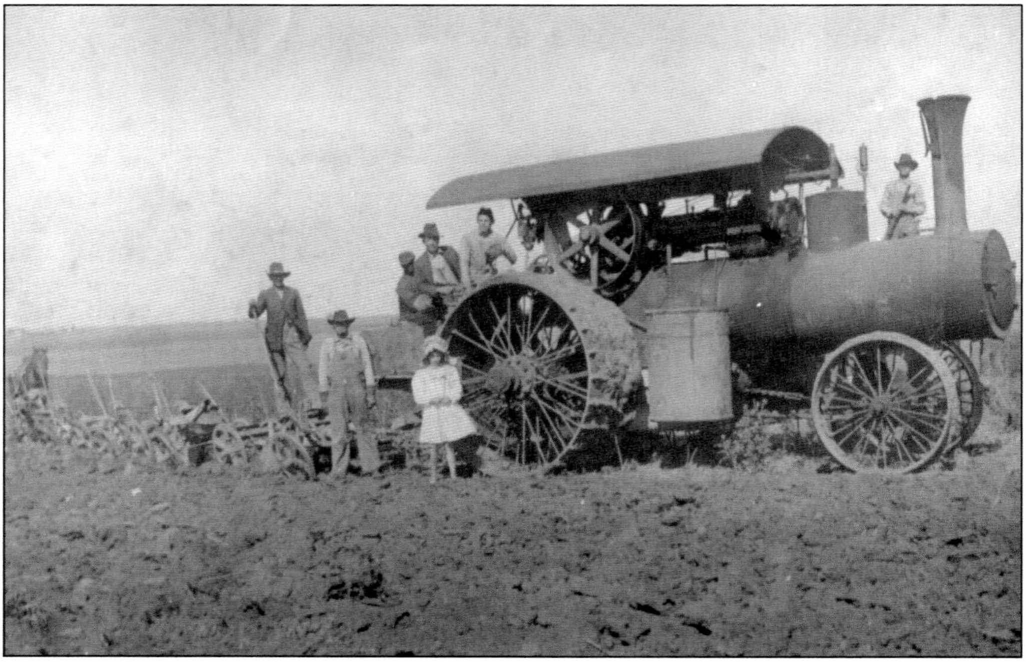

During the late 1800s and early 1900s, steam power was utilized in agriculture. There were steam-powered gristmills in the county, and some Limestone County farmers used steam power on their farms. The photograph above, from 1916, shows a steam-powered tractor that was used on the Riley Ranch between Frosa and Prairie Hill. It was bought in Dallas by the J. & J. Nussbaum Company of Mexia, owners of the Riley Ranch, and was used for plowing the area's blackland soil, which was conducive for growing cotton, corn, and oats. Below, a steam engine is being used to run a thresher on the Will Roach farm near Thornton. (Above, Limestone County Historical Museum; below, Terry Don Roach.)

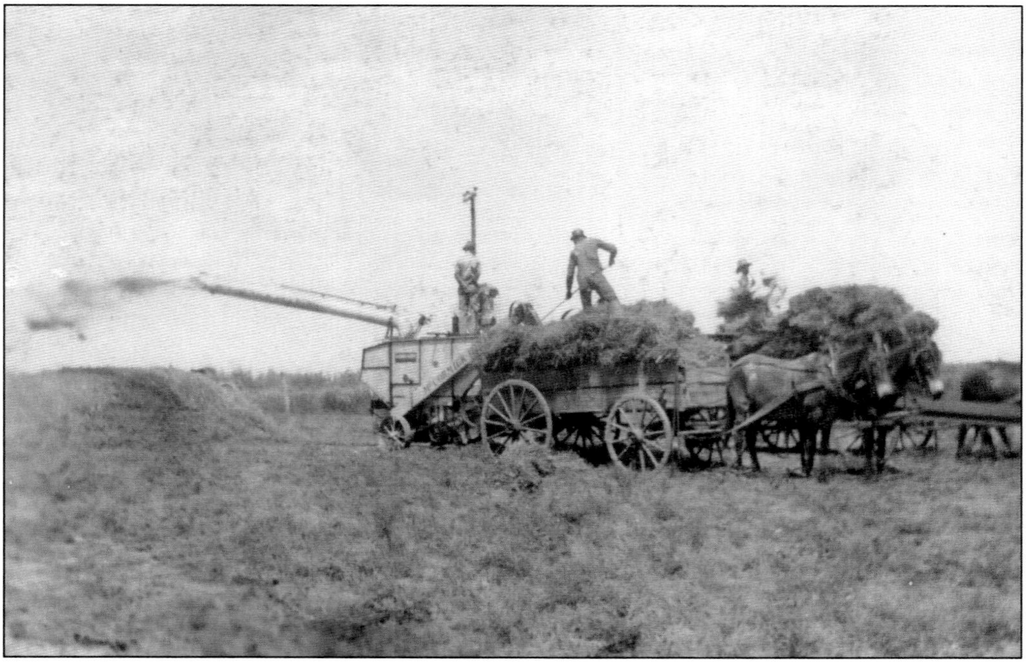

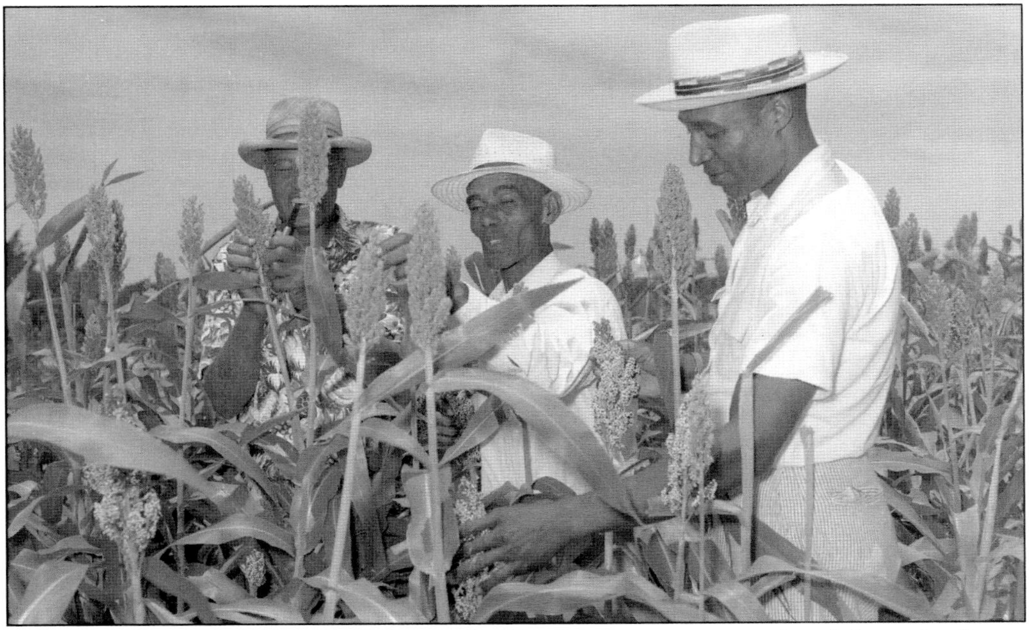

Pictured in July 1949 on the Foreman farm in the Woodland community are, from left to right, district agricultural agent H.S. Estelle, Jim Foreman, and Limestone County agriculture extension agent J.W. Booker. Foreman is showing the two agricultural agents his crop of maize. Well known for raising hogs, Foreman grew his own grain to feed them. (Cushing Library, Texas A&M University.)

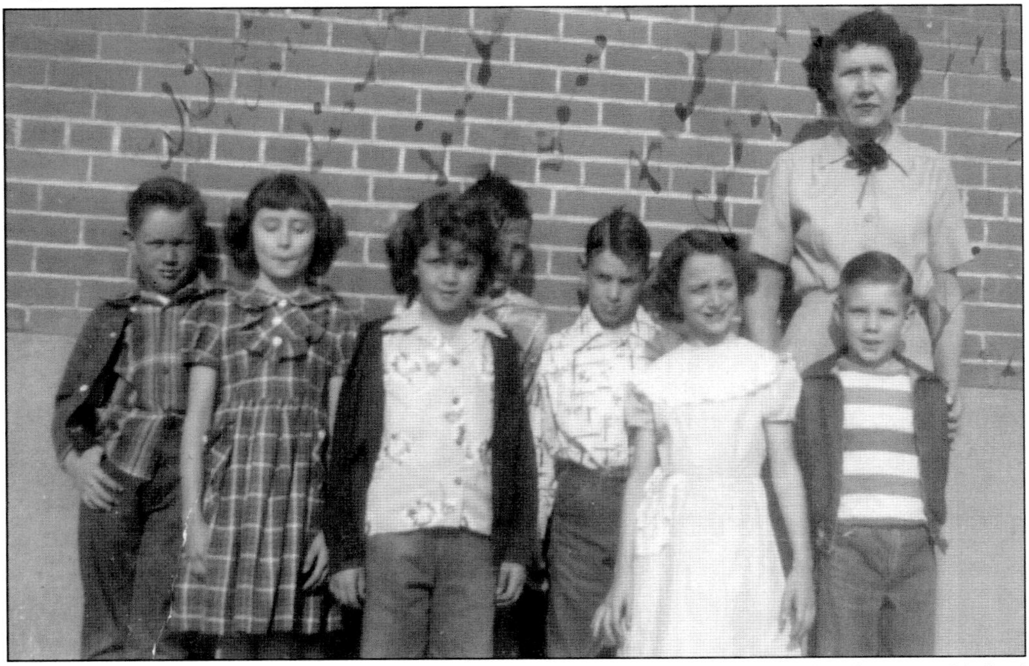

Located two miles south of Mexia, Forest Glade was settled in the 1860s. A school was established as early as 1872, and the Forest Glade School District was created in 1899. The second grade class of the Forest Glade School poses in the 1950–1951 school year. Shown here are, from left to right, Winston Worley, Linda Miller, Linda Slade, unidentified, Don Posey, Judy Matthews, a Mrs. Fowler, and Jimmy Waters. (Judy Lipsey.)

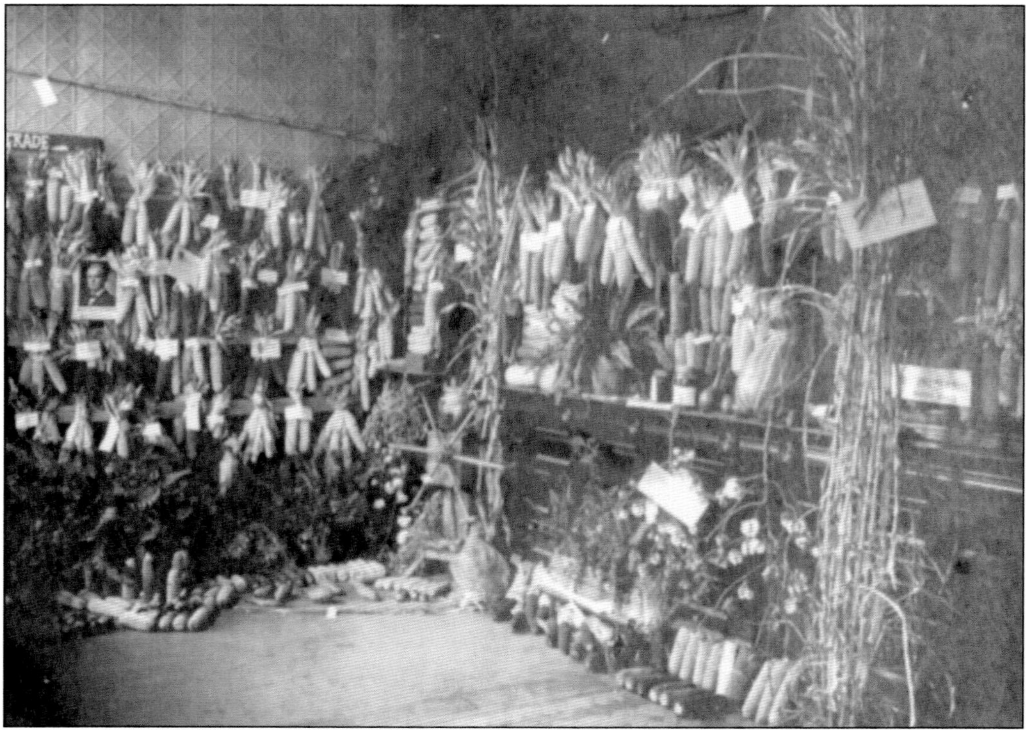

In 1892, the Limestone County Fair Association was incorporated. The early county fairs were held in Groesbeck and centered on horse racing. Many county farmers participated in the showing of livestock, agricultural crops, and garden produce. Blue and red ribbons were given to those judged the best. Shown above is a display of corn grown by Limestone County farmers during the 1916 fair. In 1928, the fair was held in Point Enterprise. Pictured below are participants waiting to have their poultry entries judged. (Above, Limestone County Museum; below, Helen Matthews.)

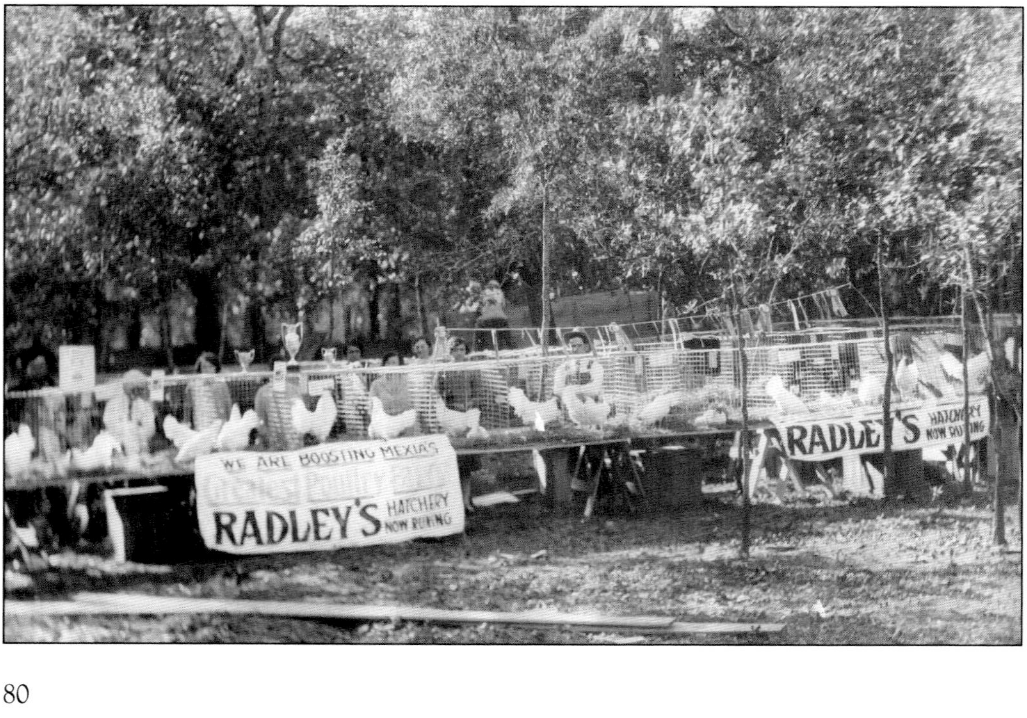

Five

County Government

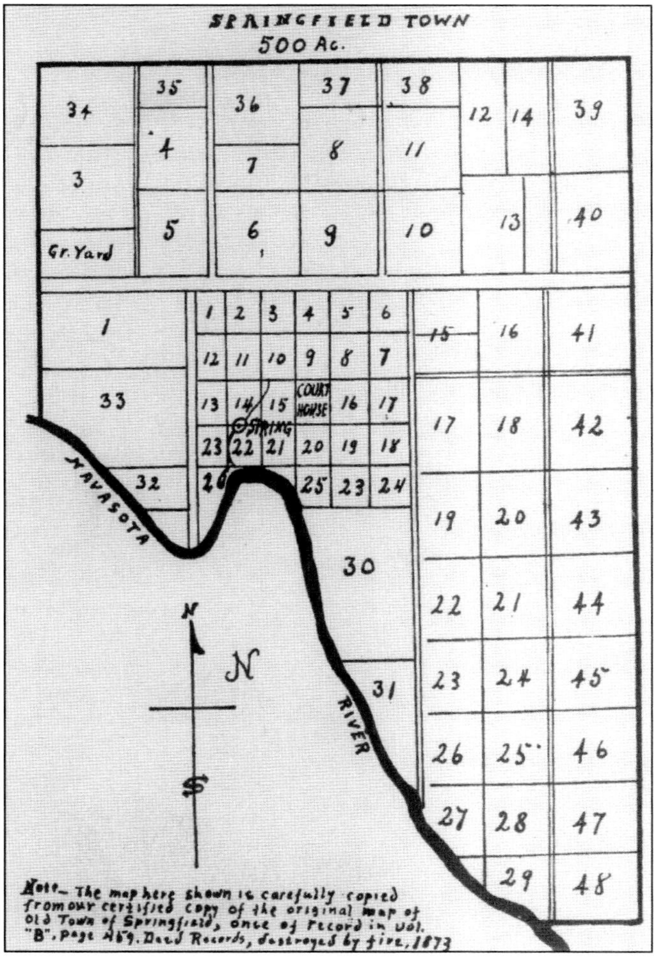

Limestone County was created on April 11, 1846, and Springfield was designated as the county seat on April 18. The first courthouse was a wooden building measuring 30 feet by 20 feet. In 1856, a two-story, brick courthouse was erected. It was condemned following a fire in June 1873. Another building was purchased but was destroyed by fire on October 24, 1873, along with all county records. (Limestone County Historical Museum.)

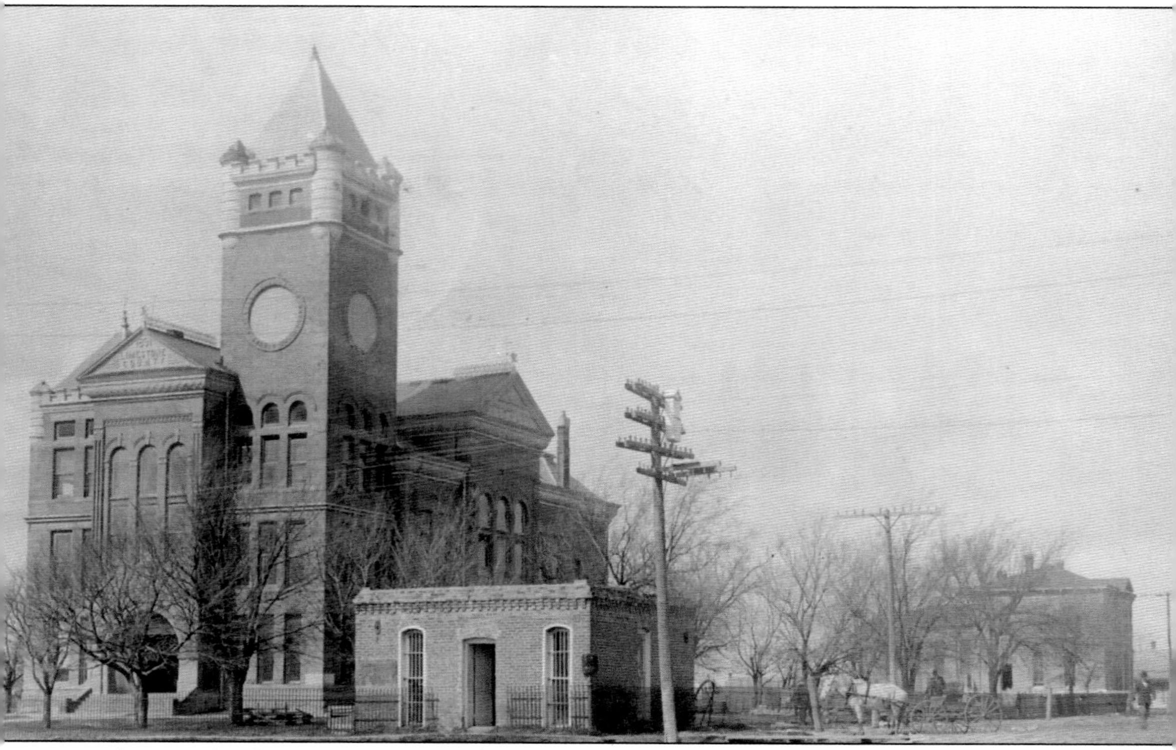

As a result of petitions to move the county seat, the railroad bypassing Springfield, and the destruction of the courthouse by fire, the county seat was moved to Groesbeck in December 1873. A brick building with a mansard roof was completed in 1878 at a cost of $23,000. Unfortunately, the building had many structural problems. The construction of the second courthouse in Groesbeck was completed in May 1889, but it was destroyed by fire on February 1, 1891. In March 1891, the county began the process of building another courthouse, which was completed in 1892 at a cost of $66,729. This third courthouse, shown here, was built in Groesbeck. The large building in the background is the county jail. (William Reagan.)

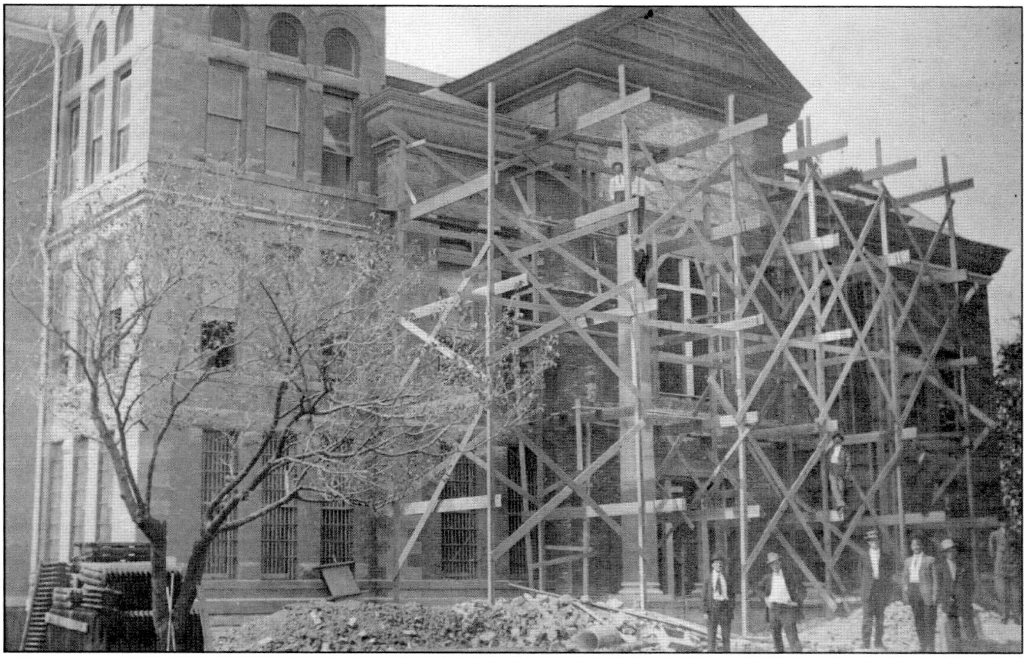

Structural defects began to appear shortly after the courthouse was finished in 1892. In 1909, the building underwent extensive repairs and remodeling. More offices were created, other offices were enlarged, the district courtroom's seating capacity was increased, steam heat and sewage were installed, and a clock and a 2,000-pound bell were placed in the tower. (Logan D. Wilson.)

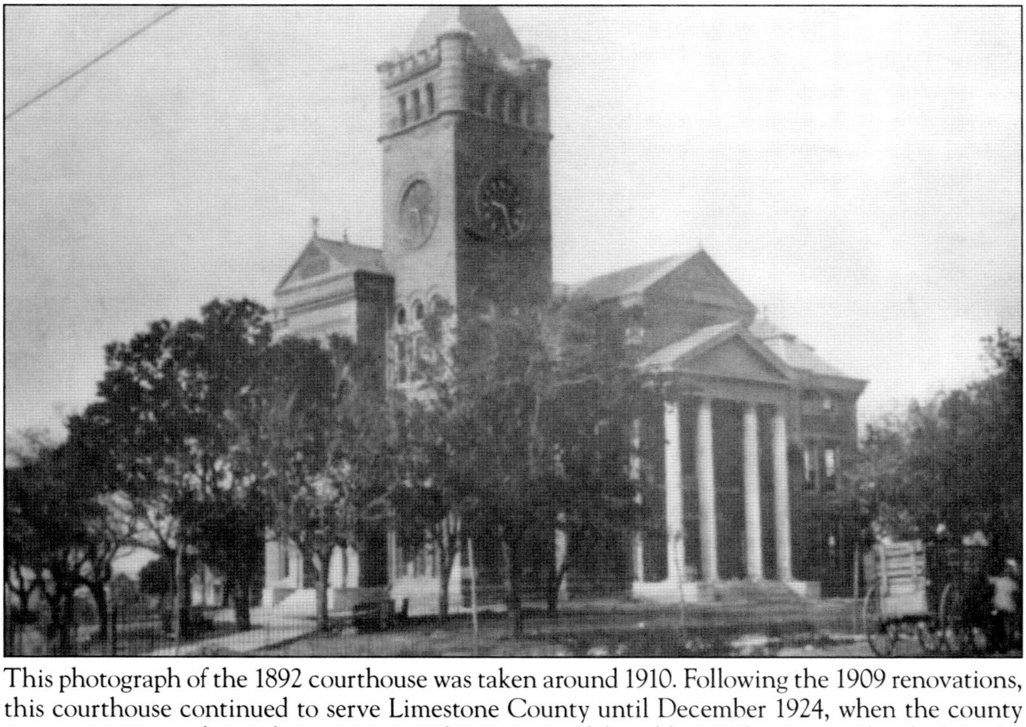

This photograph of the 1892 courthouse was taken around 1910. Following the 1909 renovations, this courthouse continued to serve Limestone County until December 1924, when the county government moved into the present courthouse. Two of the additions from 1909, the clock in the bell tower and the columns, can easily be seen. (Gibbs Memorial Library.)

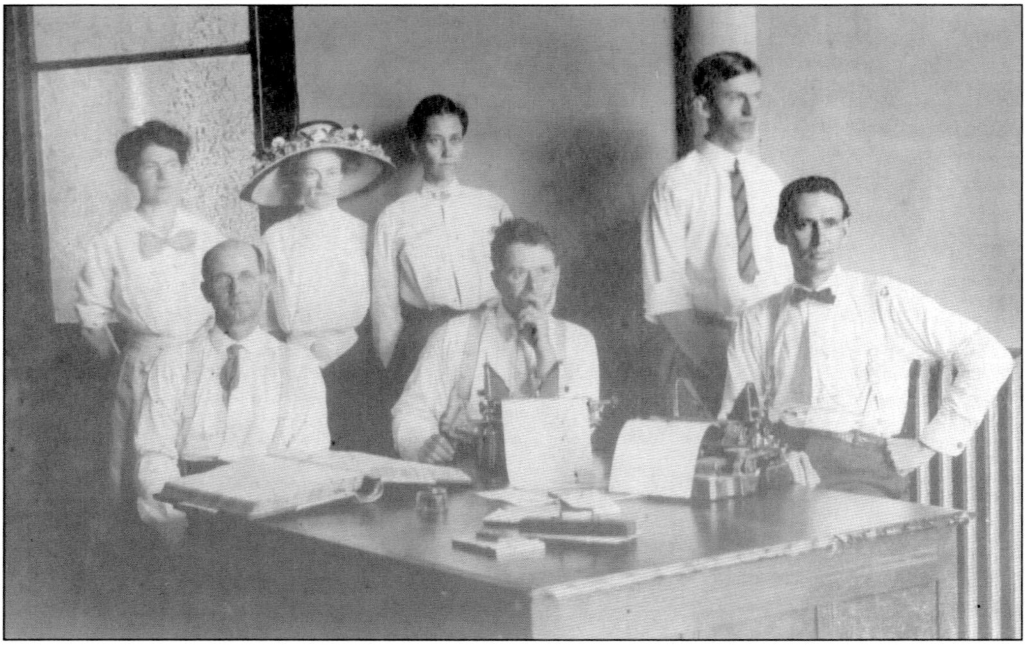

Pictured is the Limestone County Clerk's office. Sam A. Thomas was county clerk, and this photograph was taken sometime during his term in office (1910–1914). Shown here are, from left to right, (first row) Walter Carley, Sam A. Thomas, and Jim Franklin; (second row) Nell Basden, Ruby Lawley, a Ms. Phillips, and Ira Lawley. (Limestone County Historical Museum.)

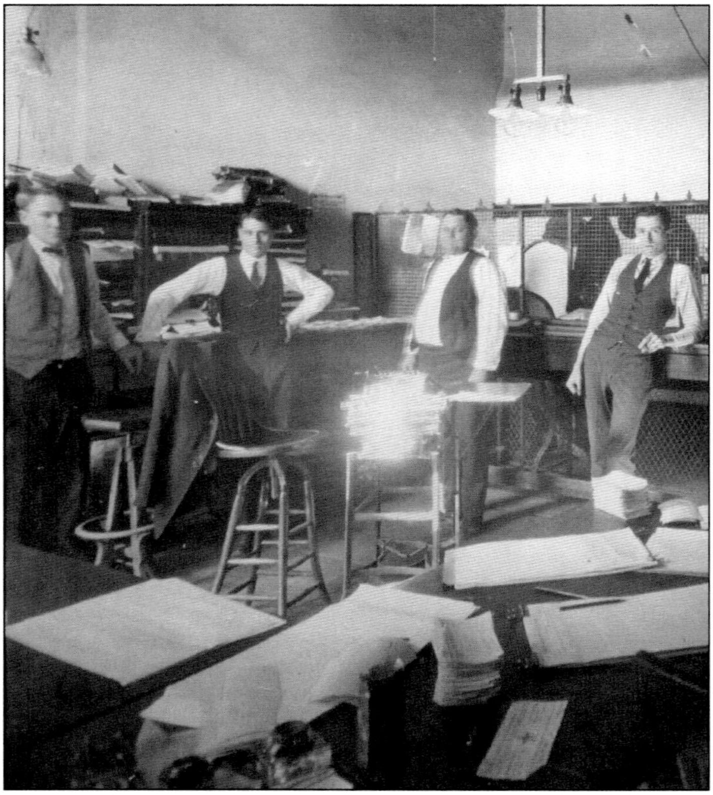

This photograph shows the Limestone County Tax Collector's office in 1921. Melvin Thetford served as tax collector from 1918 to 1922. Pictured here are, from left to right, a Mr. Thetford, F.J. Shultz, a Mr. Priddy, and Fred Kimbell. Currently, Limestone County has a tax assessor/collector, but during the time of this photograph, the assessor and collector were two separate offices. (Limestone County Historical Museum.)

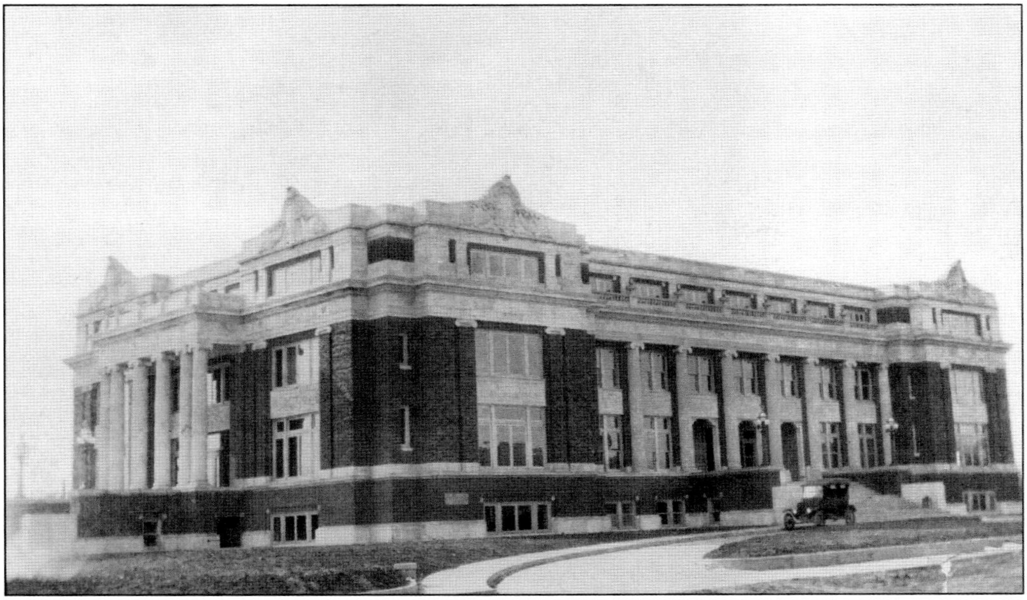

In December 1922, the Limestone County Commissioners' Court voted to build a new courthouse. The cornerstone was laid on December 20, 1923, and construction took about one year. The county officially moved into the new courthouse on December 22, 1924. It was designed in the Classical Revival style with Beaux-Arts influences. Reinforced concrete was used for the structural system, and the exterior was covered with terra-cotta and mingled shades of Oak Bark Face brick. Though the front of the courthouse faces State Street, it was designed to be viewed from all sides. On each side, classical columns flank the entrances and windows, and the upper floors are adorned with balustrades and elaborate cornucopia moldings. The above photograph was taken not long after the courthouse was completed, and the one below was taken in the 1940s. (Both, Limestone County Historical Museum.)

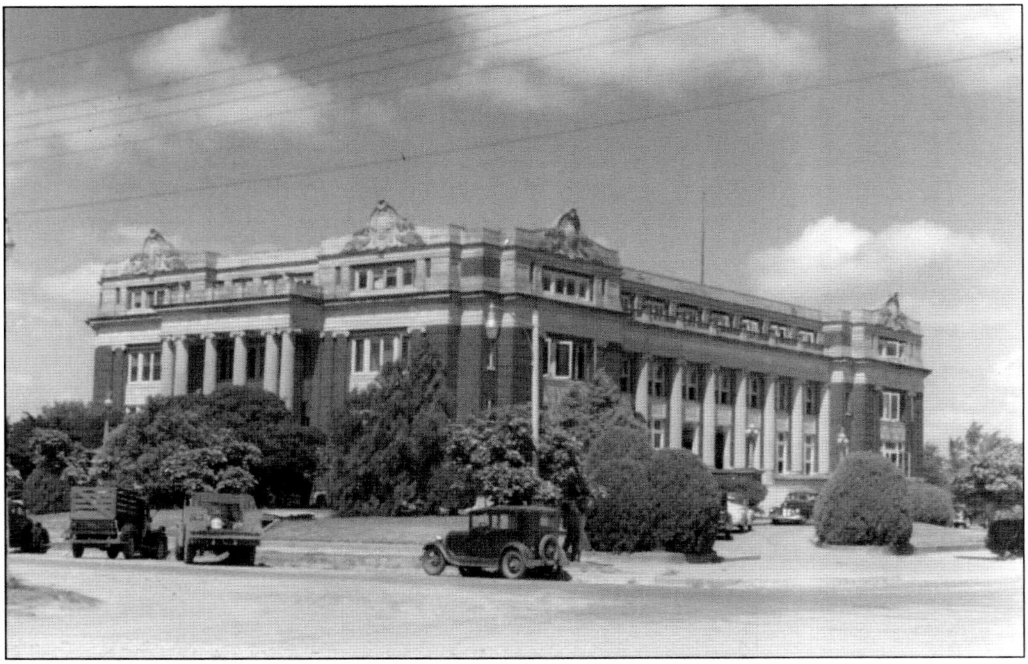

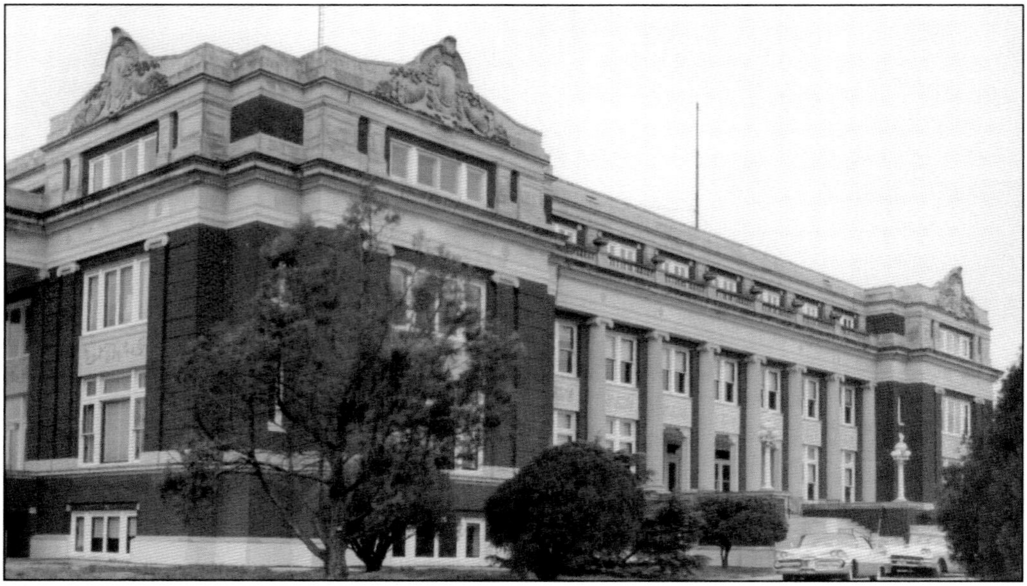

The Limestone County Courthouse has served the citizens of the county for almost nine decades. Although many of its offices have been renovated for modern use, the exterior of the building retains its elegant prominence and structural integrity. The interior retains elaborate moldings, marble walls and stairwells, elegant tiles, and many original fixtures and furnishings. Some areas of the courthouse, such as the two district courtrooms, look the way they did in 1924. Major changes to the courthouse include the addition of air-conditioning in 1971 and the installation of an elevator in 1986. The above photograph of the courthouse was taken during the 1960s, and the one below was taken during the 1970s. (Both, Limestone County Historical Museum.)

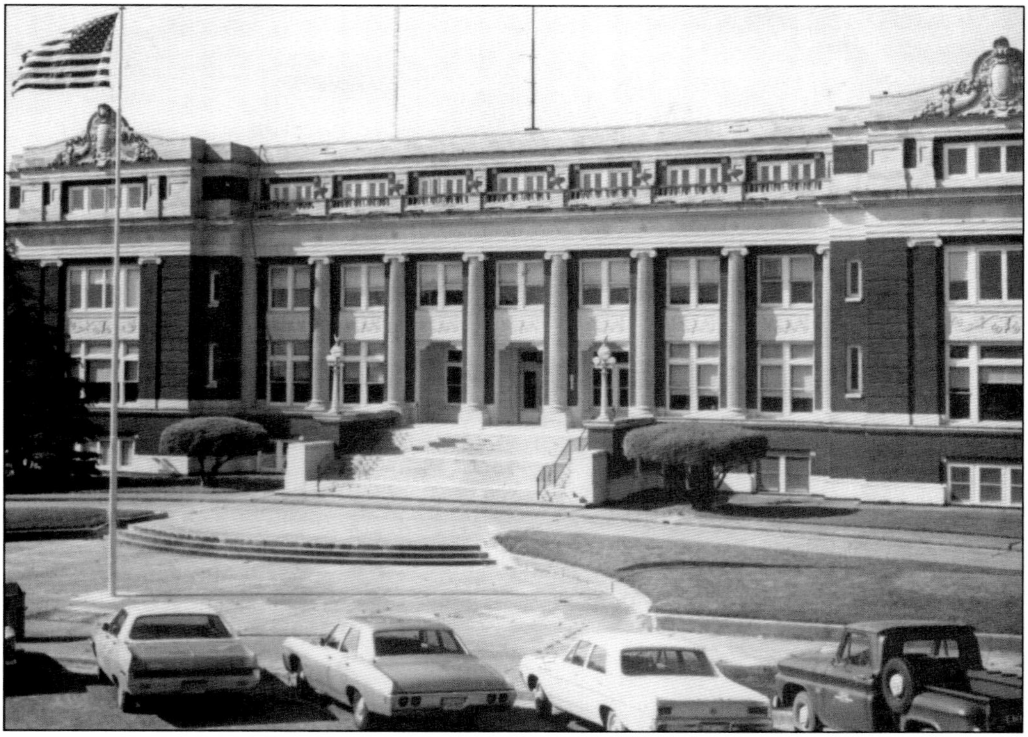

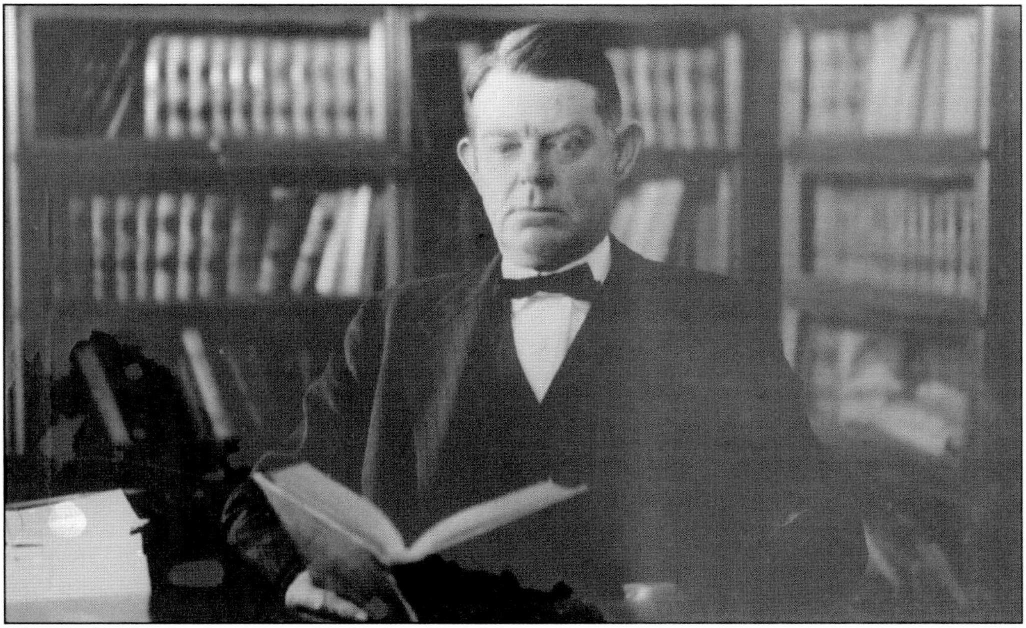

H.F. Kirby was elected county judge in 1920 and served in that position until 1928. The next year, he became the 77th district judge, serving in that position until 1952. "Fairness and justice with a slight tilt toward the 'underdog' administered without fear or prejudice was the hallmark of his public service," according to the *Groesbeck Journal.* (Limestone County Historical Museum.)

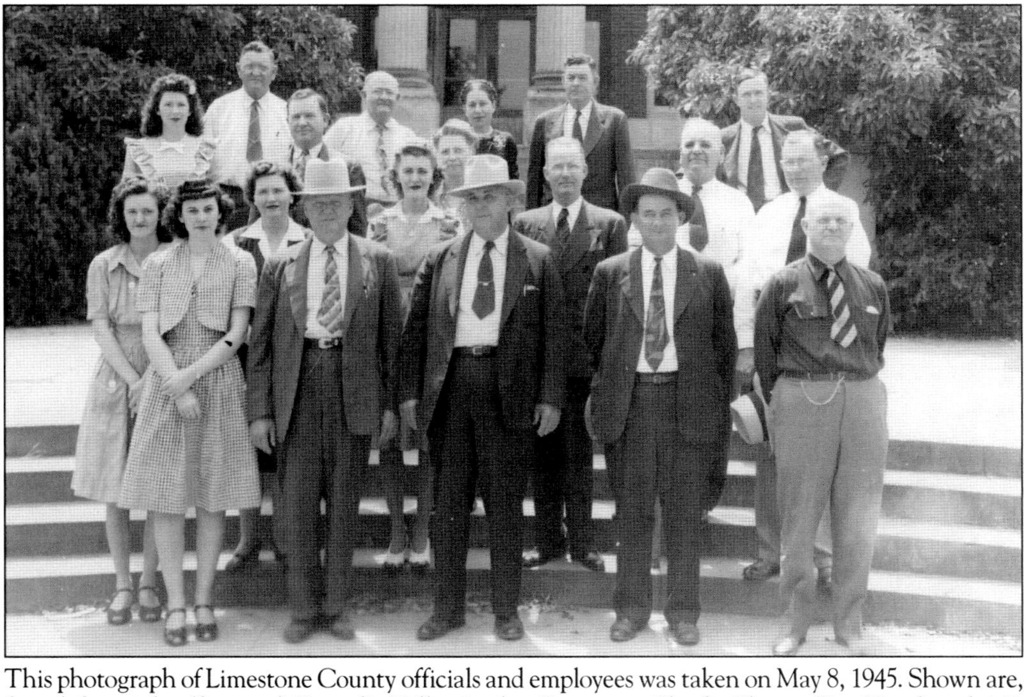

This photograph of Limestone County officials and employees was taken on May 8, 1945. Shown are, from left to right, (first row) Cornelia Kelley, Luther Simmons, Charlie Shreve, Roy Hand, and A.Y. Easterling; (second row) Mary Jo Baker, Annie Gallaher, Jimmy Ruth Taylor, Henry Jackson, Wes Coker, and John Kidd; (third row) Starlene Hughes, E.E. Prichard, Norton Fox, Red Seale, Nell Basden, Martha England, Lewis Williams, and A.B. Sims. (Limestone County Historical Museum.)

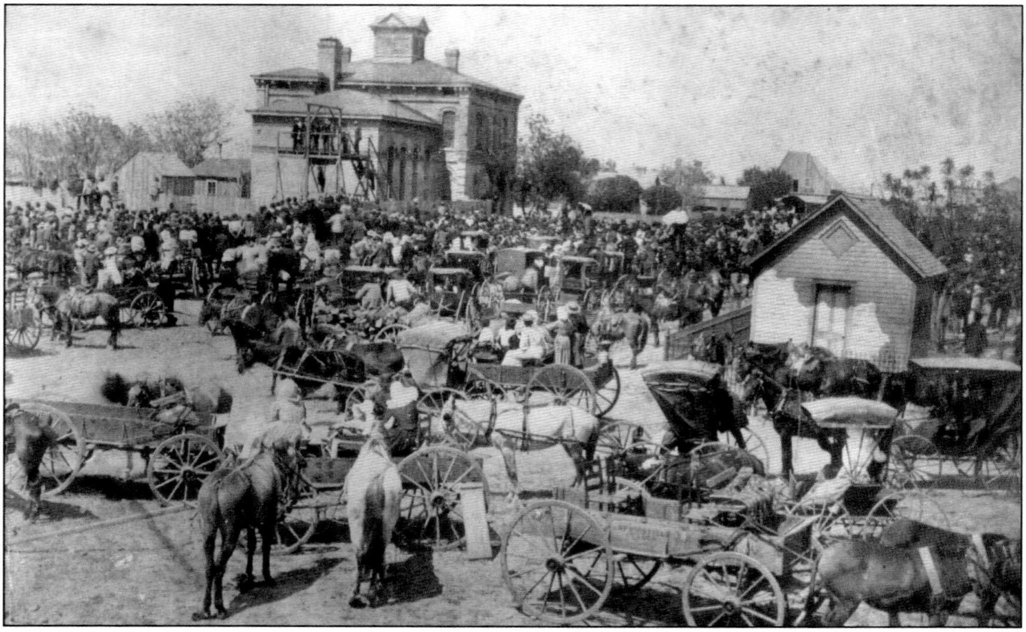

The county jail in Springfield was torn down and rebuilt in Groesbeck in 1874. A new jail was later built in 1881. Stones from the foundation of the old courthouse at Springfield were used in its foundation. In 1901, this jail was torn down, and a new one was built on the same foundation and, except for some minor changes, was constructed according to the same plans. If comparing these two photographs, one can see slight differences in the two buildings. Above, a large crowd gathers around the jail to witness the last hanging in Limestone County. On April 12, 1895, Richard Burleson was executed for the May 3, 1894, murder of J.G. McKinnon. Below is a 1920s photograph of the 1901 jail. This building was used by the county until 1989. (Both, Limestone County Historical Museum.)

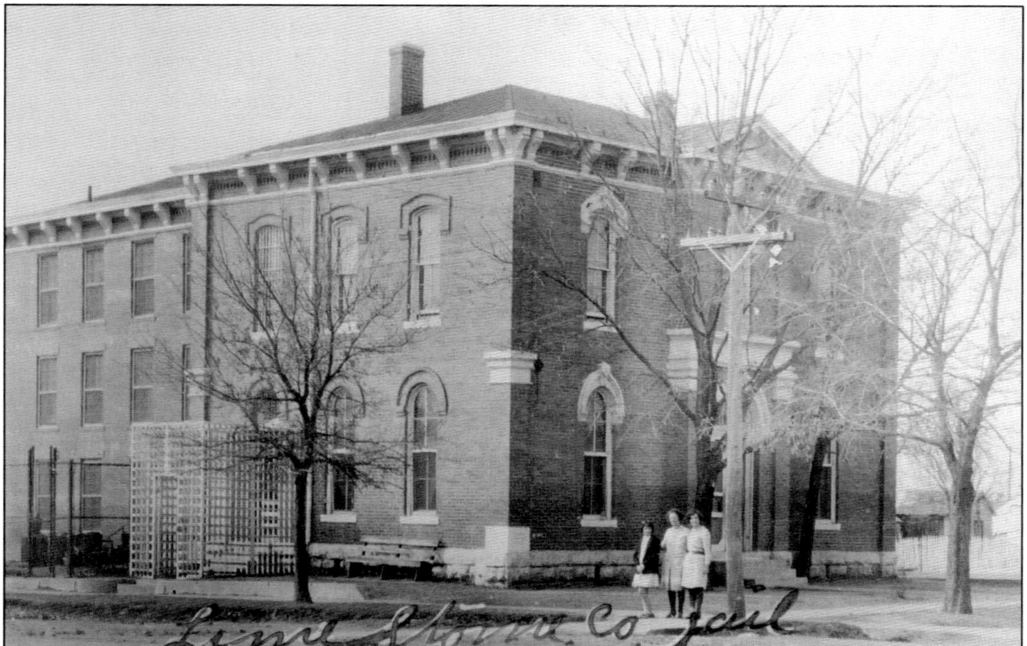

Six

Boom and Bust

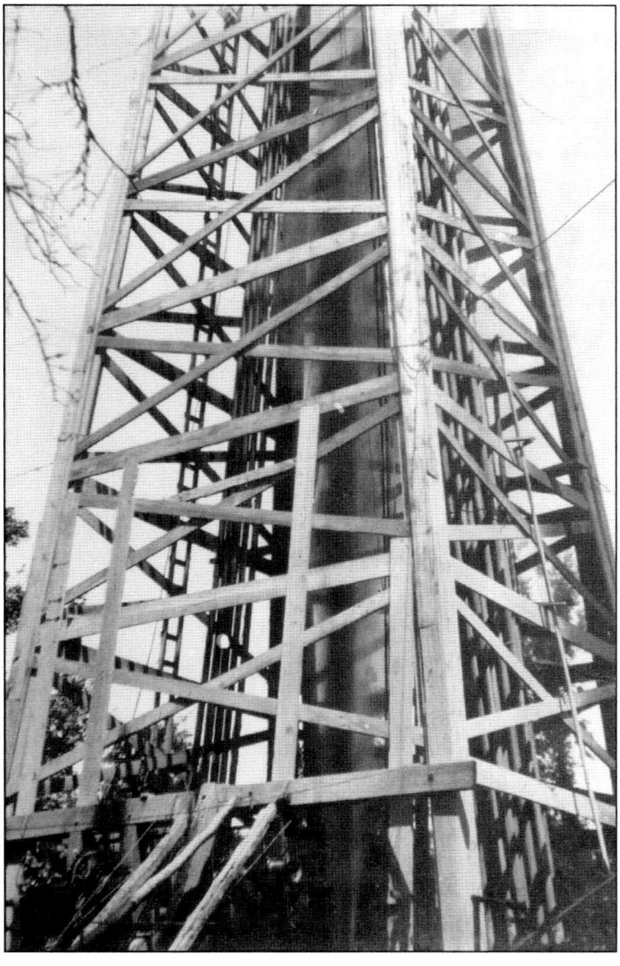

During the first part of the 20th century, gas and oil production brought prosperity to Limestone County. James Robert Stroud helped pioneer the area gas industry by constructing a distribution center in Groesbeck to furnish natural gas from wells he owned and leased. The Stroud Gas Company operated until 1945, when the family sold it to the Lone Star Gas Company. One of Stroud's wells is shown here. (Logan D. Wilson.)

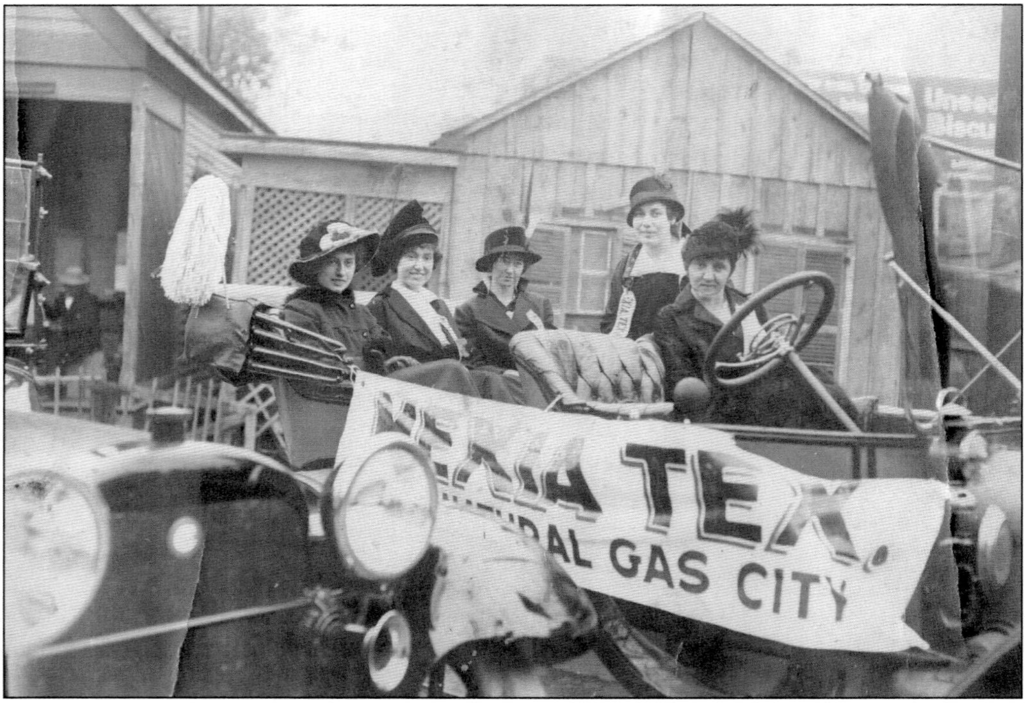

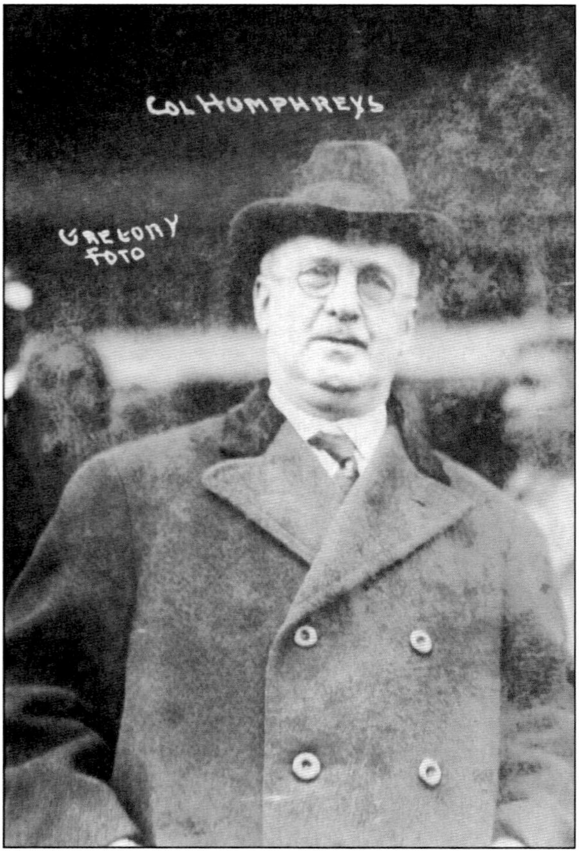

The Mexia Gas & Oil Company was established in 1912. After its 11th test well proved to be a commercial producer, lines were laid throughout Mexia, providing natural gas for heating and cooking. Within two years, Mexia was supplying natural gas to several surrounding towns within a 40-mile radius. The five ladies above were promoting Mexia's natural gas industry in Houston in November 1914. (Gibbs Memorial Library.)

After World War I, the gas began to play out, but many believed that oil existed beneath the depleted gas fields. The Mexia gas company offered half interest in its 2,000-acre lease to anyone willing to drill a test well. Col. Albert E. Humphreys arrived on the scene and brought in the Rogers well in November 1920. It only produced 50 barrels a day, but it encouraged continued exploration. (Gibbs Memorial Library.)

Colonel Humphreys and others continued drilling. In anticipation of a big strike, Humphreys bought 352 acres south of Mexia on which to build a refinery. Before 1921, total oil production in the Mexia area was less than 50,000 barrels per year. Pictured is Humphreys's Berthelson No. 1 well. It was brought in on May 22, 1921, and began producing 4,000 barrels daily. (Limestone County Historical Museum.)

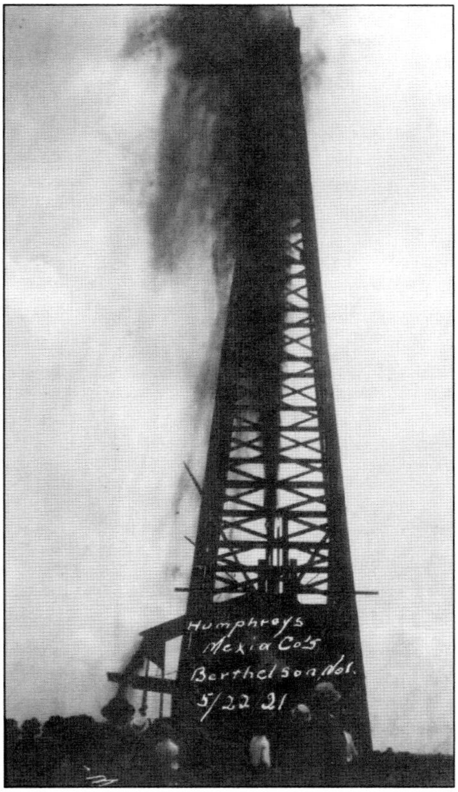

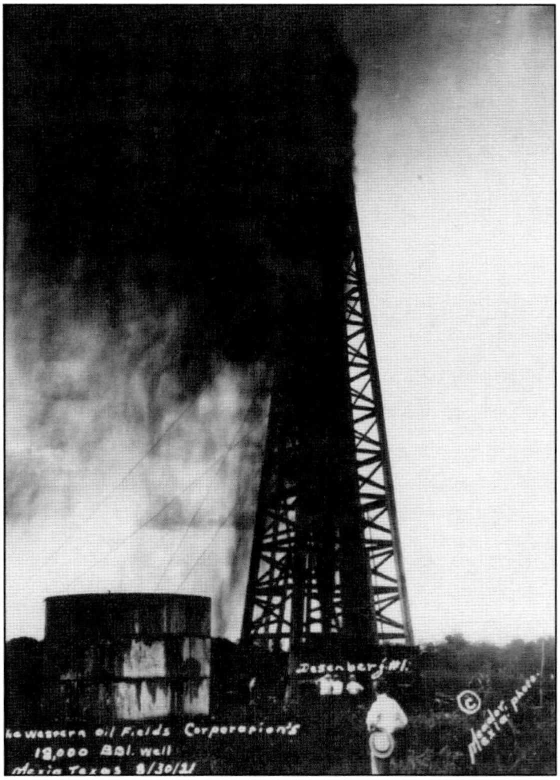

On August 21, 1921, the Western Oil Corporation's Desenberg No. 1 well spouted from a depth of 3,059 feet, producing 18,000 barrels per day. On the same day, the Adamson No. 1, a 24,000-barrel gusher, blew in. As news of these two gushers spread across the country, thousands of unemployed workers and rich investors poured into Mexia. (Limestone County Historical Commission.)

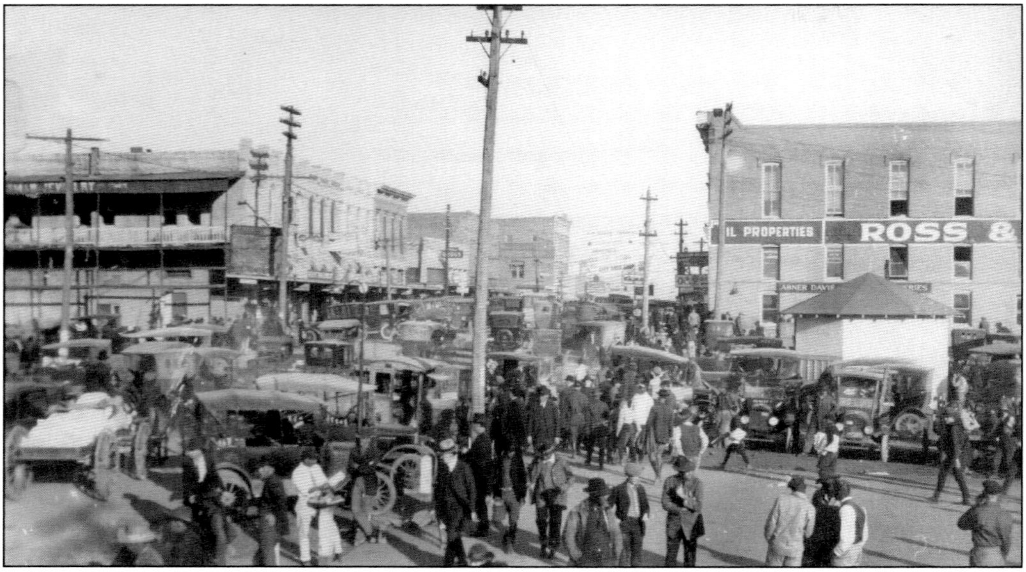

As people flocked to the town to find jobs and to make their fortunes, Mexia went from a peaceful community of 4,000 to a raucous boomtown of 50,000 in just a few weeks. Hotels, boardinghouses, and private homes could not accommodate the influx. Many slept wherever they could find a place to lie down. Transportation facilities were inadequate, grocery stores and restaurants were overwhelmed, and people had to stand in line for hours to get into the post office. These two photographs show how crowded Mexia's streets were. The above photograph was taken in December 1921, facing east on Commerce Street. The photograph below shows how busy the area around the railroad depot was following the departure of the train. (Both, William Reagan.)

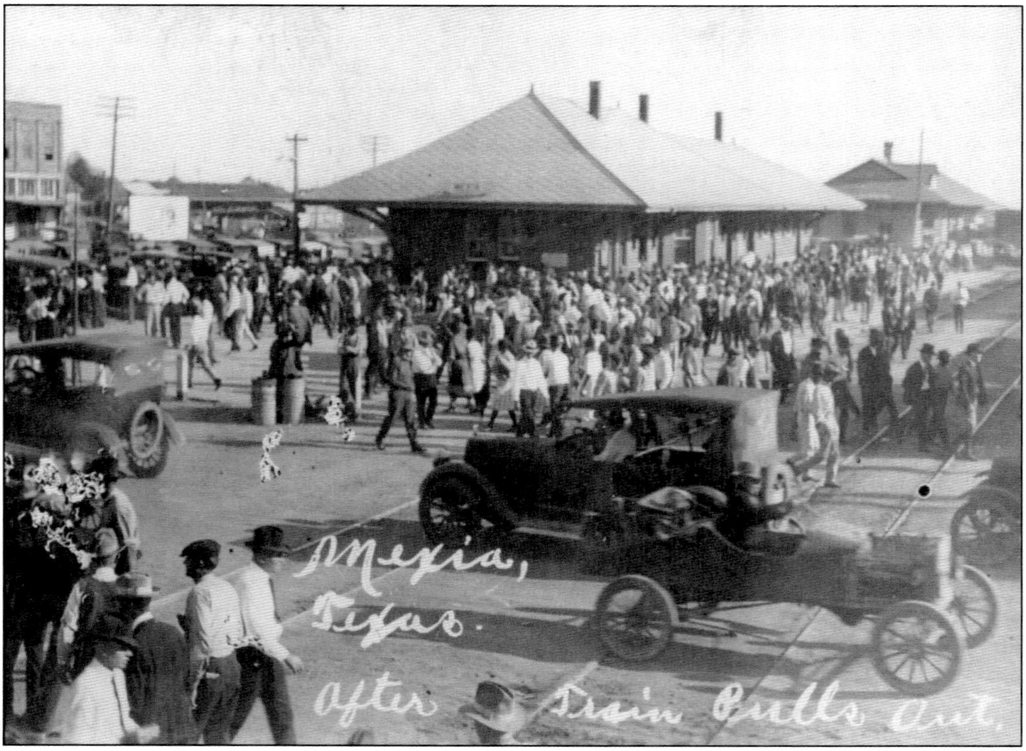

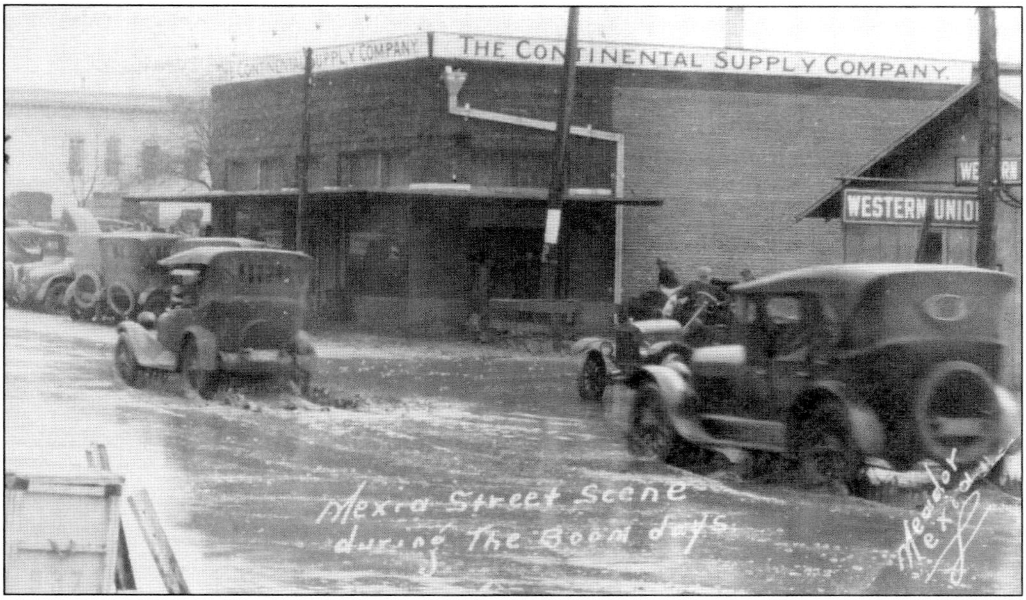

When the oil boom began, the streets of Mexia were not paved. Driving on them after a big rain was like driving down a muddy river. Shown here are the Western Union office and the Continental Supply Company, one of the many businesses that sold and rented oil-field equipment and supplies. (William Reagan.)

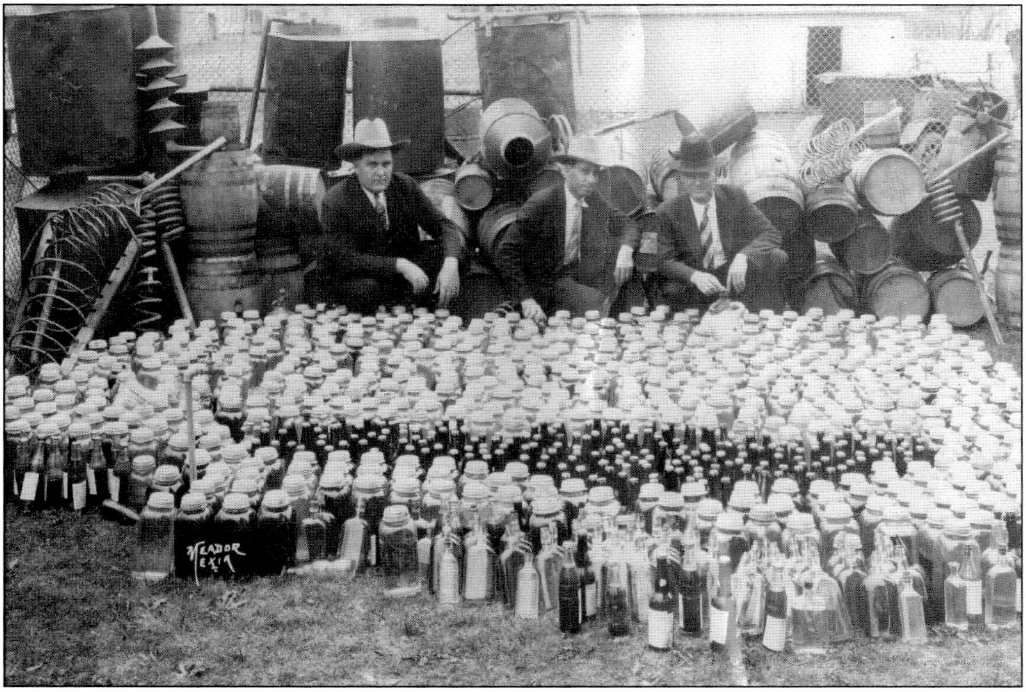

The Prohibition era began on January 16, 1919, with ratification of the 18th Amendment, which prohibited the production, distribution, and sale of alcohol. Members of the Limestone County Sheriff's Department are shown with confiscated bootlegged whiskey and distillery equipment. Pictured here are, from left to right, Sheriff A.B. "Boss" McKenzie, Will Adams, and Luther Simmons. (Gibbs Memorial Library.)

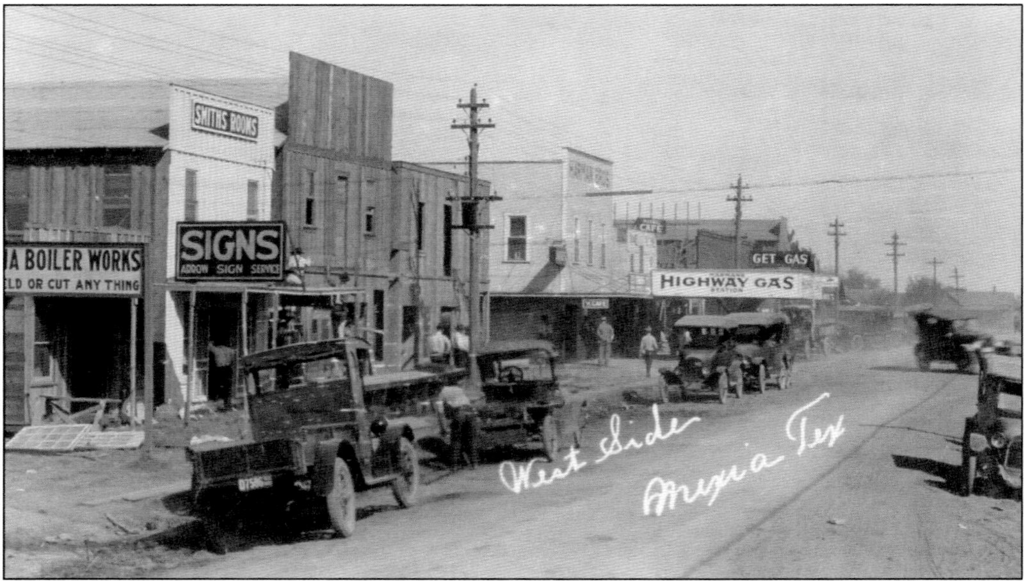

Because it was the part of town closest to the oil fields, the African American section of Mexia, located west of the railroad tracks, was overrun with gamblers, bootleggers, prostitutes, and other undesirables. From sundown to dawn, gambling, murder, and riotous behavior became the norm along muddy and overcrowded Belknap Street. Several families actually moved their houses to the eastern side of town to escape the recklessness and violence. Things became so bad that Gov. Pat Neff declared martial law in January 1922 and sent Texas Rangers and National Guard troops to restore order. The above photograph was taken on the west side of Mexia. Because Rangers and troopers were patrolling the sidewalks, things were quiet and calm. Pictured below are some of the Texas Rangers and National Guard troops sent to Mexia. (Both, the Texas Ranger Museum.)

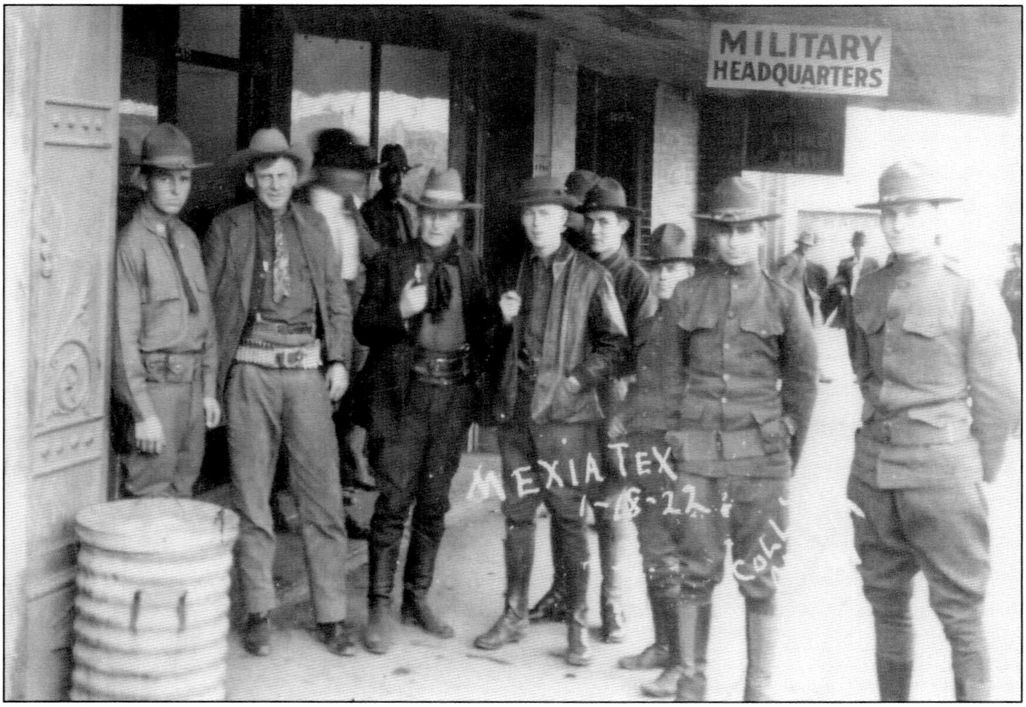

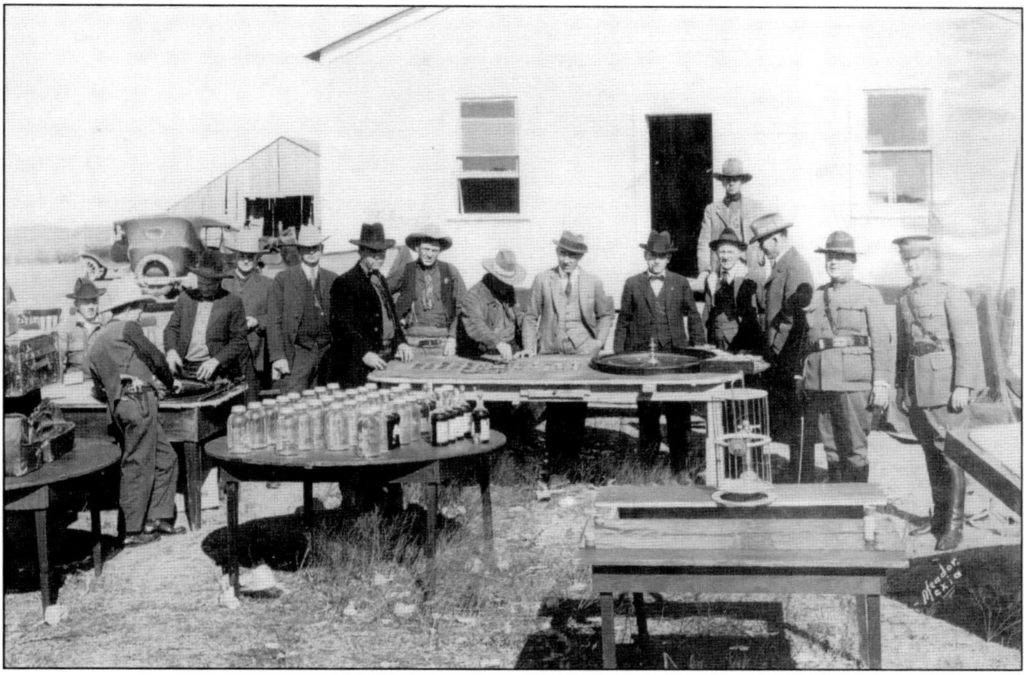

The Winter Garden and the Chicken Farm were two nightclubs that were located several miles out of town. They were guarded around the clock, inside and out, against the law and the lawless. Music, dancing, alcohol, and gambling lured many inside their doors. It took a simultaneous raid in January 1922 by Texas Rangers, the National Guard, and federal agents to close both night spots. The photograph above shows gambling paraphernalia and bootlegged whiskey that were confiscated. The Winter Garden, below, became the headquarters for the National Guard and over 150 prisoners were held here. The man standing on the far left is Capt. Frank Hamer, who was in charge of the Texas Rangers in Mexia. He would later gain fame for tracking down and killing Bonnie and Clyde. (Above, Texas Ranger Museum; below, Gibbs Memorial Library.)

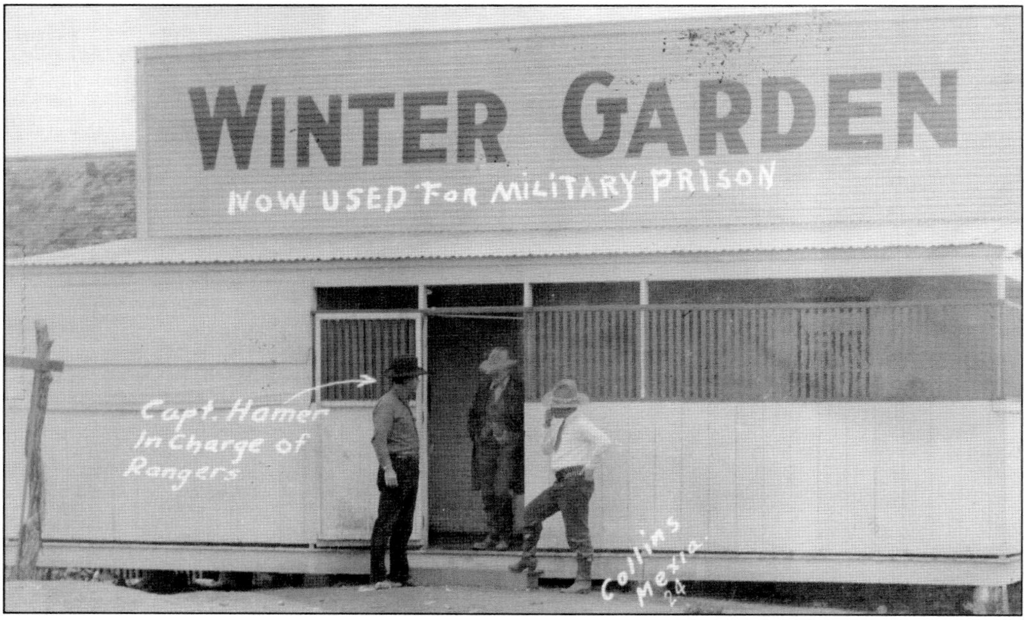

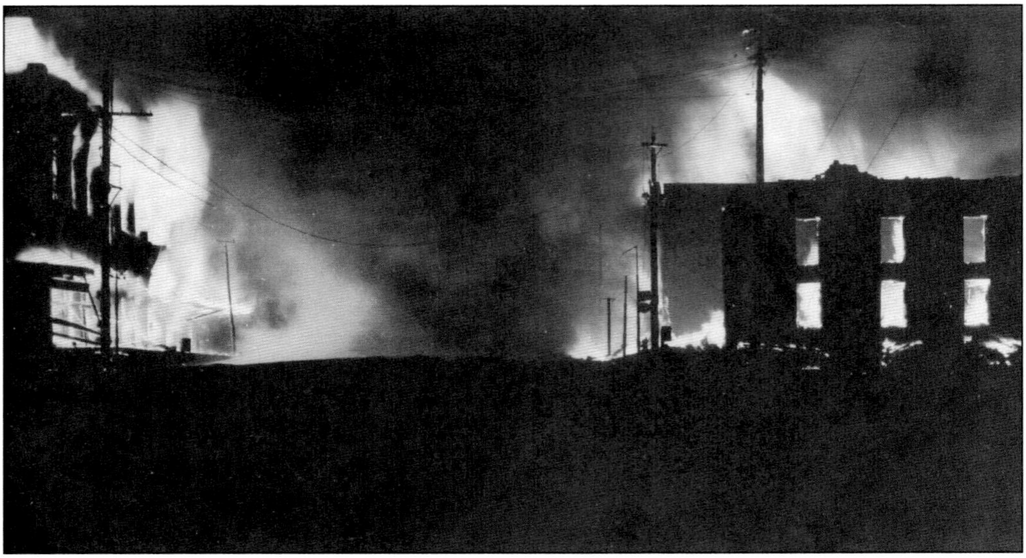

At 6:18 p.m. on January 14, 1922, a fire started in a restaurant on the ground floor of the Petroleum Building on the north side of Commerce Street. The fire soon spread, and a shortage of water hindered firemen in their efforts to control it. Telephone operators stayed on duty to complete calls to other towns for help until the roof began to fall in on them. When the fire finally burned itself out, two blocks of the business district lay in ruins, with losses estimated at $500,000. The photograph above shows the fire raging out of control on the night of January 14. The devastation was revealed the next morning, as seen in the photograph below. Many residents of the boom era would often say, "It took the Rangers, the National Guard, and a fire to clean Mexia up!" (Both, Gibbs Memorial Library.)

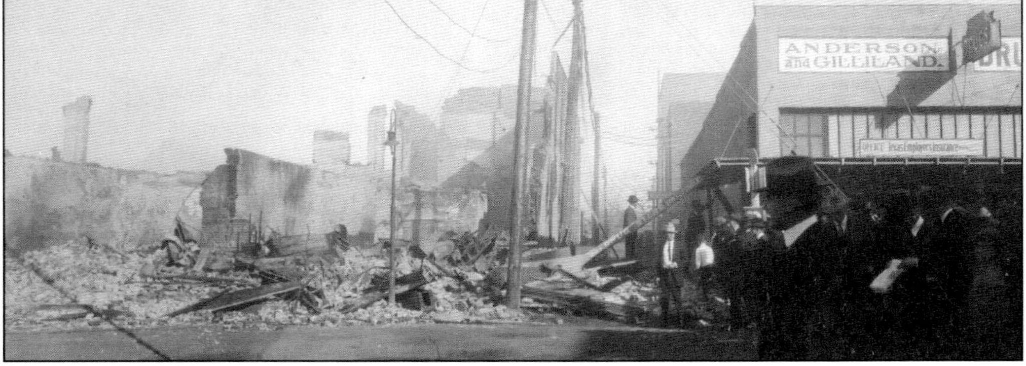

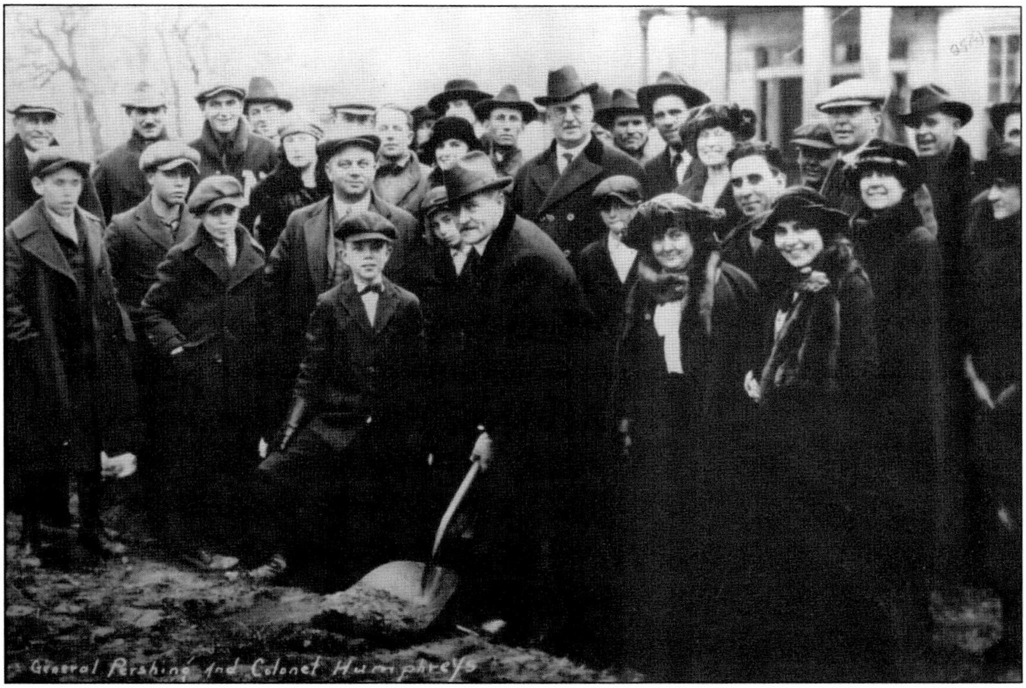

Pershing Way, the first paved road in Limestone County, was constructed by Colonel Humphreys. It stretched from the public highway in Mexia to the Confederate Reunion Grounds, where he had built a swimming hole, bathhouse, and the Poco Clubhouse for area residents. Pershing Way went past the Henry House, a Civil War–era mansion where Humphreys lived. In the photograph above, Gen. John J. Pershing, commander of American Expeditionary Forces during World War I, is turning the first shovel of dirt during the dedication ceremony on January 6, 1922. Afterward, he delivered a speech from the front porch of the Henry House, which was followed by the singing of Negro spirituals by some of Humphreys's oil-field workers. In the photograph below, Humphreys (second from right) and Pershing (far right) stand on the porch as the men perform. (Both, Gibbs Memorial Library.)

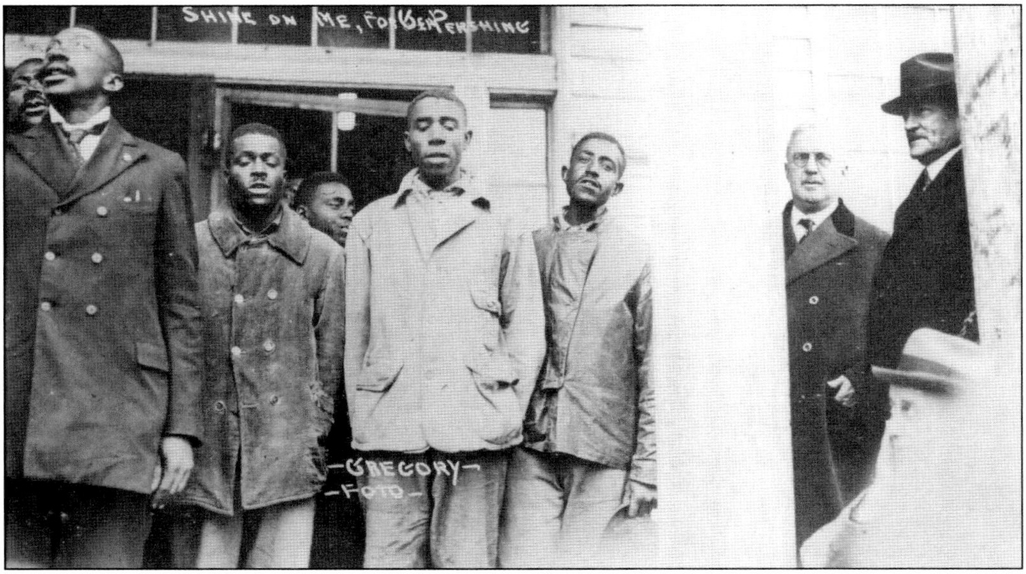

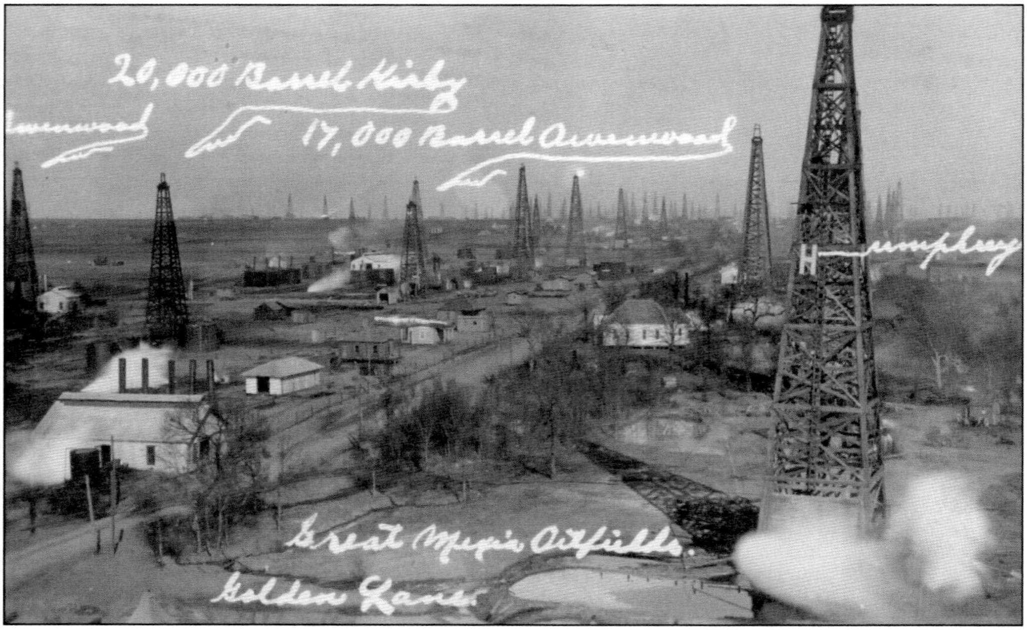

In 1921, the Mexia oil fields produced about five million barrels. That number increased to over 35 million barrels in 1922. The peak day's production of 176,000 barrels came on February 12, 1922. The area of heaviest production was the Golden Lane, a one-half-mile-wide strip that ran along the Mexia Fault. These photographs provide two different views of the Golden Lane. Note the *H* on the derrick in the above photograph. Colonel Humphreys had all of his wells marked in this way. After the record production of 1922, oil output began to decline, dropping to about 20 million barrels in 1923, 15.6 million in 1924, and 7.5 million in 1925. By the 1940s, Mexia's oil fields had become stripper fields, with pumpers producing a few dozen barrels daily. (Above, William Reagan; below, Limestone County Historical Museum.)

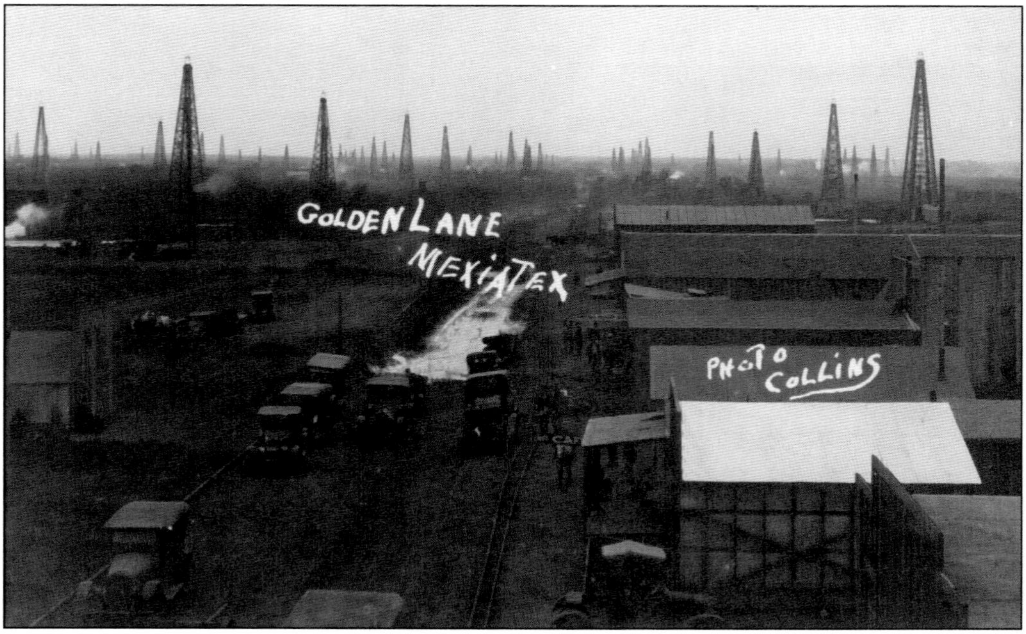

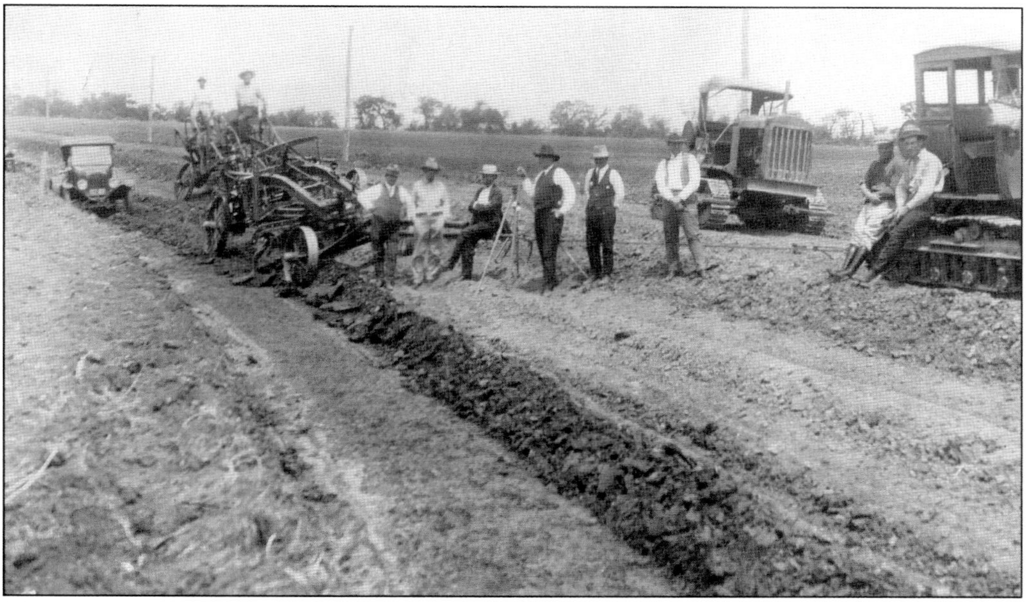

The prosperity that the oil boom brought greatly benefited Mexia and Limestone County. Mexia was able to build 38 miles of paved streets, a new city hall, a new high school, and a new library. It was also during this time that the county built a new courthouse. Here, workers construct a new road in the Mexia area. (Gibbs Memorial Library.)

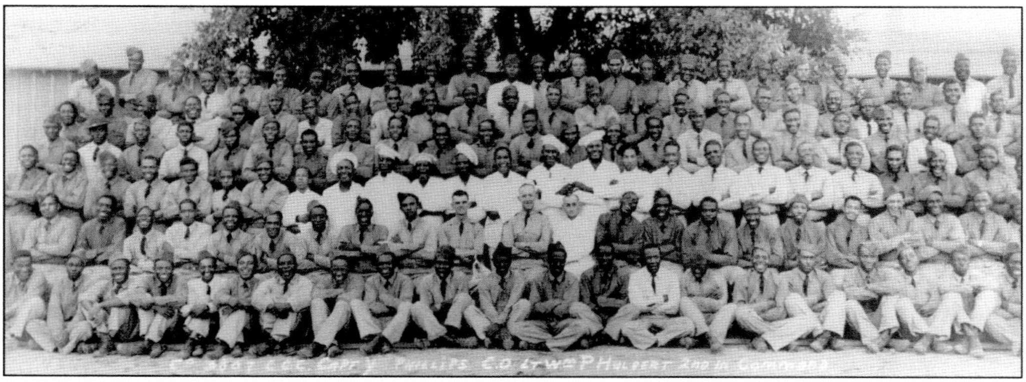

One of the programs implemented by President Roosevelt to put people back to work during the Great Depression was the Civilian Conservation Corps (CCC). Shown here is the African American CCC Company 3807(c), which from 1933 until 1942 constructed Fort Parker State Park. These men were paid $30 monthly but were allowed to keep only $8 for personal spending. The rest was sent to their families. (Fort Parker State Park.)

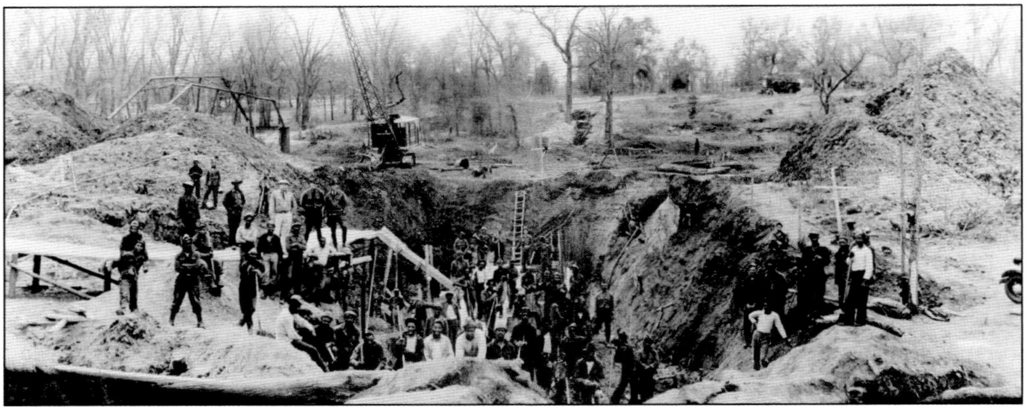

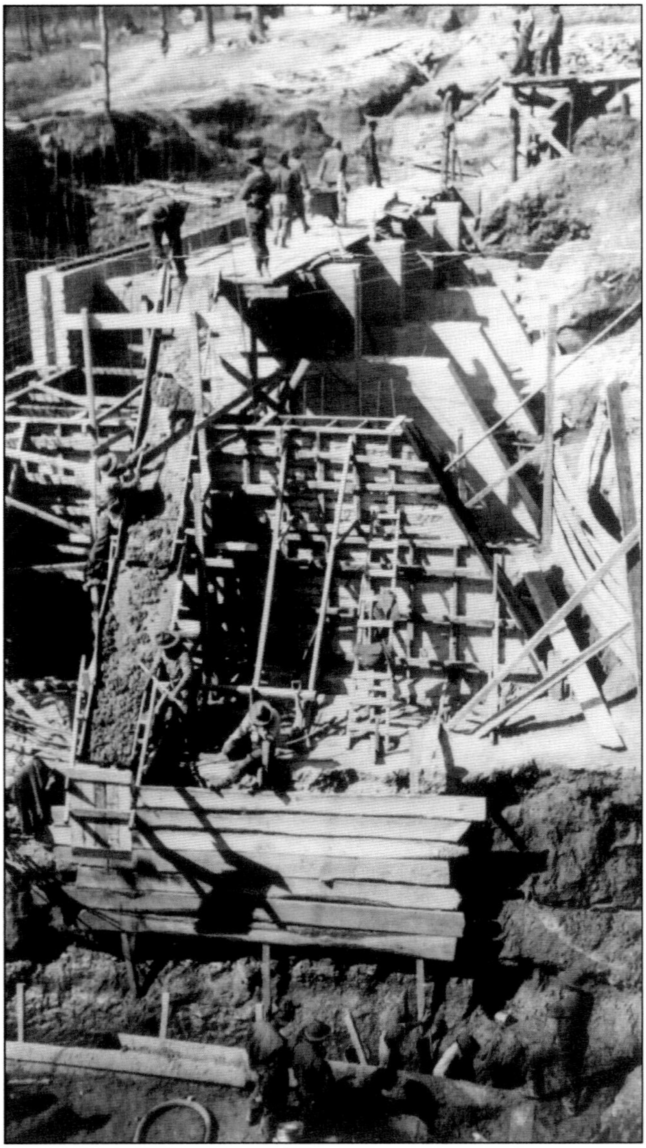

As the CCC crews began work at Fort Parker State Park, major tasks included building a dam across the Navasota River, building roads, and constructing buildings and recreational facilities. All CCC projects were labor intensive. Heavy equipment was used to haul rock and timber, but most of the work was done by hand with shovels, picks, and sledgehammers. The most ambitious project was the dam. It entailed digging out the dam's footings, as shown in the photograph above, breaking and hauling rock for cement, and pouring the cement for the dam, spillway, and wing walls. In the photograph at left, cement is being poured into wooden forms during construction of the dam. (Both, Fort Parker State Park.)

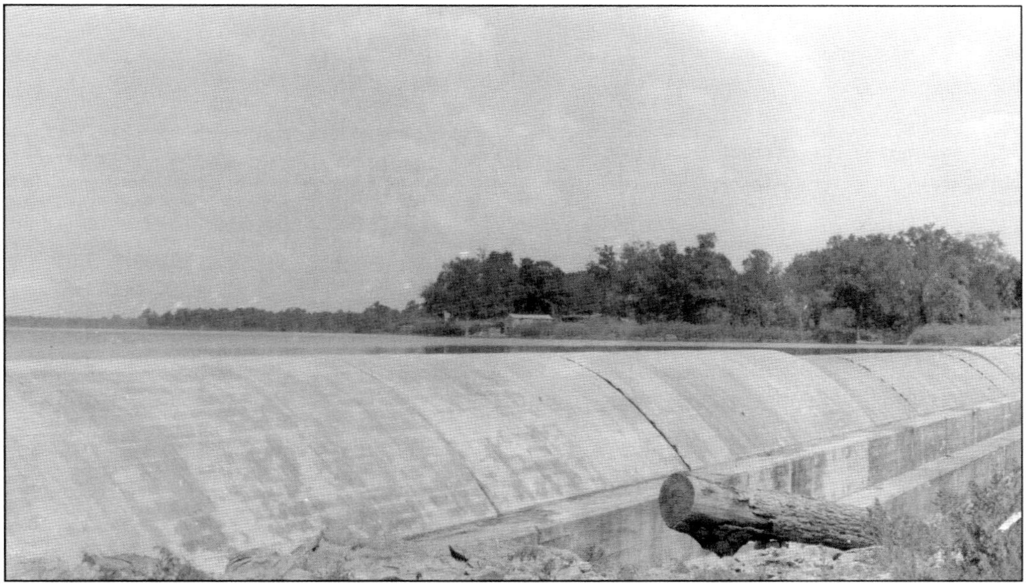

The construction of the Fort Parker Dam began on September 1, 1935. The project, delayed because of flooding on the Navasota River, was completed in November 1938. This photograph shows the completed dam. Engineers originally believed that it would take two to three years for the lake to fill, but the 750-acre lake filled after a single rain. (Mary Marcotte.)

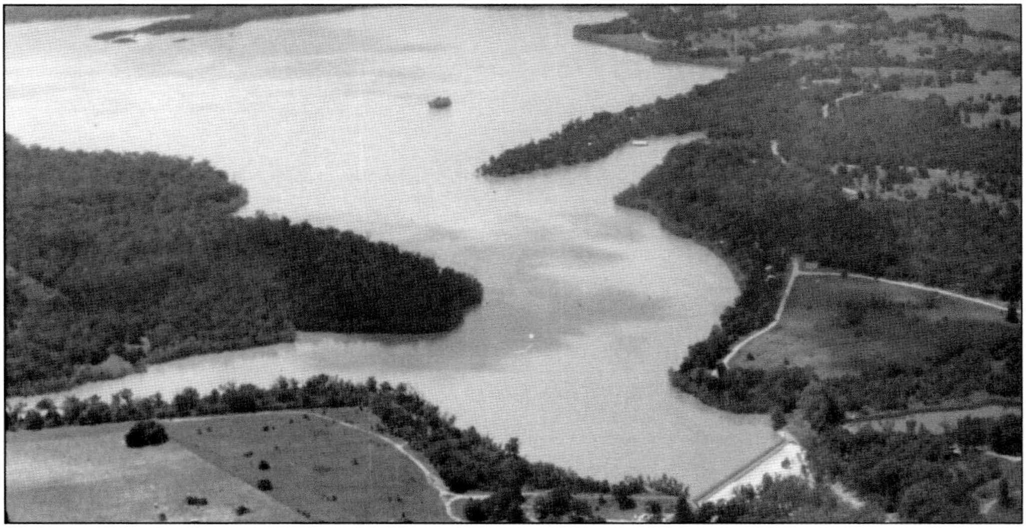

The CCC was assigned to construct a clubhouse, boathouse, bathhouse, roads, picnic tables and benches, swings, wading pools, sandlots, walks, drinking fountains, and parking lots. The men also cleared, cleaned, and partially landscaped the park. In January 1942, the projects were finished and the company was transferred to Zavala to do forestry work. This aerial photograph shows the completed lake and state park. (William Reagan.)

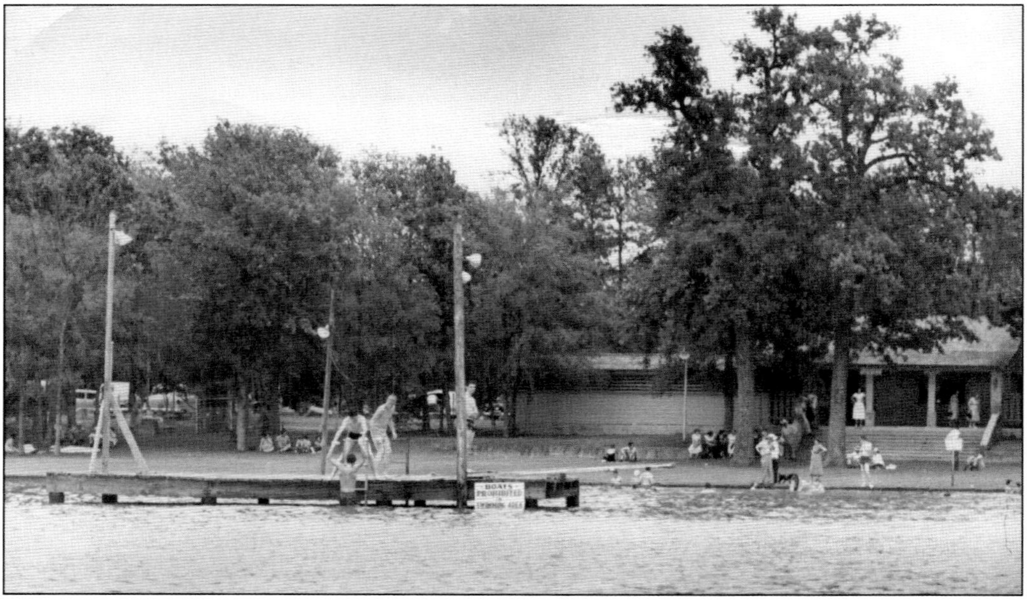

Fort Parker State Park opened to the public on May 1, 1941. Pat Neff, former governor, president of Baylor University, and creator of the Texas State Park System, officially opened the park. Recreational facilities included boating, fishing, swimming, and nightly dances on the terrace overlooking the lake. Here, park visitors swim in the lake. The clubhouse is in the background. (Fort Parker State Park.)

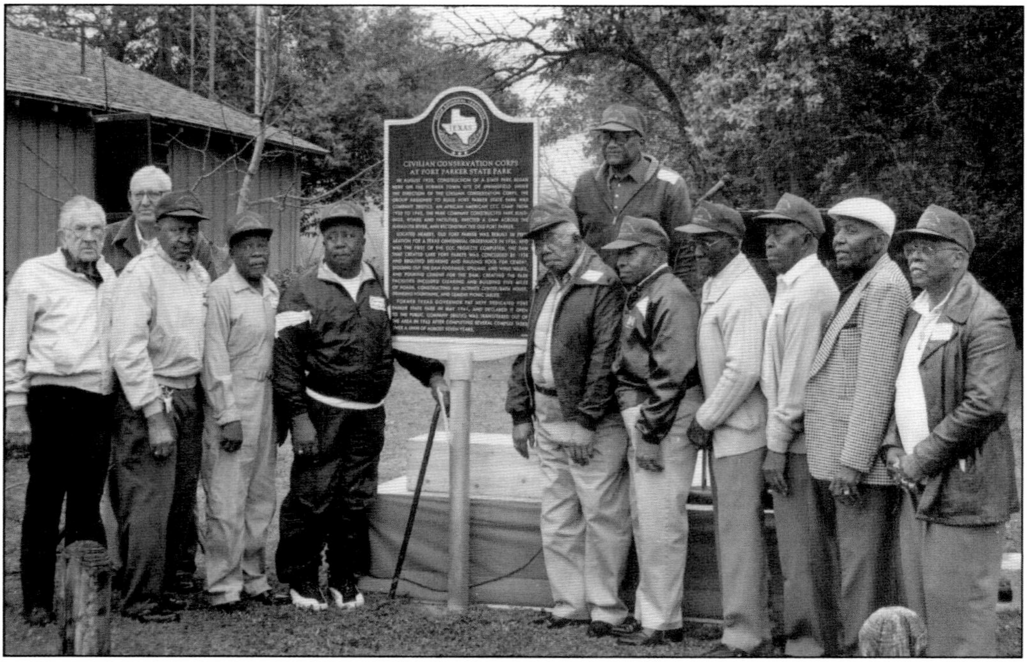

Several of the men from CCC Company 3807(c), which built Fort Parker State Park, are shown with a Texas Historical Marker describing the project. The marker was dedicated on March 7, 1998. Posing here are, from left to right, Vastine Fritsch, M.F. Rutherford, W.E. Chrisner, Calvin Burnett, Fletcher Mooney, Lawrence Daniel, Willie Lansford, James Sweeney, Willis Slaughter, Zeke Rhodes, Harold Curry, and Grady Rubbles. (Fort Parker State Park.)

Seven

WORLD WAR II

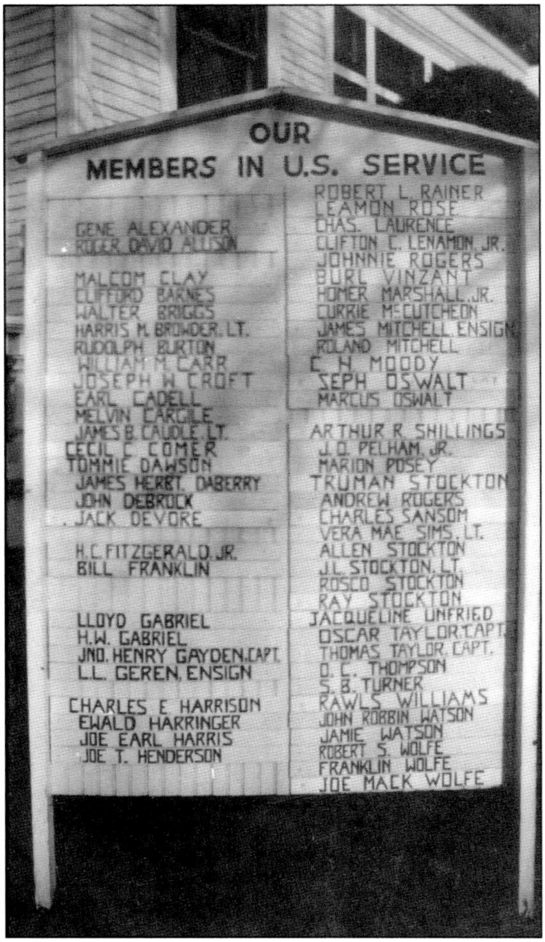

After the United States entered World War II in 1941, the residents of Limestone County stepped up to do their part for the war effort. Many able-bodied men proudly served in the armed forces. This 1944 photograph shows a sign on the lawn of the Groesbeck Baptist Church. It gives the names of the church's members who were serving in the military. (Limestone County Historical Museum.)

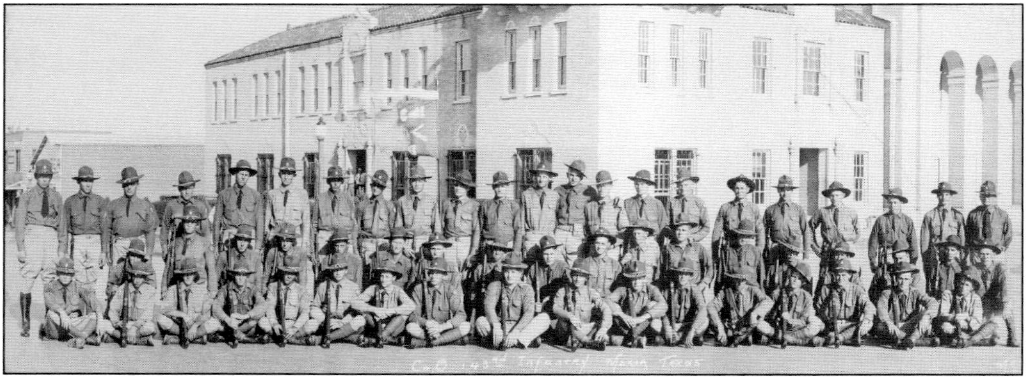

Company B of the 143rd Infantry, 36th Infantry Division, a Texas National Guard unit, was organized in Mexia on April 17, 1928. It was mobilized into federal service on November 25, 1940. During World War II, the 36th Infantry saw combat in North Africa, Italy, and western Europe. The Mexia Company suffered many casualties, but only 5 of the original 125 men were killed. (Limestone County Historical Museum.)

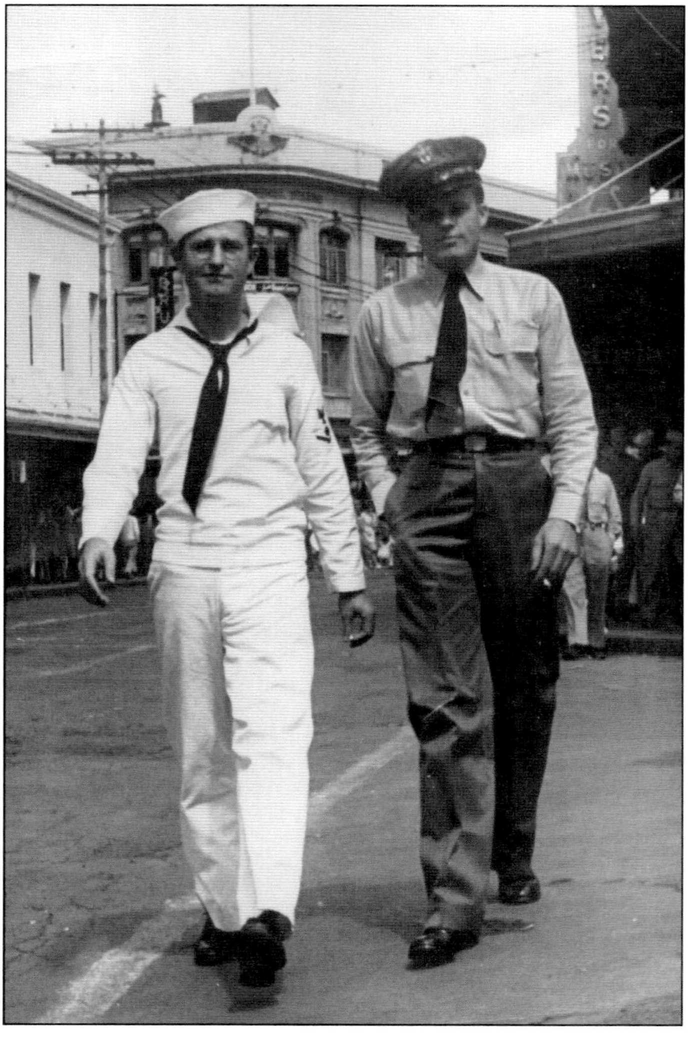

Photographed in Hawaii during World War II are Limestone County natives and brothers-in-law Onys T. Curlee (left) and H.C. Fitzgerald. Both men served in the Navy, Curlee in the Seabees and Fitzgerald on the battleship *South Dakota*. (Logan Wilson.)

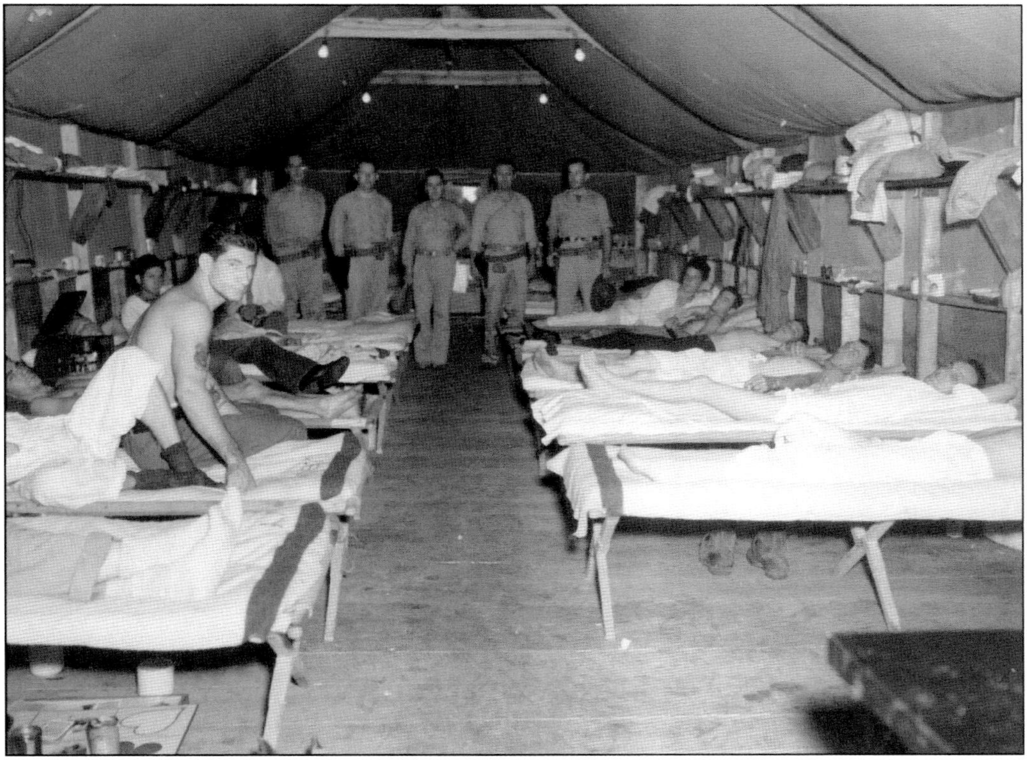

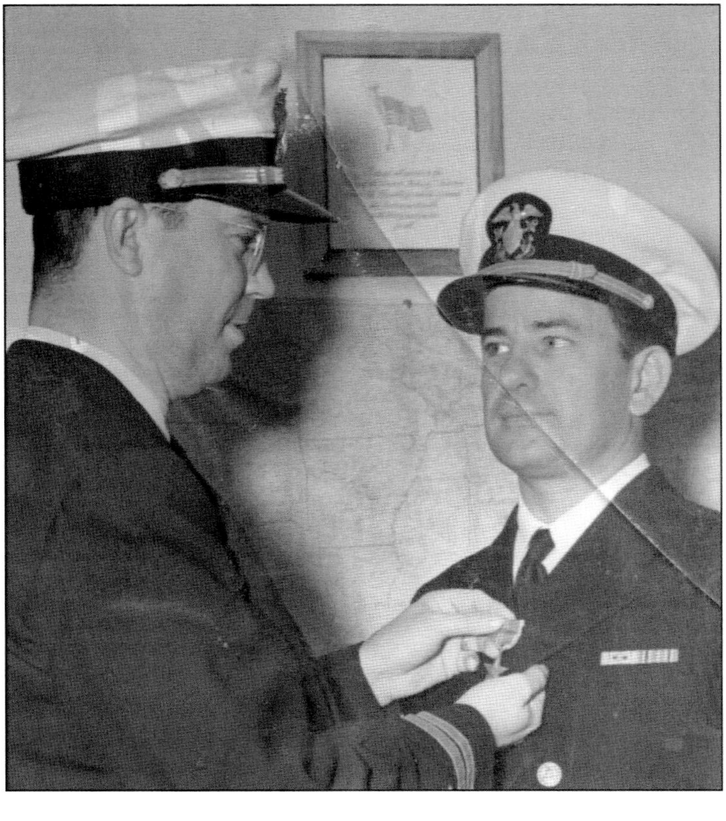

Lt. Stanley Cox of Groesbeck, Medical Corps, United States Naval Reserve, served in the Pacific during World War II. The above photograph was taken on January 10, 1943, on an unidentified island where Cox was stationed at the time. Lieutenant Cox stands at far right with his fellow doctors in one of the medical wards. At right, at a ceremony in Dallas on December 11, 1944, Cox is awarded the Bronze Star for extraordinary heroism during the invasion of Guam. He reported to Houston the next day as senior medical officer at the office of naval officer procurement. (Both, Limestone County Historical Museum.)

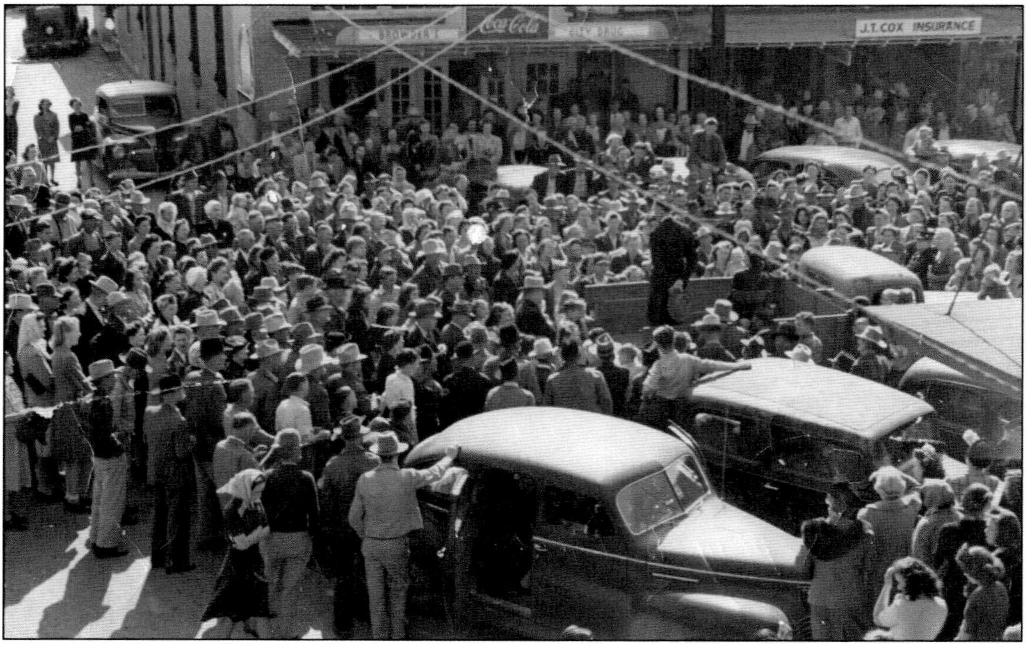

A large crowd gathered on Navasota Street in Groesbeck to welcome home Lt. Earlyn Black Harding, United States Army Nursing Corps. She was captured by the Japanese on Corregidor on May 6, 1942, and spent 33 months in Santo Tomas Prison in Manila. She was liberated by American forces on February 3, 1945. (Limestone County Historical Museum.)

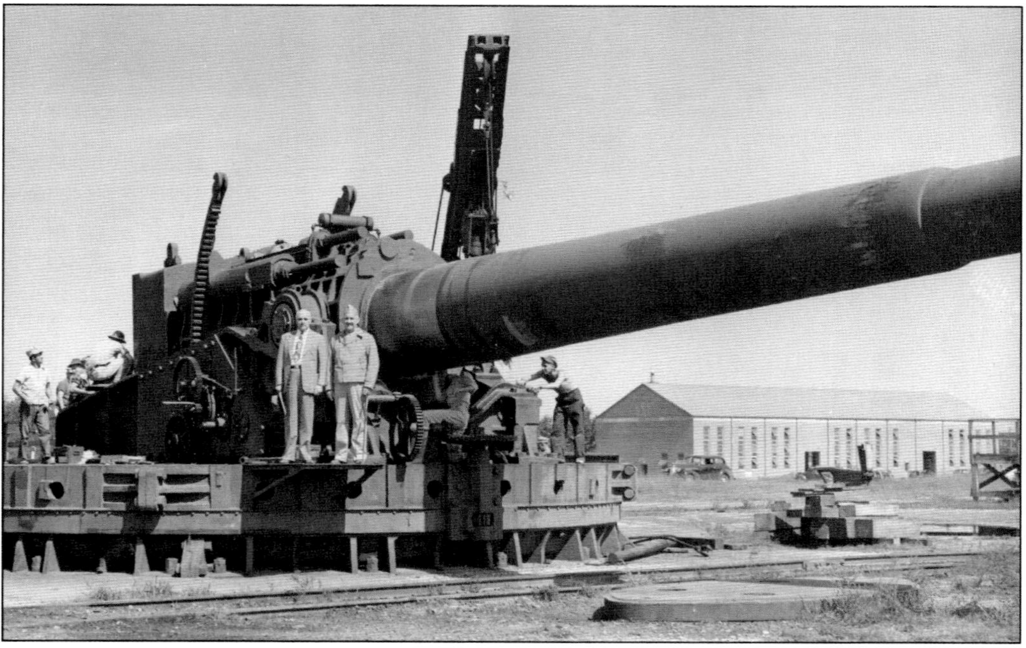

Gen. Charles T. Harris Jr. of Mexia was author of the first Industrial Mobilization Plan, presented to Congress prior to World War II. From 1942 to 1946, he served as commanding general of the Aberdeen Proving Ground in Maryland. In this 1943 photograph, he and Congressman Andrew J. May, chairman of the Military Affairs Committee, stand in front of a 16-inch seacoast gun. (Gibbs Memorial Library.)

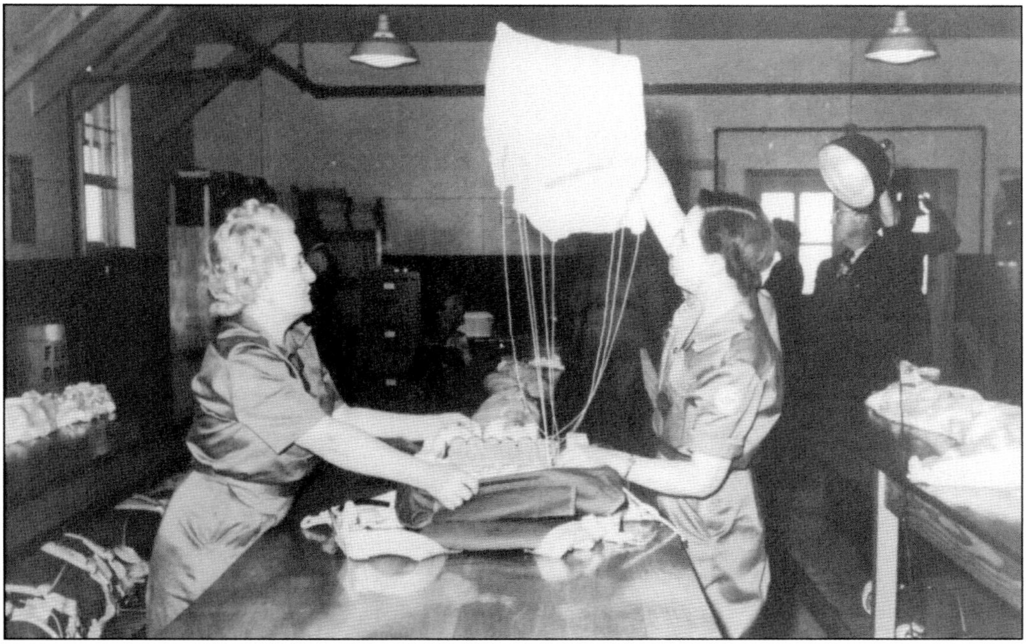

Many women entered the workforce during World War II to fill vacancies left by men serving overseas and to perform jobs vital to the war effort. In the above photograph, Edith Wilson Scroggins (left) of Groesbeck and Myrtle Dickey work on Christmas Day 1944, packing parachutes for the Air Transport Command at Love Field. Scroggins also served as an airplane mechanic. Below, Scroggins (third from right) and her fellow workers make repairs to the "Suzy Q," the famous B-17 Flying Fortress. It was assigned to the 93rd Bomb Squadron, 19th Bomb Group, and participated in all of the early Pacific battles except Midway. It was credited with destroying 93 Japanese planes and ships. (Both, Logan D. Wilson.)

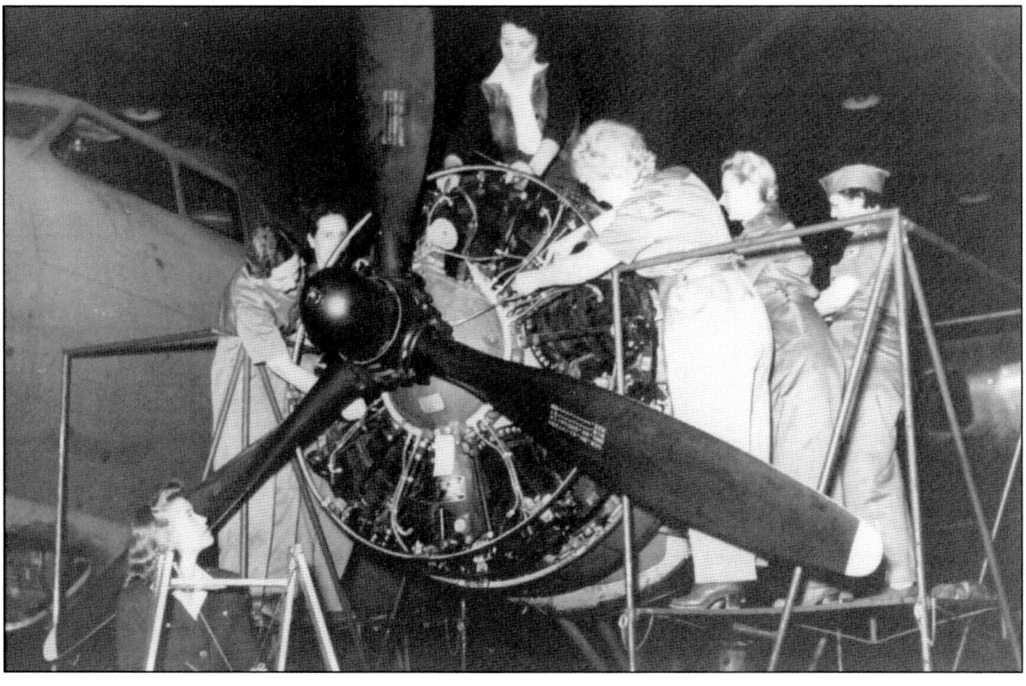

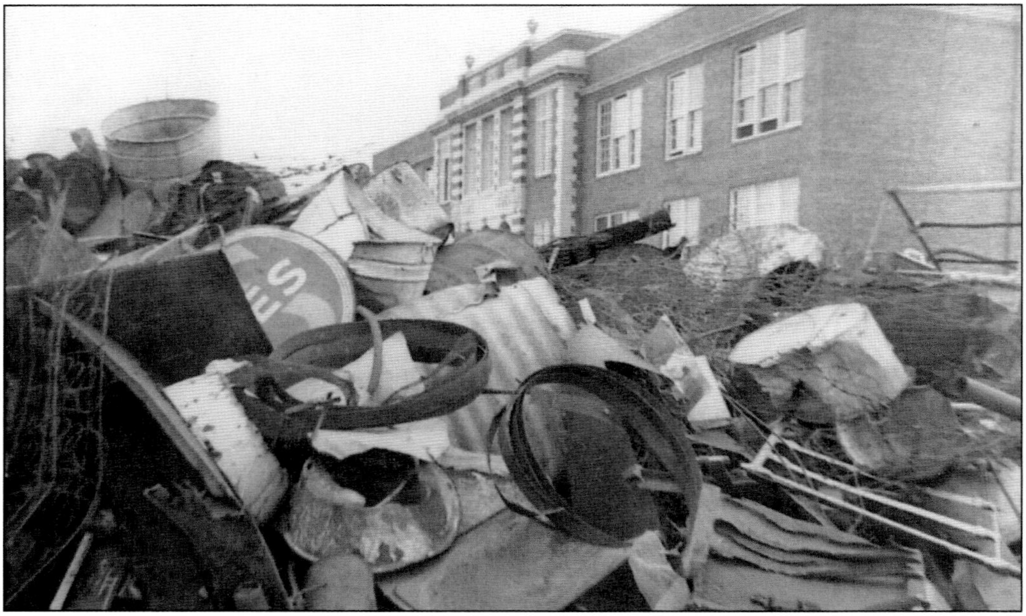

On the home front during World War II, Limestone County residents did their part for the war effort. They bought war bonds, raised gardens, and canned their own food. Having to make do with less, they conserved vital resources. During 1942, the students of Mexia High School conducted a scrap metal drive. The result of their efforts is shown here in front of the school. (Mexia School Museum.)

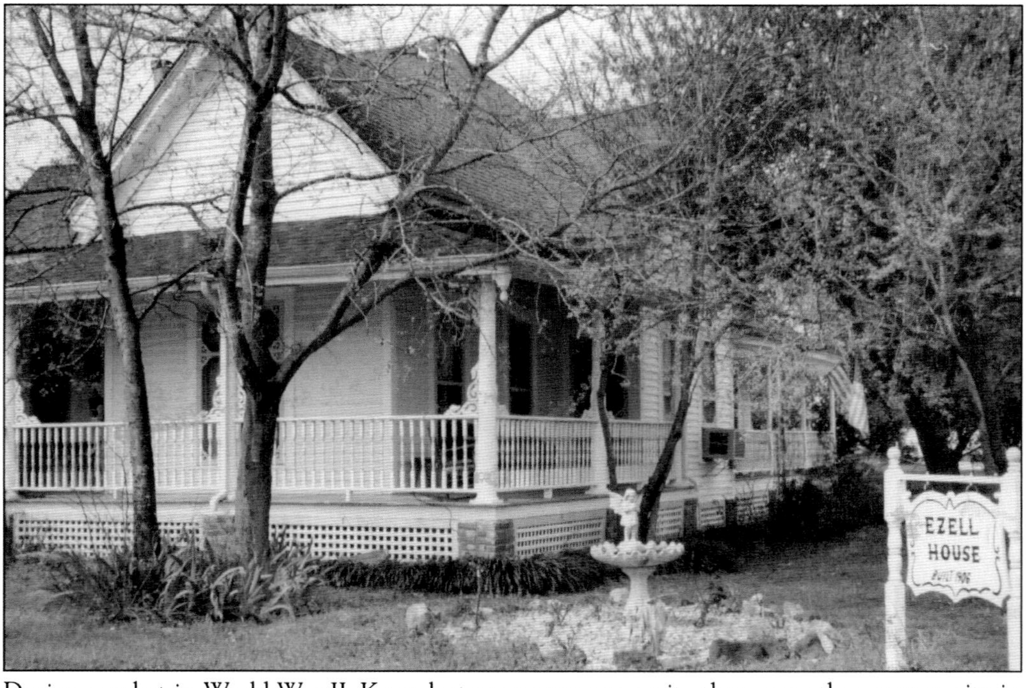

During combat in World War II, Kosse lost more men per capita than any other community in the United States. The Ezell Home, built in 1906, was once called the "Widows' Corner" because several of Kosse's World War II widows moved their families into the house in order to pool their resources. (Karen Parten.)

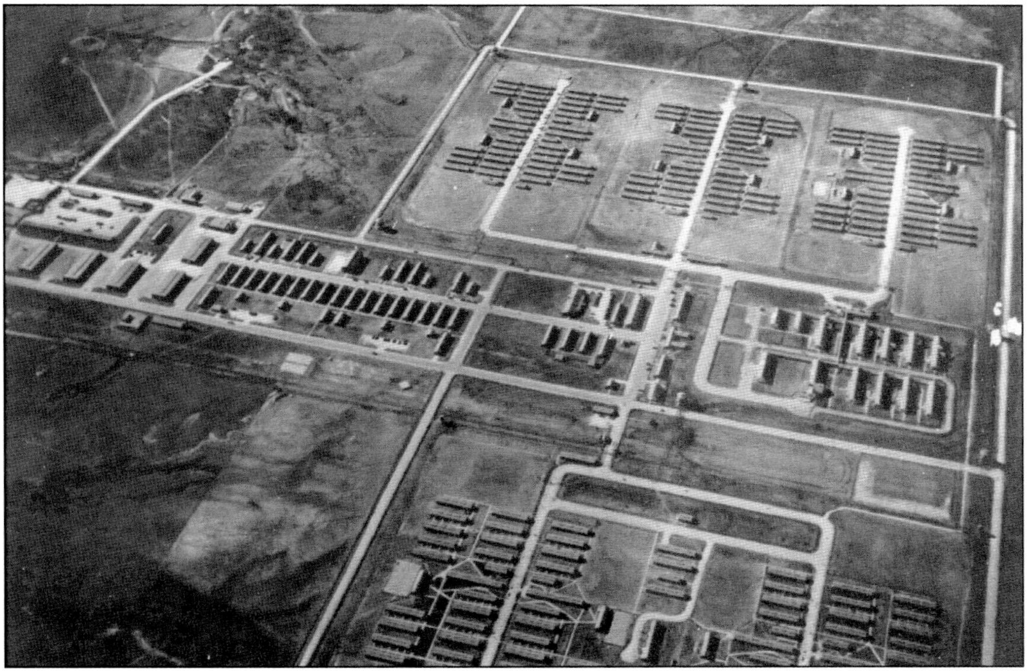

During World War II, Mexia was home to the largest German internment camp in Texas. In 1942, Camp Mexia was constructed three miles west of Mexia on 1,200 acres. It once held as many as 8,500 prisoners, the first of which arrived on June 4, 1943. The POWs at Camp Mexia were members of Gen. Erwin Rommel's Afrika Korps, which surrendered in April 1943. (History Room, Mexia State Supported Living Center.)

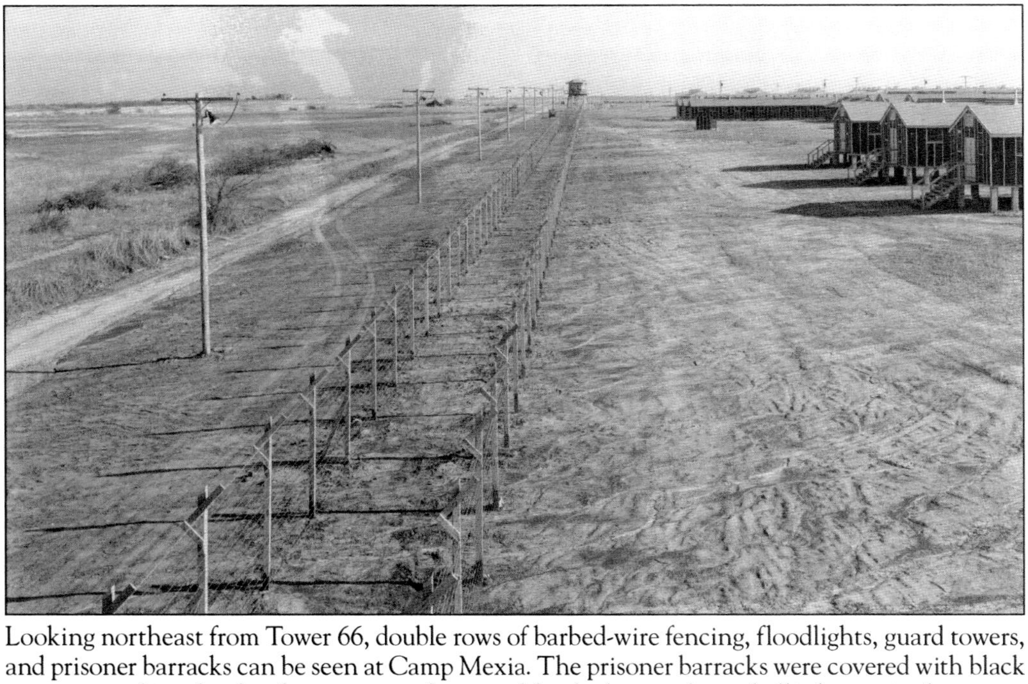

Looking northeast from Tower 66, double rows of barbed-wire fencing, floodlights, guard towers, and prisoner barracks can be seen at Camp Mexia. The prisoner barracks were covered with black tar paper and inside of each were rows of cots and footlockers and a potbellied stove in the center aisle. (History Room, Mexia State Supported Living Center.)

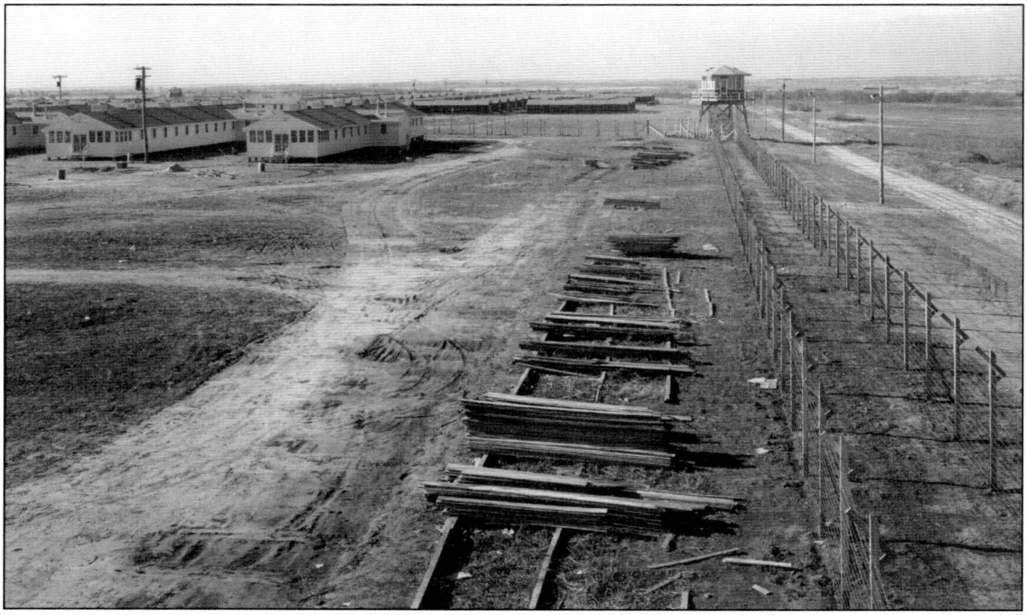

Many of the prisoners at Camp Mexia worked in the community, performing such tasks as picking cotton, pruning trees, picking peaches, and cutting hay. The employer would pay the government, and each prisoner was given credits to purchase cigarettes, writing paper, soft drinks, and other items. Most of the German prisoners felt that they were treated very well, and many left Mexia after the war with fond memories. A few returned in later years to visit Mexia, and in more recent years, children of former prisoners have also started visiting. Looking south from Tower 60, the above photograph gives a general view of the hospital area, where prisoners were given top medical care. Below, four former prisoners are rehashing memories of Camp Mexia during a visit in the early 1990s. (Both, History Room, Mexia State Supported Living Center.)

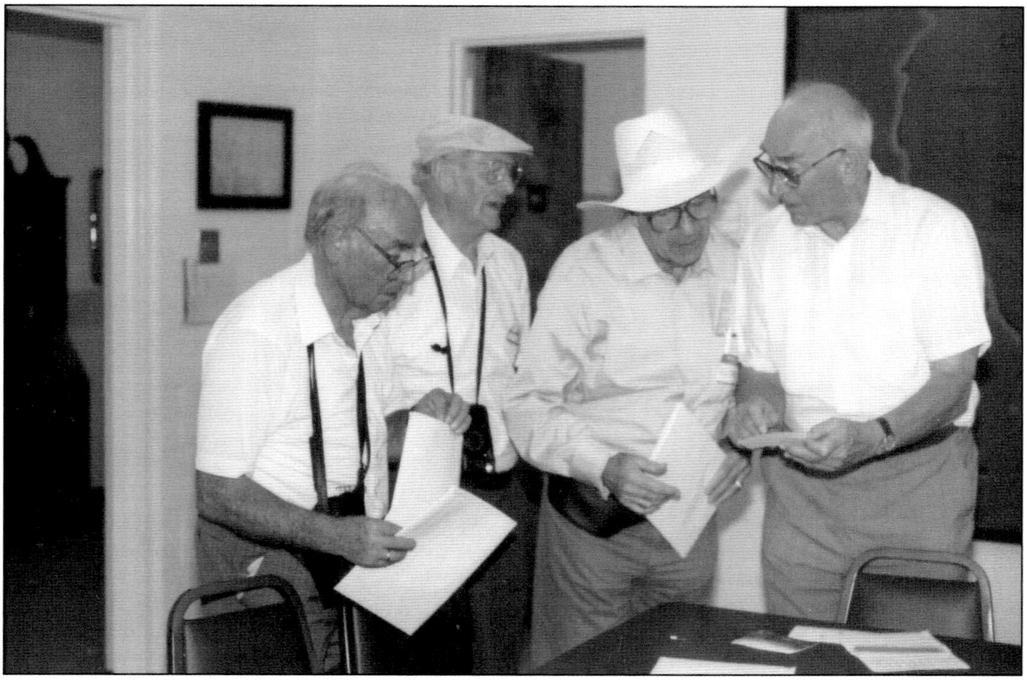

Eight

1945 to the Present

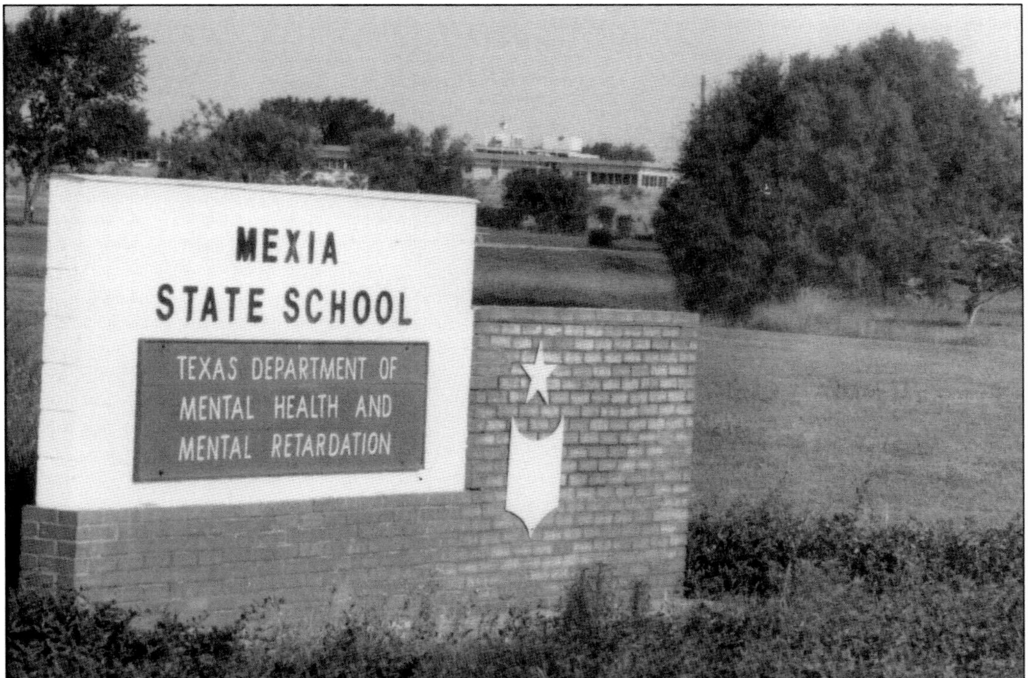

The Mexia Prisoner of War Camp was closed in May 1945. After much negotiation, the property was transferred to the State of Texas. The Mexia State School, a residential facility for individuals with mental disabilities, was opened on April 24, 1946, with the transfer of 48 residents from Ink's Lake Branch of the Austin State School. (History Room, Mexia State Supported Living Center.)

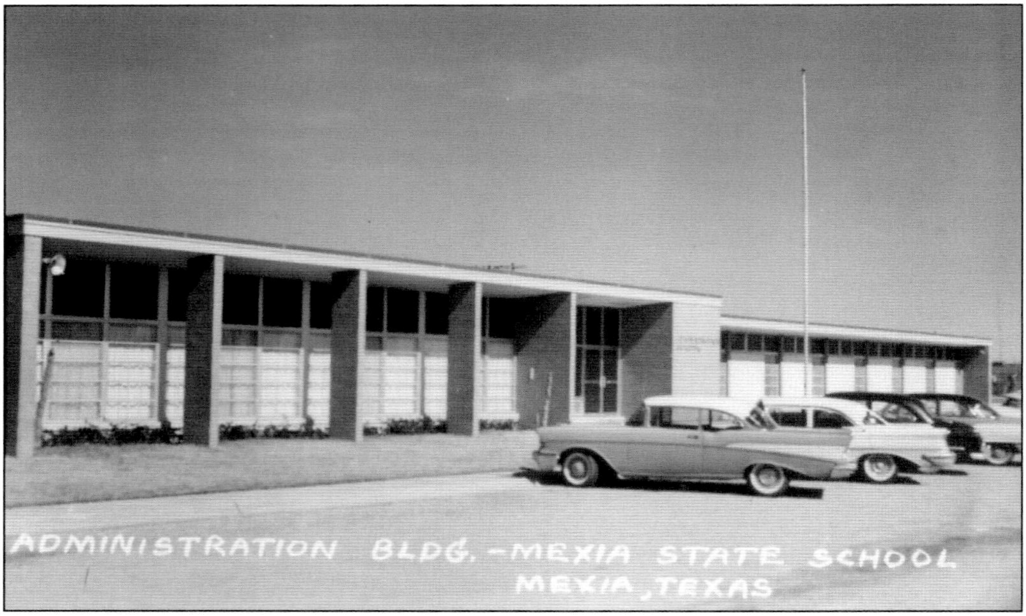

In the beginning, the buildings from the POW days were used by the Mexia State School. The first permanent dorms were completed in 1951 and 1952. The Administration Building, shown here, and a 60-bed hospital were constructed in 1957. In 2009, the facility had an annual budget of $68 million and employed about 1,700 people, making it the county's largest employer. (William Reagan.)

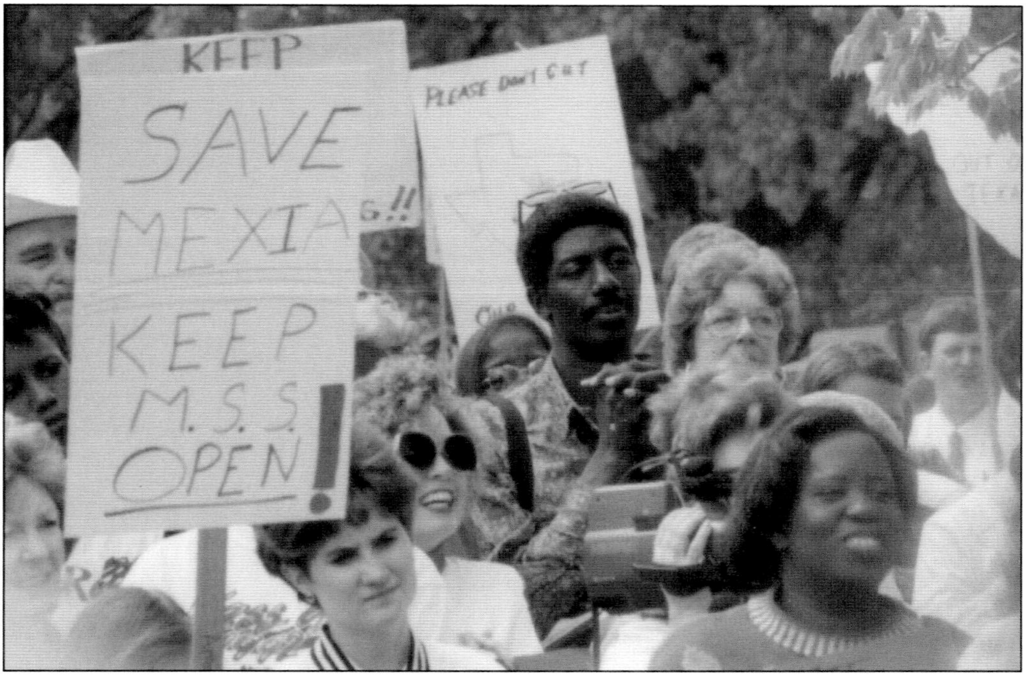

In 1991, the state considered closing the Mexia State School, threatening the area's economic stability. On March 24, 1992, more than 5,000 individuals traveled to Austin in protest. The governor's office received over 61,000 letters. On March 26, Gov. Ann Richards announced that the Mexia State School would remain open. In 2009, the facility's name was changed to the Mexia State Supported Living Center. (Gibbs Memorial Library.)

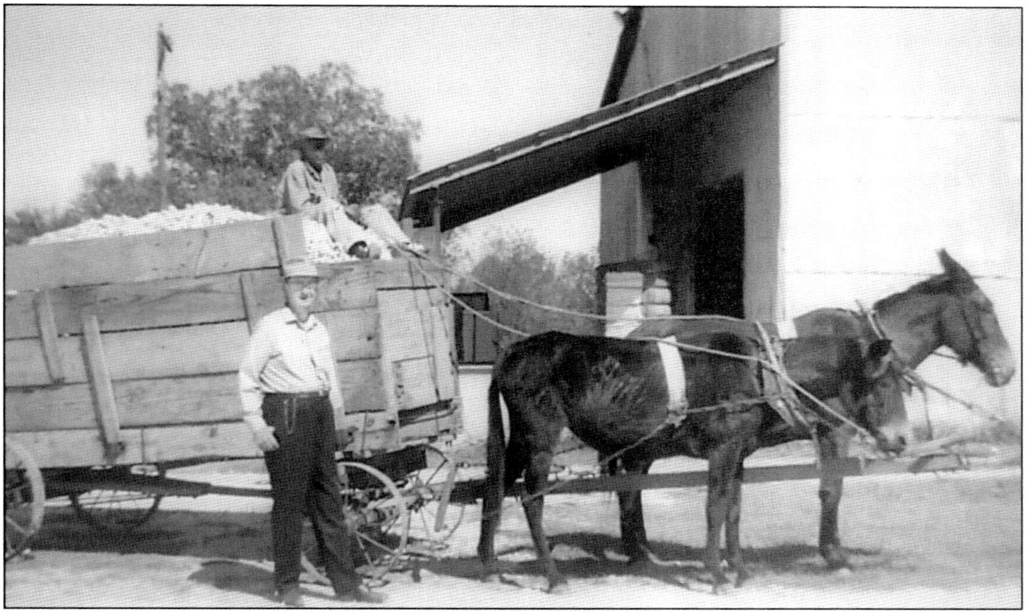

Cotton farming in Limestone County declined following World War II. Cotton production went from 64,956 bales in 1930, to 31,245 bales in 1953, to 2,608 bales in 1969. At one time, there were over 50 cotton gins in the county. Today, there are none. This 1968 photograph, of the Kling and Weatherspoon Gin in Kosse, depicts the last load of cotton to be ginned in Limestone County. (Kosse Heritage House.)

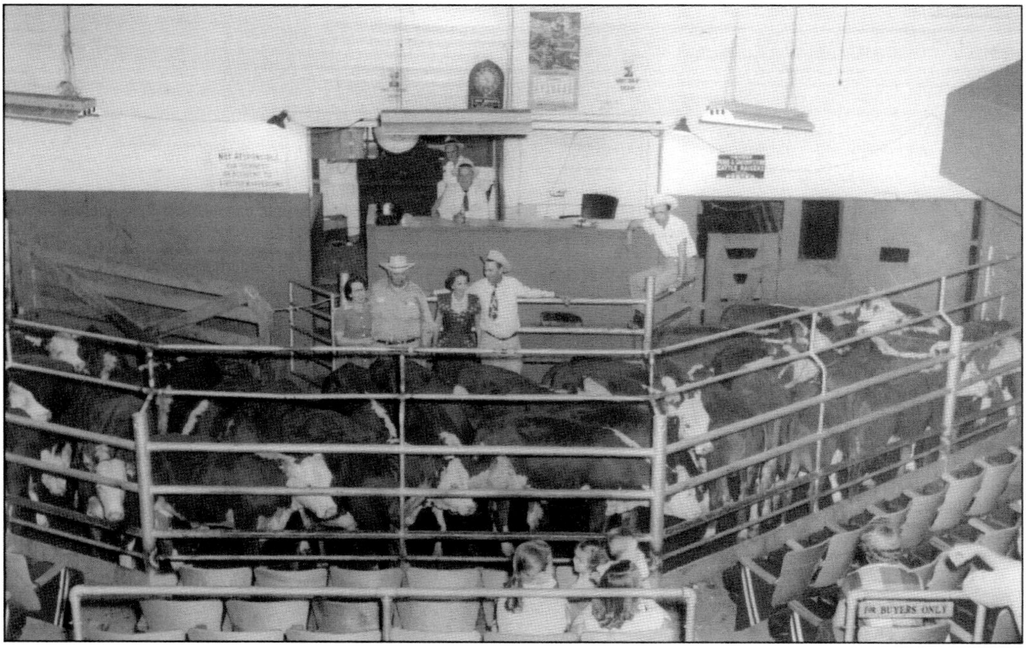

Cattle ranching became the primary agricultural activity in Limestone County following World War II. This photograph from the early 1950s shows a special cattle sale at the Groesbeck Commission Company. Standing in the livestock auction arena are, from left to right, Ruth and Franklin Jackson and Lucille and Irwin (June) de Cordova. In 1969, there were over 74,000 head of cattle in the county. (Peggy de Cordova Champion and Ethel de Cordova Porter.)

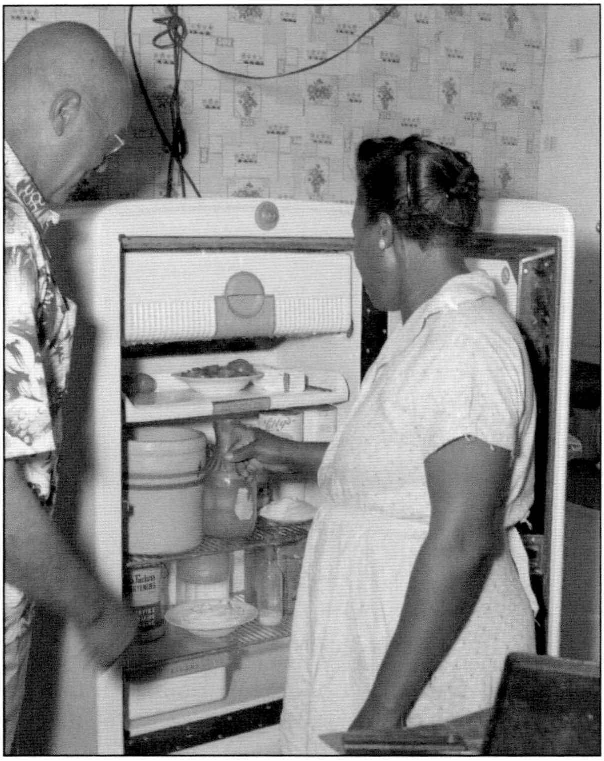

Life for many rural residents of Limestone County improved immensely after electrical service reached their homes during the postwar years. These two photographs were taken in July 1949 on the Foreman farm, located in the Woodlands community. At left, Lula Foreman shows her new refrigerator to Limestone County extension agent J.W. Booker. Below, Jim Foreman is pictured with a new electric well pump and tank, which allowed his family to enjoy indoor plumbing. They no longer had to carry water from the well to the house or needed the use of an outhouse. (Both, Cushing Library, Texas A&M University.)

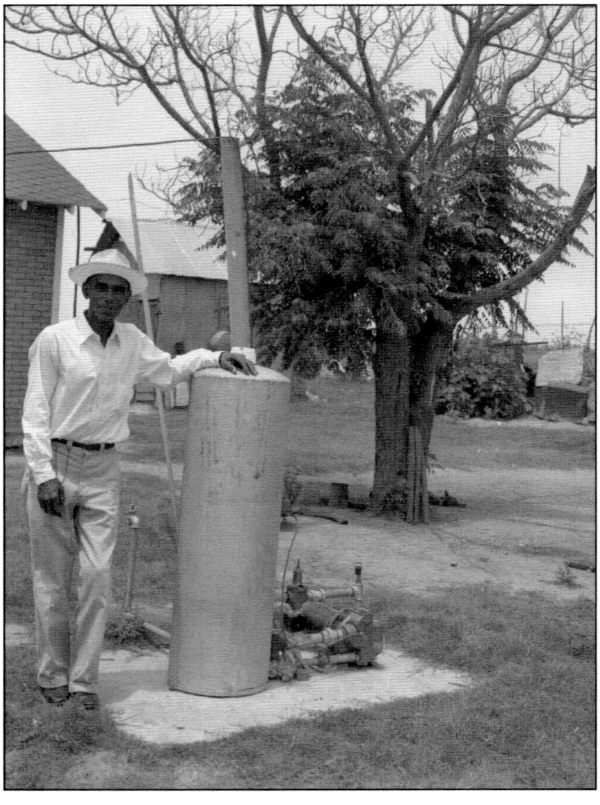

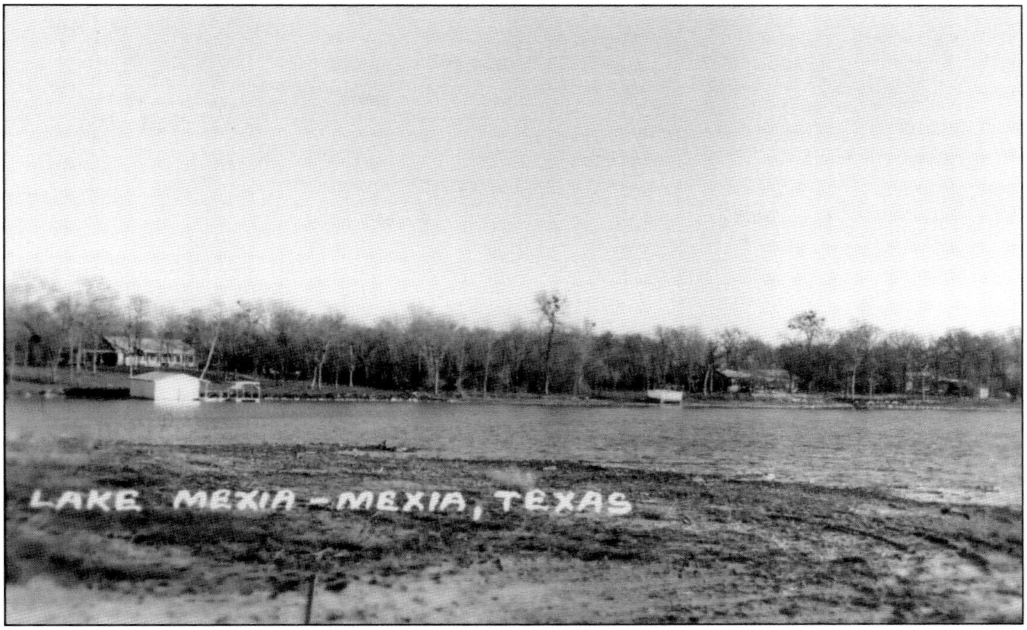

Located seven miles southwest of Mexia is Lake Mexia. Construction of the Lake Mexia Dam on the Navasota River began in July 1960 and was completed in June 1961. The 1,200-acre lake is owned and operated by the Bistone Municipal Water Supply District. The area has several subdivisions with many attractive lakeside homes. Camping, fishing, and boating are popular recreational activities at the lake. (William Reagan.)

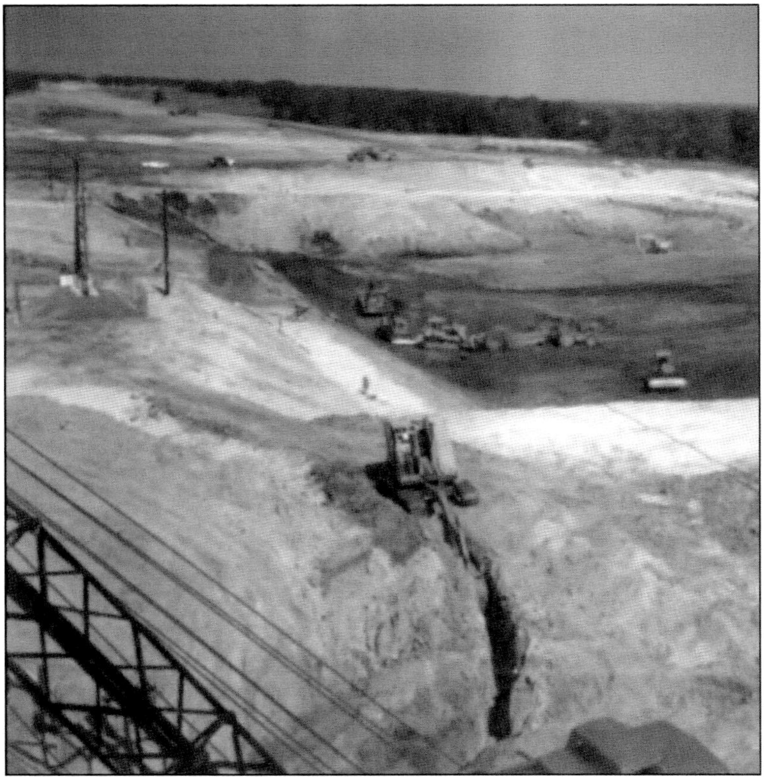

In January 1974, the Brazos River Authority announced its plan to create Lake Limestone. Construction of the Sterling C. Robertson Dam, just across the county line in Robertson County, began in November 1975. Taken in May 1976 from atop the concrete batch plant, this photograph provides a view of the excavation work for the dam's service spillway. (Brazos River Authority.)

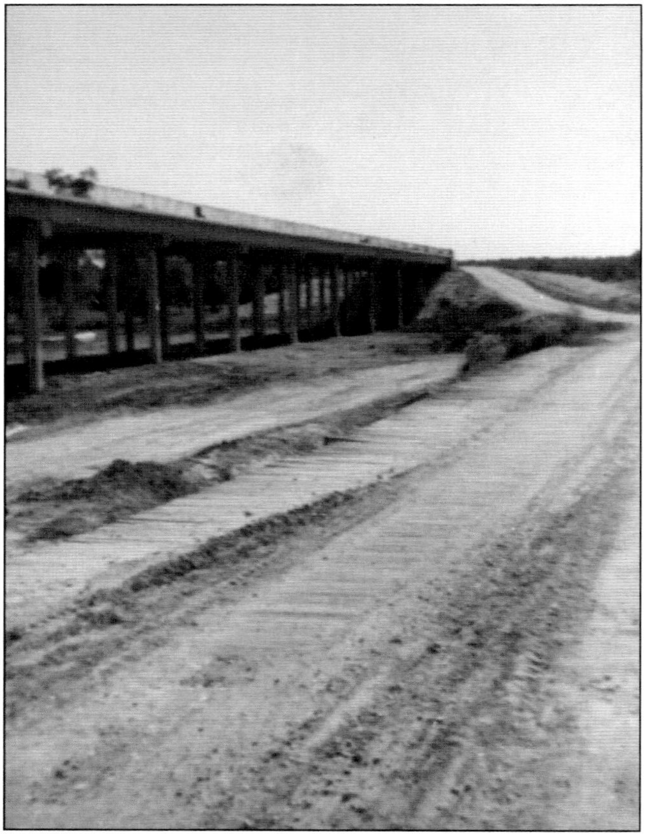

In February 1976, the county commissioners requested that the Lost Prairie & Old Union crossing on the Navasota River be retained across Lake Limestone. Using a $490,000 settlement from the Brazos River Authority, Limestone County built the only public crossing on Lake Limestone. Originally dedicated as Jacobs Crossing in December 1977, it was later renamed Henderson Crossing. Shown here is the crossing's bridge as it neared completion in 1977. (William Reagan.)

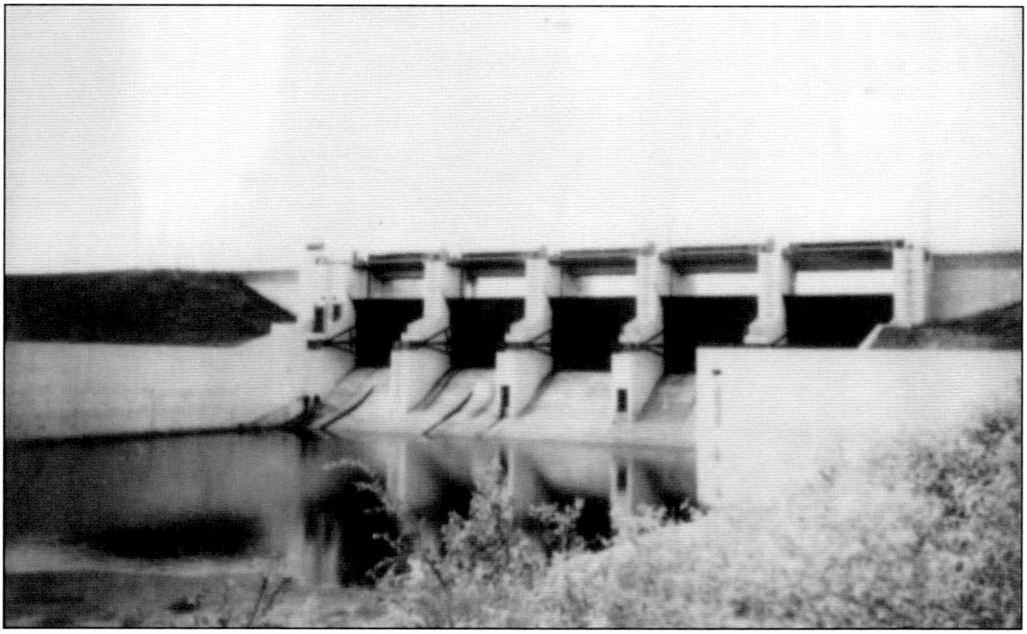

The gates to the Sterling C. Robertson Dam were closed on October 16, 1978. Due to heavy rains and flooding in the spring of 1979, Lake Limestone reached its full level on May 12, 1979. The sudden filling of the lake was a surprise to many. (Brazos River Authority.)

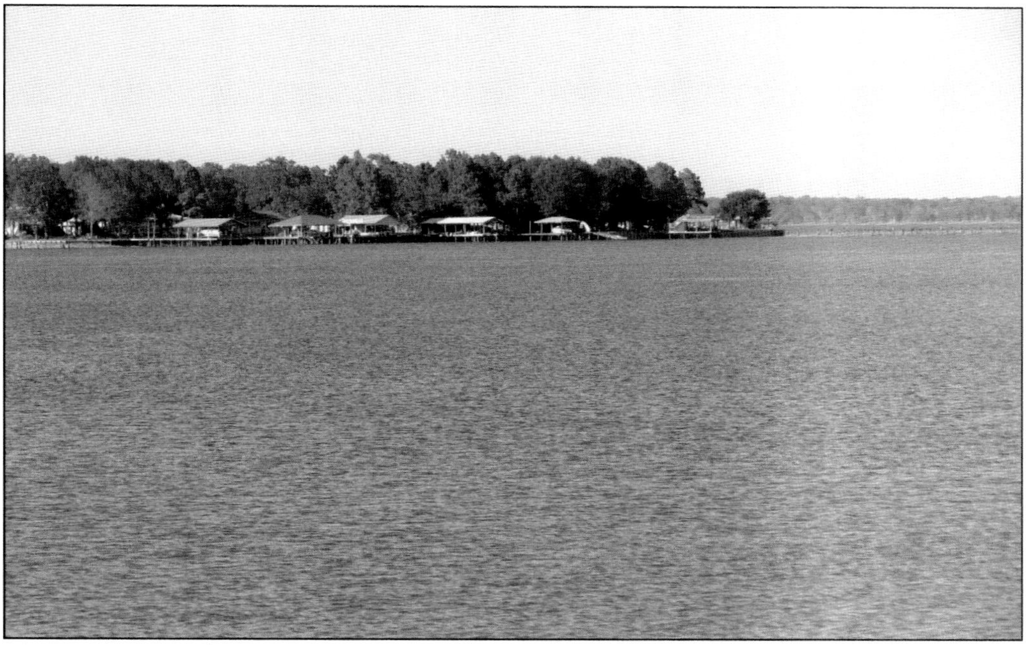

The 13,680-acre Lake Limestone is a popular recreational spot for both local residents and tourists. Fishing, boating, skiing, and swimming are popular activities on the lake. The subdivisions along the shores of Lake Limestone contain numerous homes that serve as both permanent residences and weekend getaways. (William Reagan.)

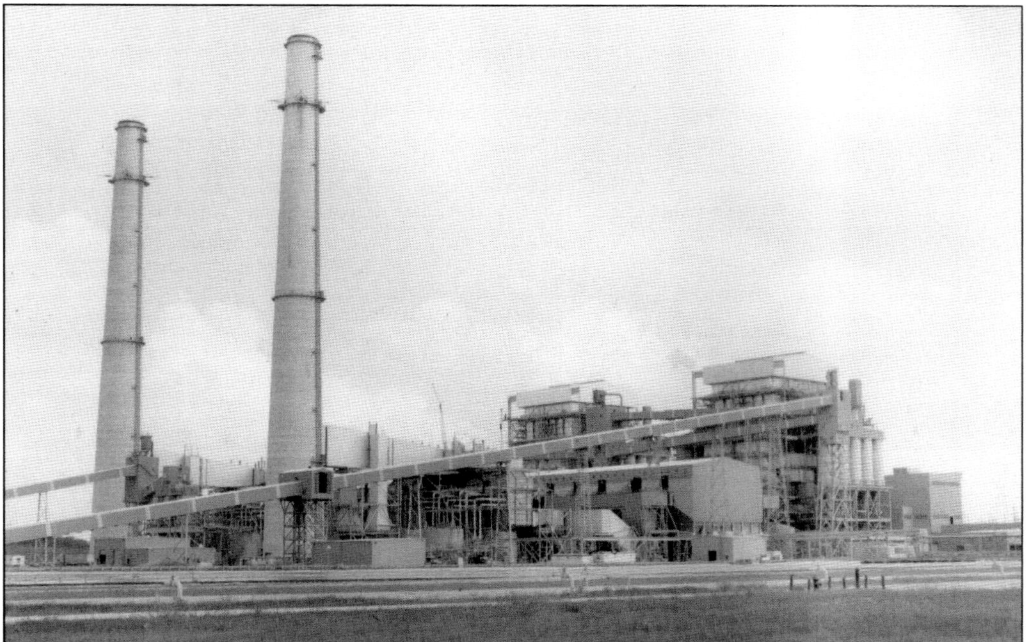

Energy production in Limestone County over the last three decades has brought prosperity reminiscent of the oil boom days. The construction of a two-unit power plant in the southeastern corner of the county during the early 1980s created numerous jobs and generated additional taxes. (Limestone County Historical Museum.)

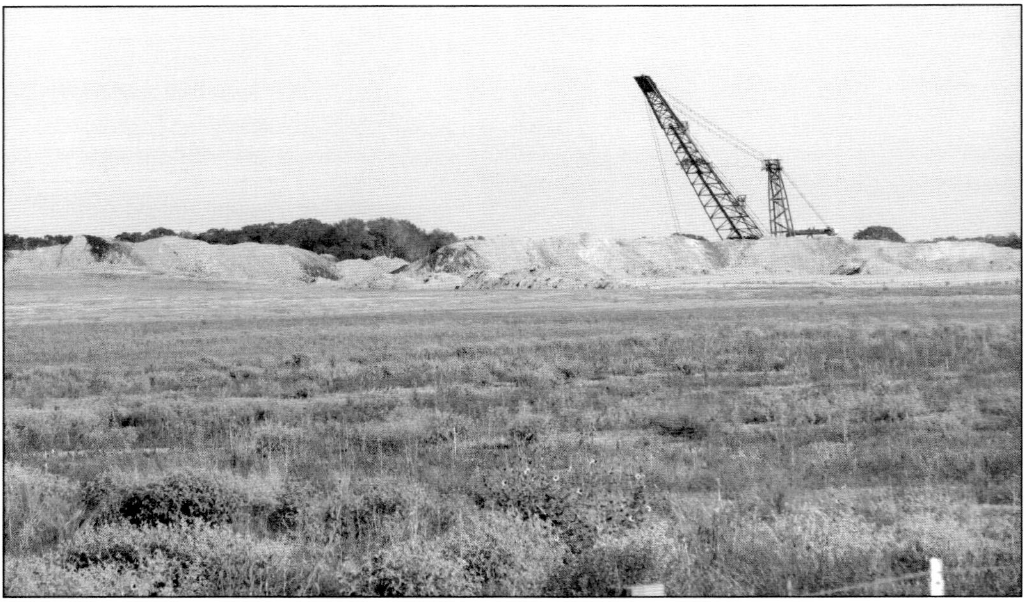

Lignite coal deposits are found under much of southern Limestone County. Mining operations in the county, and in neighboring counties, provide lignite to area power plants. Pictured is Luminant Energy's Kosse Mine, located eight miles east of Kosse. It provides fuel to a two-unit power plant near Franklin in neighboring Robertson County. (William Reagan.)

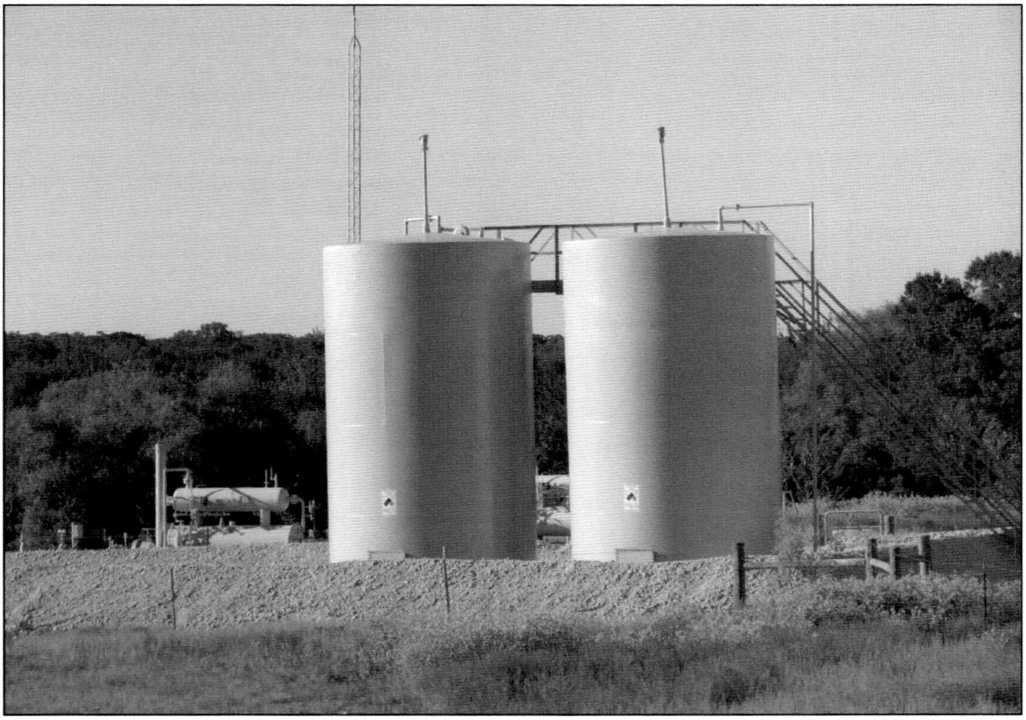

Limestone County also sits above huge deposits of natural gas. Shown here is one of almost 3,000 natural gas wells in Limestone County. The royalty and lease payments to individuals, the creation of jobs, and the taxes generated from the production of natural gas greatly impact the county's economy. (William Reagan.)

Nine

NOTABLE PERSONALITIES

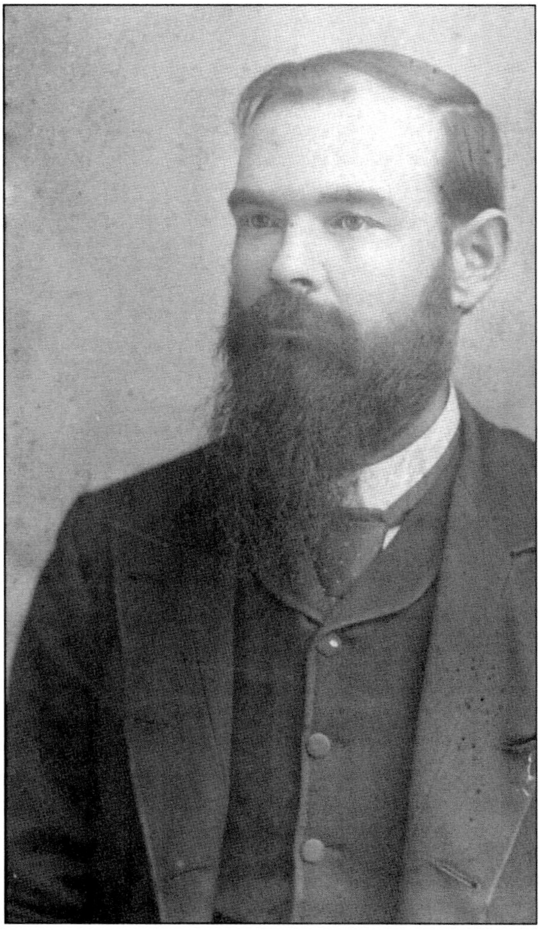

Born in Georgia in 1851, Lafayette Lumpkin Foster moved to Limestone County when he was 18 years old, and he settled at Horn Hill. After attending Waco University, he moved to Groesbeck in 1873 and started a newspaper called the *Limestone New Era*. He was elected representative for two terms and in 1884 became the youngest Speaker of the House. He served on the first railroad commission and was president of Texas A&M College from 1898 until his death in 1901. (Cushing Library, Texas A&M University.)

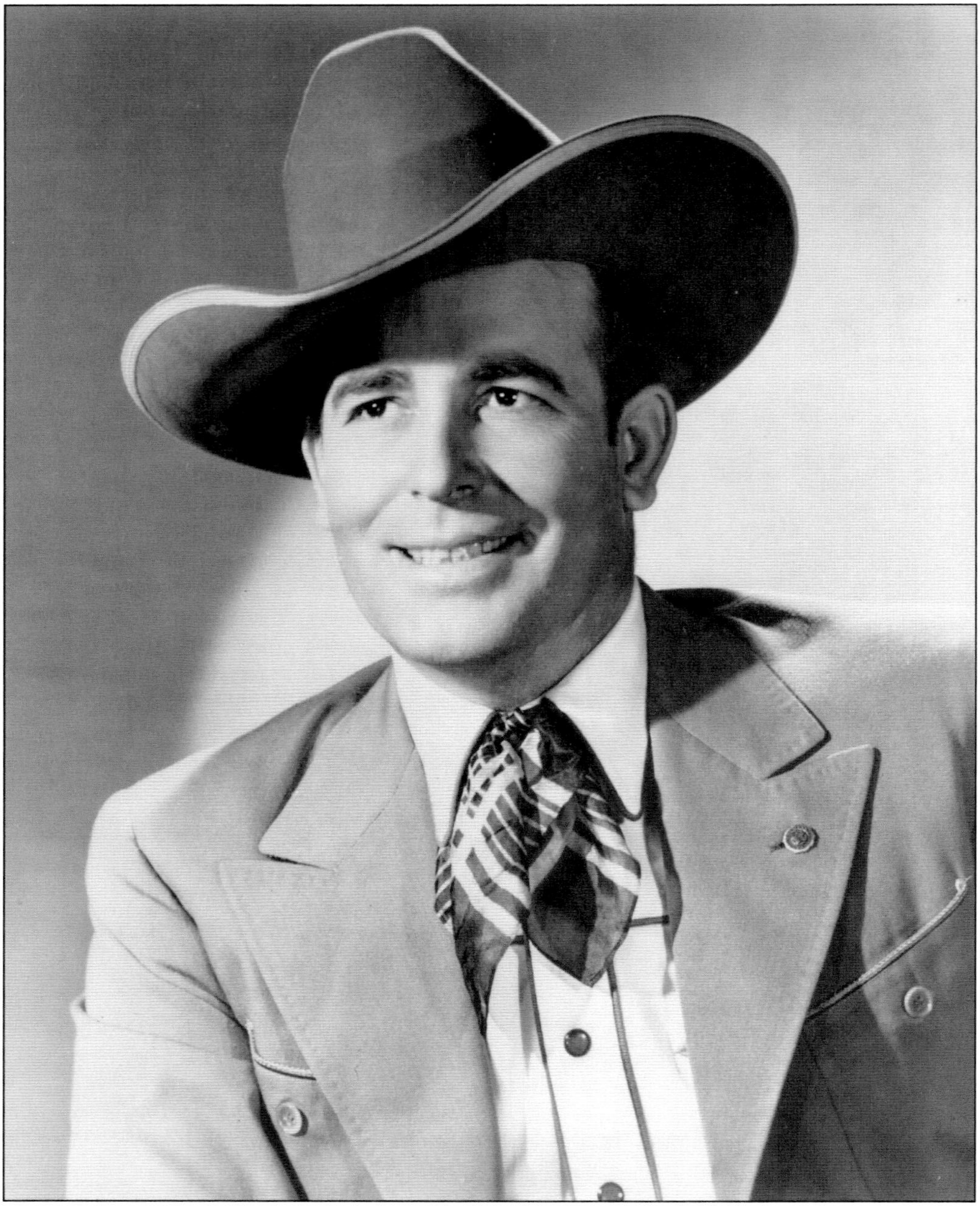

James Robert (Bob) Wills was born on March 6, 1905, on a farm near Kosse. He was the eldest of 10 children born to John and Emmaline Foley Wills. In 1913, the Wills family moved to Hall County in West Texas. Becoming a proficient fiddle player at an early age, he played at his first dance in 1915. Bob Wills developed a new style of music called western swing, a blend of western fiddle music, blues, and jazz. He learned frontier fiddle music from his father and grandfather and learned blues and jazz from black playmates and coworkers in the cotton fields of Limestone County and West Texas. In 1934, he formed his own band, Bob Wills and His Texas Playboys, and gained national popularity in 1940 when he recorded his composition "New San Antonio Rose." He was inducted into the Country Music Hall of Fame in 1968. Bob Wills died on May 13, 1975, and was buried in Tulsa, Oklahoma. (Oklahoma Historical Society.)

Cindy Walker was born on July 20, 1918, near Mart, Texas. After living in Los Angeles for 13 years, she moved in 1954 to Mexia, where she lived until her death. A prolific songwriter, she published over 500 songs. Her songs have been recorded by over 375 different recording artists, including Ray Charles, Jim Reeves, Elvis Presley, Roy Orbison, Willie Nelson, and Eddy Arnold. Bob Wills alone recorded over 50 of her songs. In 1970, she became the first woman inducted into the Nashville Songwriter's Hall of Fame. She was also inducted into the Country Music Hall of Fame in 1997, the Texas Country Music Hall of Fame in 1998, and the National Cowgirl Hall of Fame in 1998. Walker died in Mexia on March 23, 2006. Her grave in the Mexia Cemetery is pictured below. (Both, Dick Flatt.)

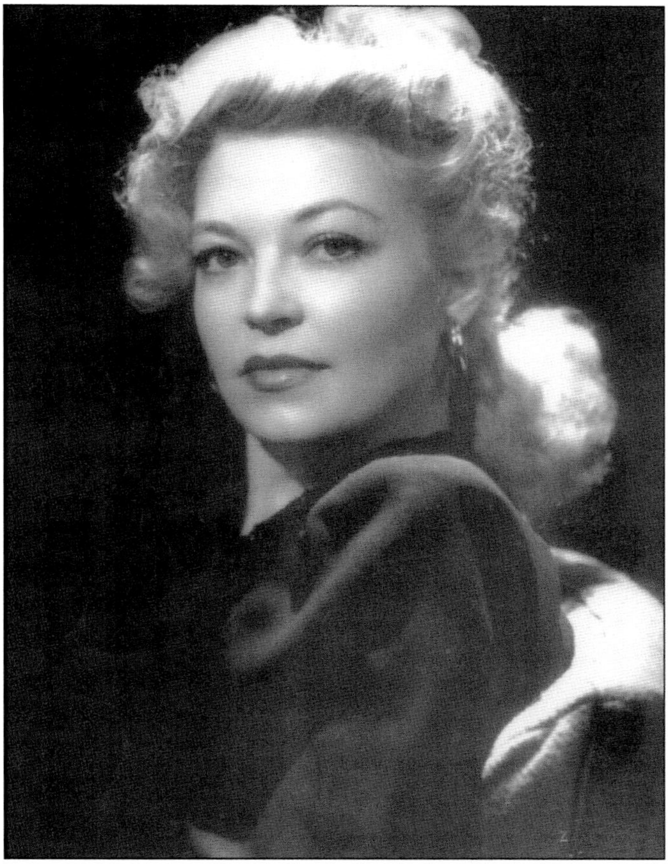

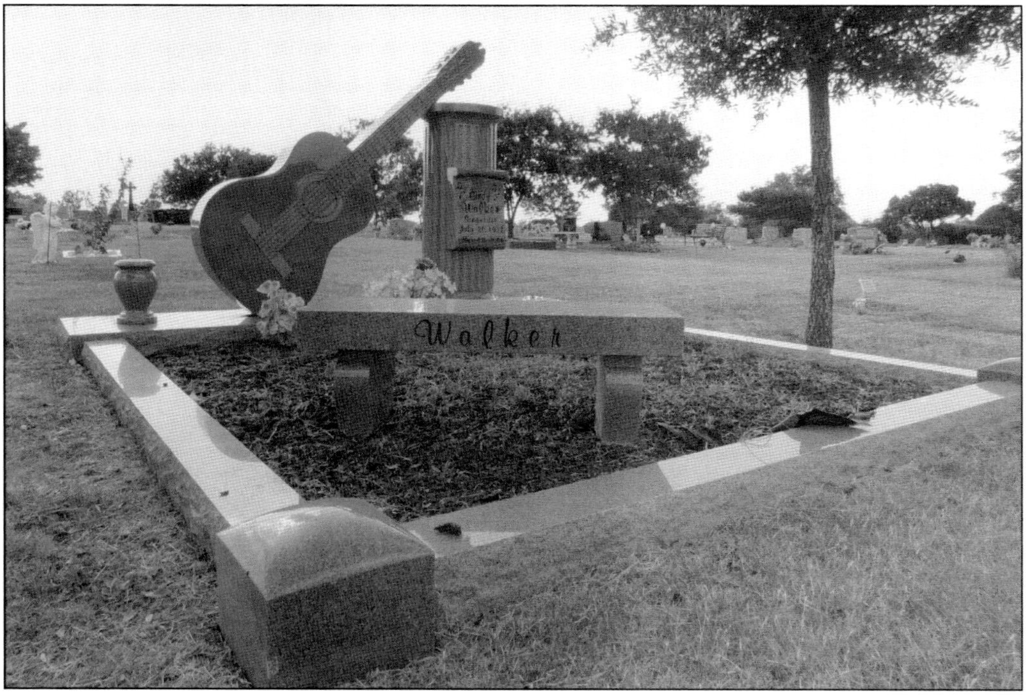

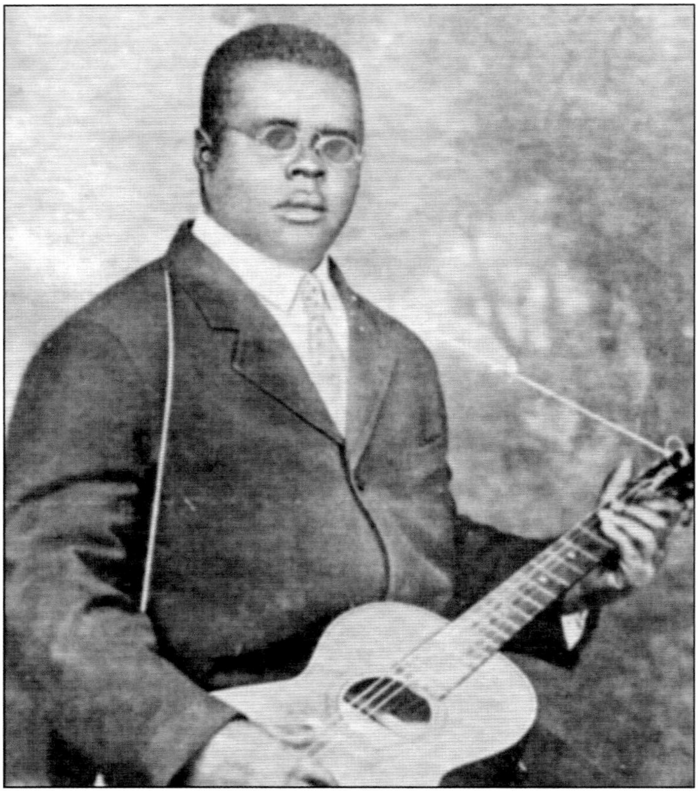

Blind Lemon Jefferson was a nationally known blues guitarist and singer. He was born in Freestone County in 1893 but performed throughout the local area, including Mexia and Groesbeck. One of his songs, "Penitentiary Blues," was written about Groesbeck. He began performing around Dallas in 1912, was discovered by a Paramount recording scout in 1925, and went to Chicago, where he recorded 110 songs. He died in 1929. (Limestone County Historical Museum.)

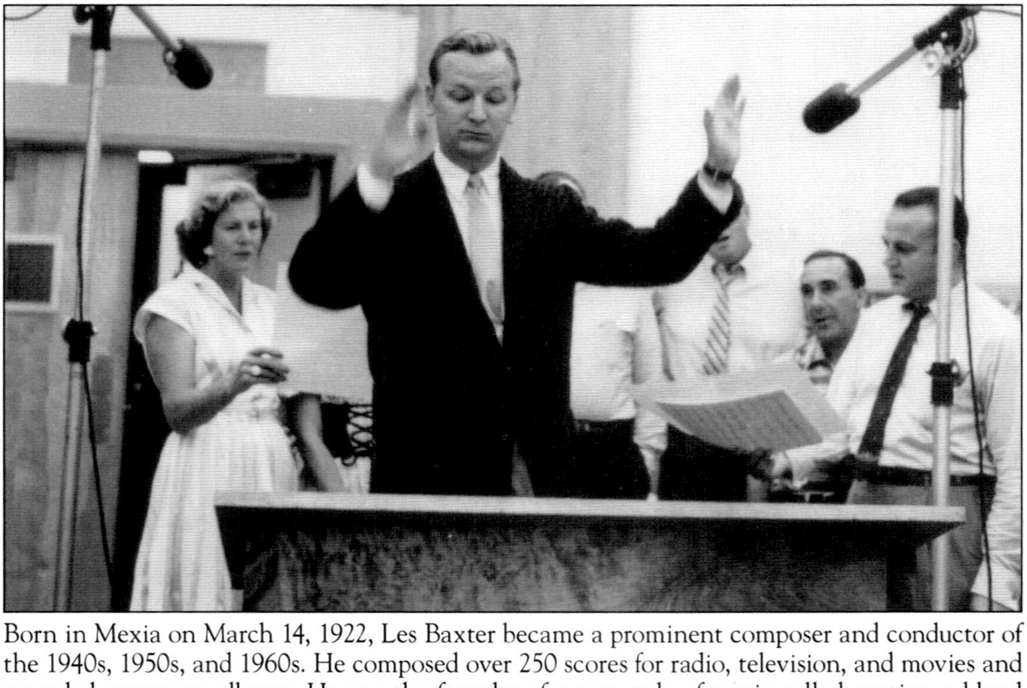

Born in Mexia on March 14, 1922, Les Baxter became a prominent composer and conductor of the 1940s, 1950s, and 1960s. He composed over 250 scores for radio, television, and movies and recorded numerous albums. He was the founder of a new style of music called exotica, a blend of easy listening and the sounds and styles of South America, Africa, and Polynesia. (Limestone County Historical Museum.)

Joe Don Baker was born in Groesbeck on February 12, 1936, and graduated from Groesbeck High School in 1954. During the 1960s, he made guest appearances on shows like *Bonanza* and *Gunsmoke*. Featured in movies from the 1960s to the present, his most memorable role was Bufford Pusser in *Walking Tall*. He had the starring role in the television series *Eischeid* and was in three *James Bond* movies. (Limestone County Historical Museum.)

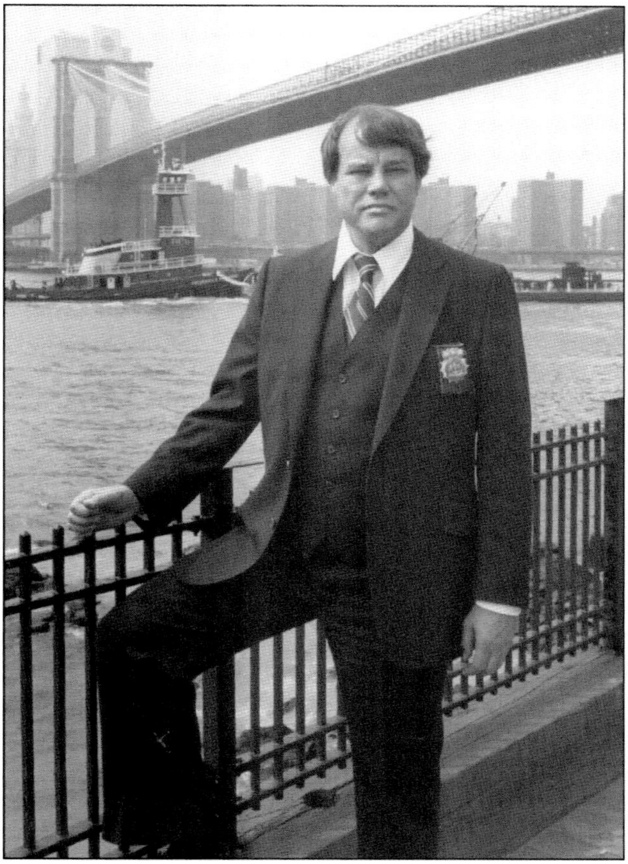

Ray Rhodes, a Mexia native, played professional football for the New York Giants from 1974 to 1978 and the San Francisco 49ers in 1980. Over his more than 30-year coaching career, he has worked as a defensive coach for several teams and has served as head coach of the Philadelphia Eagles and the Green Bay Packers. Rhodes is pictured below with his mother, Tommie, at Super Bowl XL. (Tommie Rhodes.)

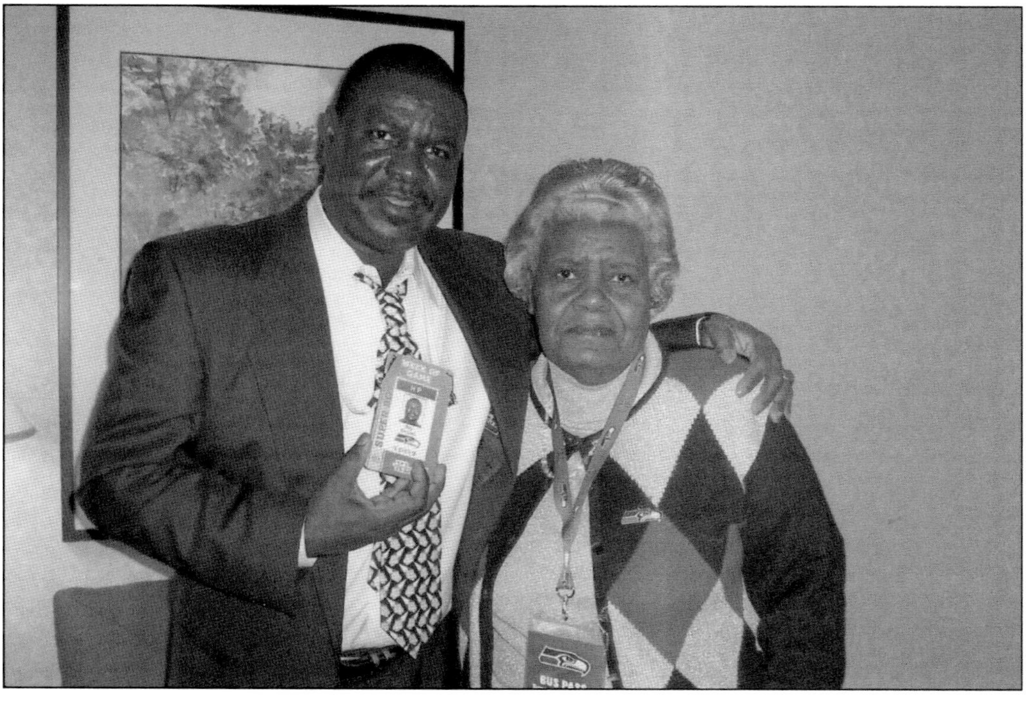

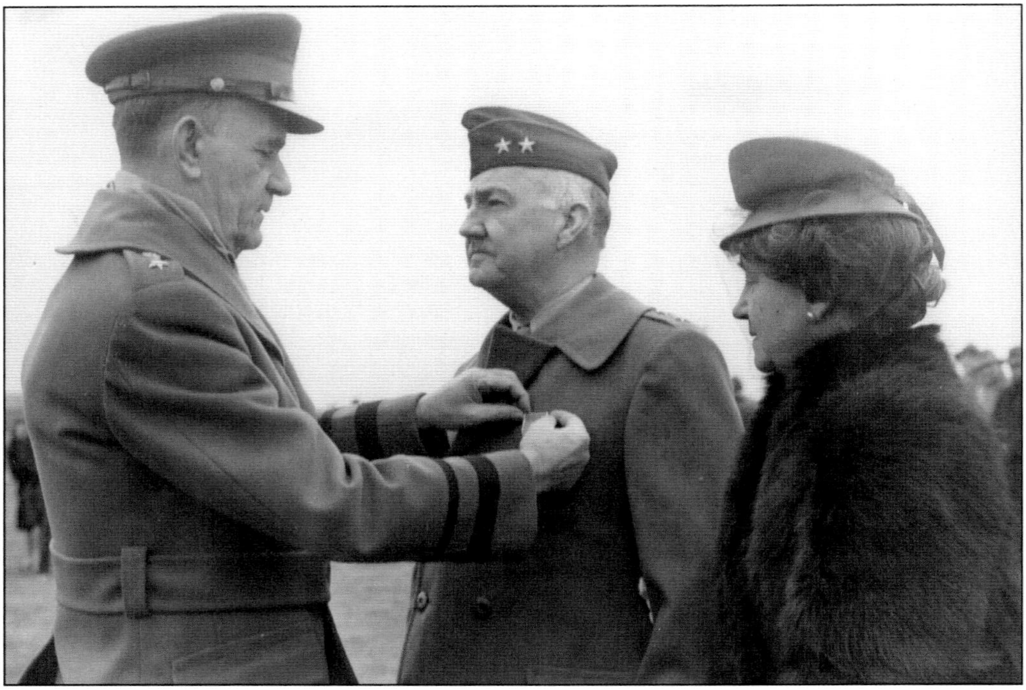

Maj. Gen. Charles Harris was born in Mexia on March 31, 1884. He graduated from Mexia High in 1900 and from West Point in 1907. He was considered the leading expert in industrial preparedness between the two world wars and was awarded the Distinguished Service Medal during both wars for his work in ordnance. He was commanding general of the Aberdeen Proving Ground from 1942 to 1944. (Gibbs Memorial Library.)

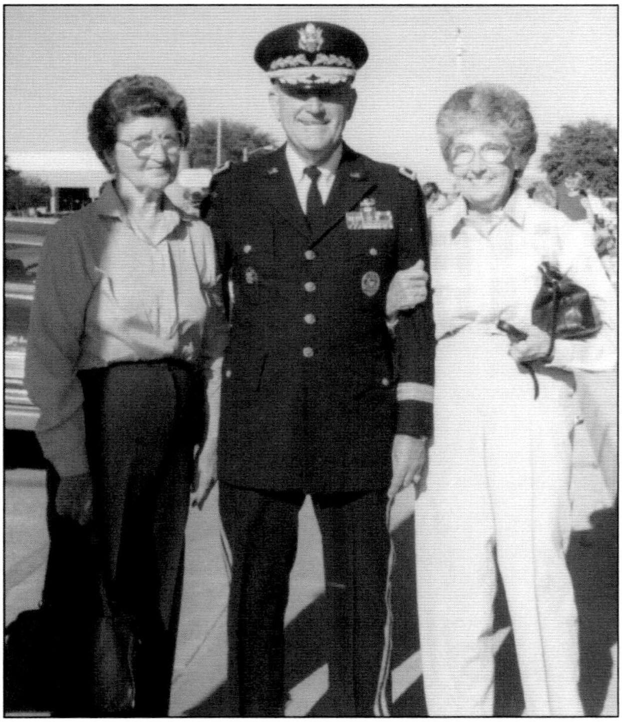

Brig. Gen. Robert Macon Mullens was born on June 19, 1928, in Thornton and was a 1944 graduate of Groesbeck High School. His military career includes combat tours in Korea and Vietnam and service at NATO Command in Germany and the Pentagon. He was commander of the Air Defense, Western Region with units in Washington, Oregon, and California. He is pictured with two of his sisters, Janice Reagan and Laverne Downs. (William Reagan.)

Dr. E. Donnall Thomas grew up in Coolidge and graduated from Coolidge High School in 1937. His father had a doctor's office in nearby Prairie Hill. A graduate of Harvard Medical School, Dr. Thomas became director of clinical research at the Fred Hutchinson Cancer Medical Research Center. He received the Nobel Prize in 1990 for pioneering bone marrow transplantation to cure leukemia. (Fred Hutchinson Cancer Medical Research Center.)

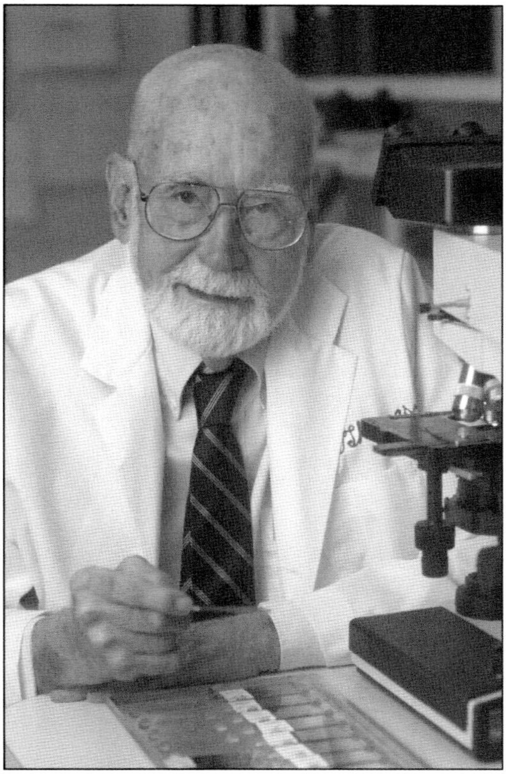

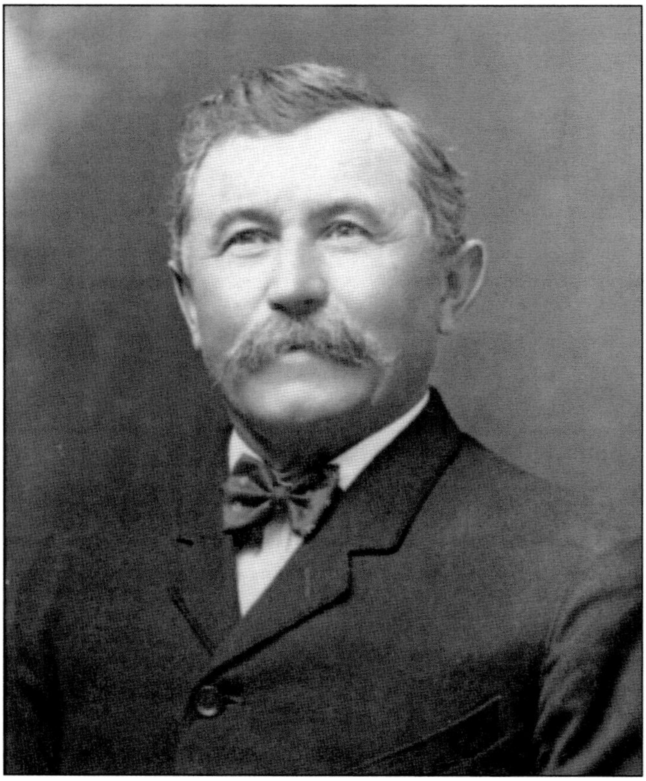

Born in Bavaria in 1852, Joseph Stubenrauch migrated to New York in 1871 and to Mexia in 1876. In an attempt to develop fruit trees better suited for Texas, he developed 100 new varieties of peaches and propagated more than 20 for commercial purposes. He practiced terracing, crop rotation, soil testing, fertilization, and irrigation. He was recognized nationally, and his practices were incorporated into many government programs. (Gibbs Memorial Library.)

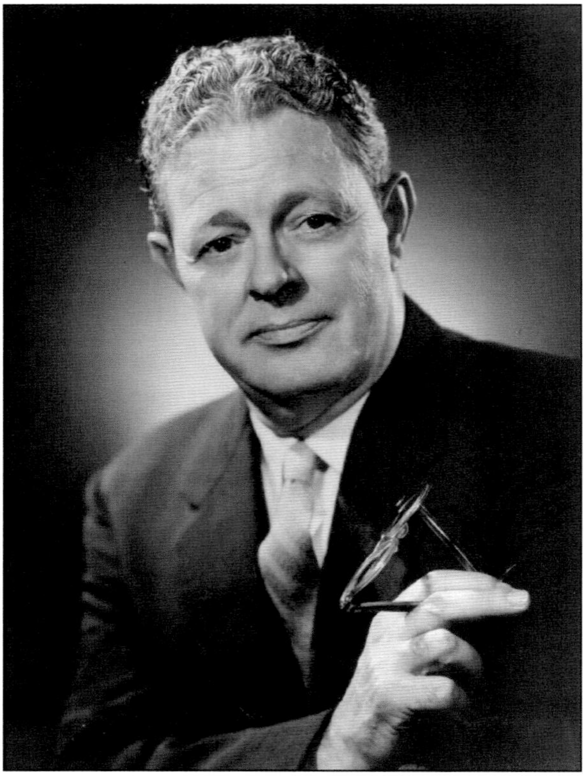

Garland Roark was born in Groesbeck on July 26, 1904. He became well known during the 1950s and 1960s as an author of seafaring adventures. Two of his works were made into movies, *Wake of the Red Witch* with John Wayne and *Fair Wind to Java* starring Fred McMurray. (Limestone County Historical Museum.)

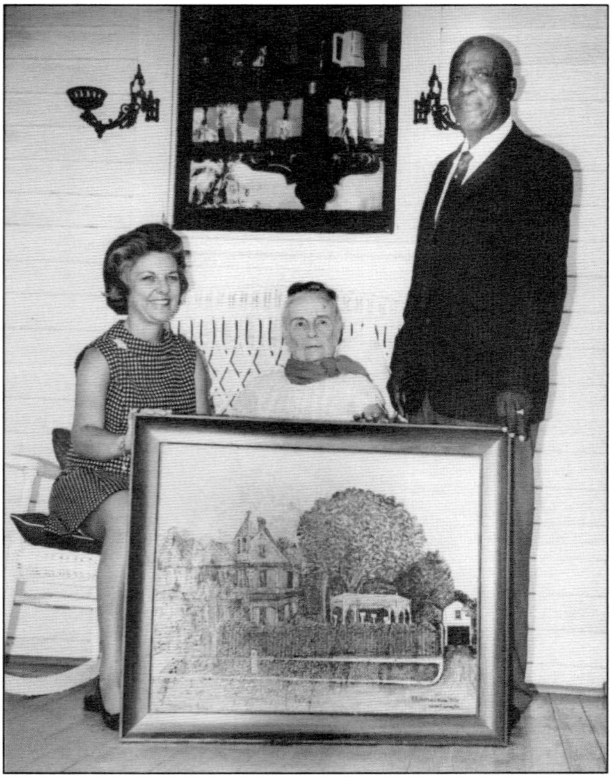

A descendant of slaves, Walter Cotton (right) was born on December 27, 1892. He picked cotton, served in World War I, and worked for the railroad before entering a long career in education. He taught history and eventually became principal of the Woodlands School. He was an accomplished artist who created numerous paintings depicting religious scenes and local history. He also authored two books about local African American history. (Gibbs Memorial Library.)

Groesbeck native Karl Shiflett learned to sing and play guitar at the age of nine. He began his professional career in bluegrass music as a side man in the 1980s and organized The Karl Shiflett & Big Country Show in 1993. Deeply rooted in traditional bluegrass music, he blends elements of classic country, western swing, and honky-tonk, creating a sound uniquely his own. (Karl Shiflett.)

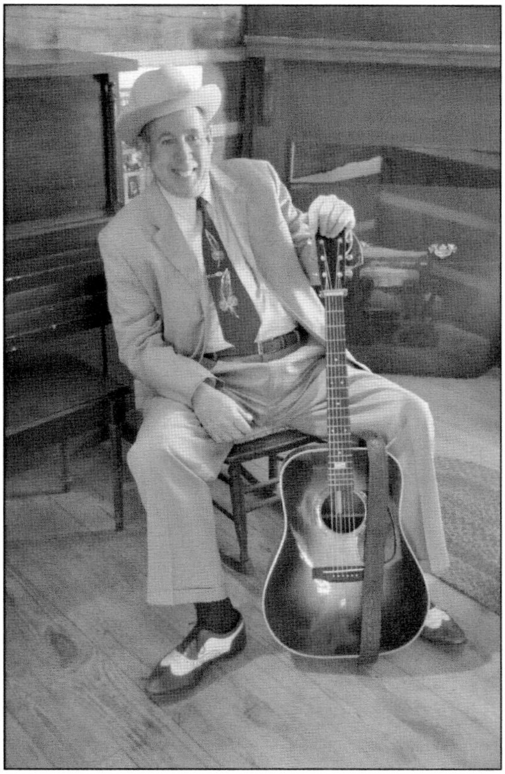

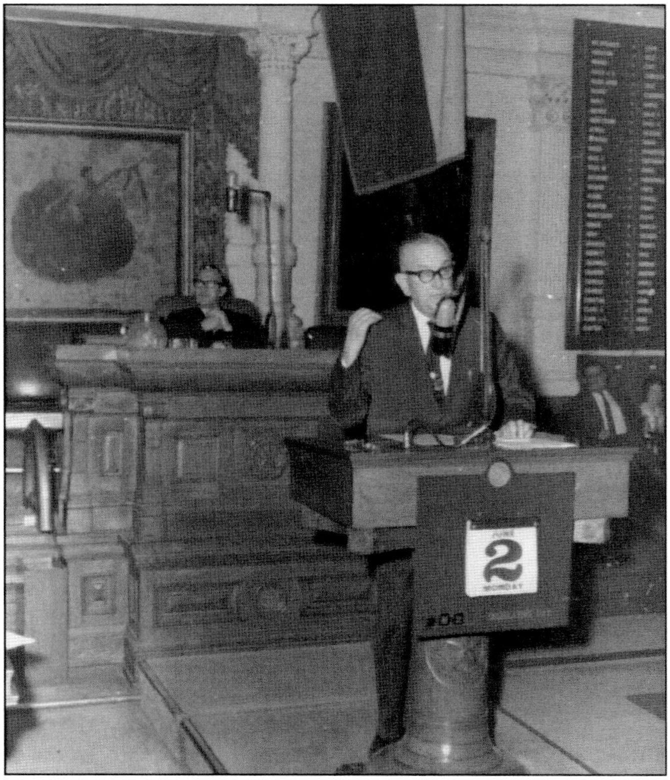

Jack Hawkins moved to Groesbeck in 1930, at which time he purchased the *Groesbeck Journal*. He married Euleta Sharp on January 29, 1931, and together they ran the newspaper. Both served in multiple civic organizations. Jack was on the first elected State Board of Education and served in the Texas Legislature from 1964 to 1972. He is seen here delivering a speech in the Texas House of Representatives. (Tom Hawkins.)

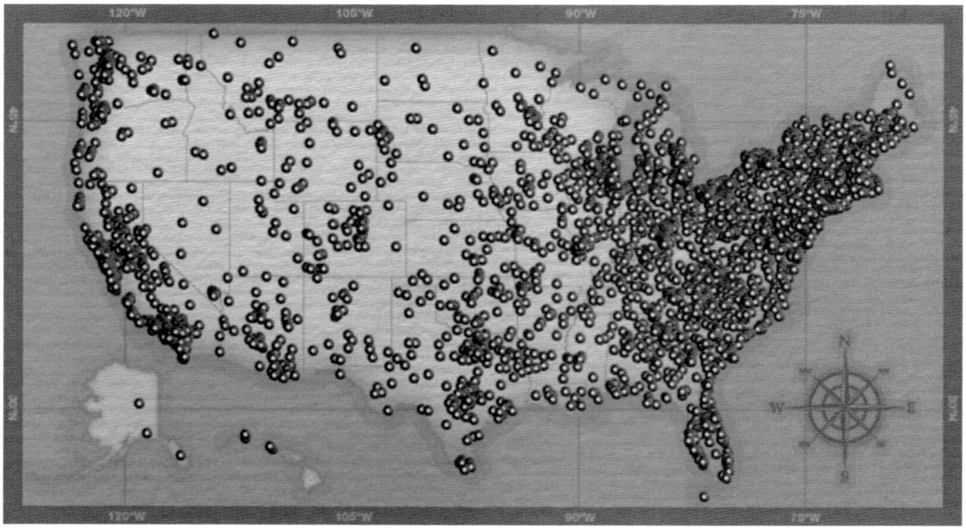